GARLAND LIBRARY OF MEDIEVAL LITERATURE
VOL. 97A

SONGS OF
THE WOMEN
TROUBADOURS

The Garland Library
of Medieval Literature

SONGS OF THE WOMEN TROUBADOURS

edited and translated by

Matilda Tomaryn Bruckner
Laurie Shepard
Sarah White

GARLAND PUBLISHING, Inc.
New York & London / 1995

Library of Congress Cataloging-in-Publication Data

Songs of the women troubadours / edited and trans-
    lated by Matilda Tomaryn Bruckner, Laurie Shepard,
    Sarah White.
        p.   cm. — (Garland library of medieval litera-
    ture ; v. 97A)
    Includes bibliographical references.
    ISBN 0-8153-0817-5
    1. Provençal poetry—Women authors—Translations
into English.   2. Women and literature—France,
Southern—History.   3. Provençal poetry—Women
authors.   4. Women—France, Southern—Poetry.
5. Troubadours.   I. Bruckner, Matilda Tomaryn.
II. Shepard, Laurie.   III. White, Sarah Melhado.
IV. Series
PC3365.E3S66   1995
849'.120809287—dc20   95-2961
                                              CIP

Printed on acid-free, 250-year-life paper
Manufactured in the United States of America

Preface of the General Editors

The Garland Library of Medieval Literature was established to make available to the general reader modern translations of texts in editions that conform to the highest academic standards. All of the translations are originals, and were created especially for this series. The translations usually attempt to render the foreign works in a natural idiom that remains faithful to the originals, although in certain cases we have published more poetic versions.

The Library is divided into two sections: Series A, texts and translations; and Series B, translations alone. Those volumes containing texts have been prepared after consultation of the major previous editions and manuscripts. The aim in the edition has been to offer a reliable text with a minimum of editorial intervention. Significant variants accompany the original, and important problems are discussed in the Textual Notes. Volumes without texts contain translations based on the most scholarly texts available, which have been updated in terms of recent scholarship.

Most volumes contain Introductions with the following features: (1) a biography of the author or a discussion of the problem of authorship, with any pertinent historical or legendary information; (2) an objective discussion of the literary style of the original, emphasizing any individual features; (3) a consideration of sources for the work and its influence; and (4) a statement of the editorial policy for each edition and translation. There is also a Select Bibliography, which emphasizes recent criticism on the works. Critical writings are often accompanied by brief descriptions of their importance. Selective glossaries, indices, and footnotes are included where appropriate.

The Library covers a broad range of linguistic areas, including all of the major European languages. All of the important literary forms and genres are considered, sometimes in anthologies or selections.

The General Editors hope that these volumes will bring the general reader a closer awareness of a richly diversified area that has for too long been closed to everyone except those with precise academic training, an area that is well worth study and reflection.

James J. Wilhelm
Rutgers University

Lowry Nelson, Jr.
Yale University

To Daniel, Louis, Malcolm, Owen, Raphael and Thomas

Tanz salutz e tantas amors
e tanz benz e tantas honors
e tantas finas amistaz
e tanz gauz com vos volriaz
e tanz ris e tant d'alegrier
Azalais d'Altier

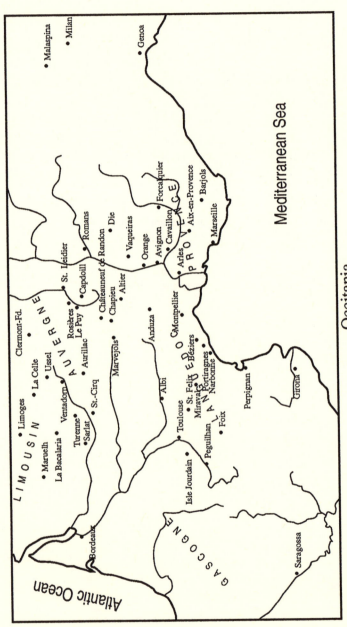

Occitania

(Places associated with the Trobairitz)

Contents

Preface

We have conceived this anthology of women troubadours or trobairitz as a performance, with all the rich possibilities that term implies. Among the songs that present a woman's voice circulating in the troubadour tradition, we have included all those whose attribution to trobairitz is strongly assured by manuscript or historical evidence. In addition, we offer access to a number of poems that are spoken in the voices of named or anonymous *domnas,* though not verifiably authored by women. Readers may thus come to their own conclusions about the distinction or coincidence of *fémininité génétique* and *textualité féminine* in any particular case.

We have not tried to be exhaustive in scope, an impossible task in any case, given the difficulty of pinning down the trobairitz repertoire (as explained below). We have designed rather a collection that brings together a broad selection of trobairitz songs that may serve general readers, poets, students, teachers, and scholars working in disciplines including medieval literature, social history, women's studies, culture studies, poetry and translation. Our newly edited texts are presented with a focused apparatus and a reliable, colloquial translation that may stand on its own or help the reader work with the original language. We have not aimed to replace Angelica Rieger's monumental critical edition for the specialist of Occitan literature, but our selection of variants and notes, as well as the Guide to the Vocabulary will help situate these songs in their social, literary, and cultural contexts.

As in any concert performance, we have arranged the selection of songs for our own and the public's pleasure. They are divided into categories according to lyric genres recognized by the poets themselves, with the *canso* first as befits its prestige. Within each category the order is subjective and aims to set up a suggestive interplay among the songs. As this edition performs and translates each of the songs, we hope the readers will find themselves enriched by their reception and equipped thereby to go farther in the study and appreciation of an exciting repertoire. Certainly the process of collaboration that produced it has been a great pleasure for the three of us, as we have probed the texts together, learning from them and each other. As the trobairitz' songs have come alive for us through our readings, translations, and discussions, we hope that they may leave the page and enter the minds, ears and hearts of our readers.

Among the many final gestures that bring a work to its conclusion, acknowledging and thanking colleagues and friends is one of the most plea-surable. In some sense, the seeds for this project were first planted in the late seventies, when an NEH Summer Seminar brought to Princeton Don Monson and Sarah White, who were thus able to join Sylvia Huot and my-self in a weekly study group on troubadour poetry. I am grateful to all of them for the many hours we spent together in my Gothic-shaped office, reading, translating, and analyzing a series of poems by troubadours and trobairitz. That initial shared acquaintance with the troubadour repertoire led subsequently to my first project on Castelloza and a written correspon-dence with Angelica Rieger, who has been most generous over the years in sharing her perspectives, suggestions and extensive work on the trobairitz. My ongoing involvement with the women troubadours through a number of lectures, papers and articles was put in a new light when Don Maddox was kind enough to tell me about Garland's interest in an edition and trans-lation of their songs. With the agreement of my colleagues, Laurie Shepard and Sarah White, whose expertise in textual criticism and translation gave me the courage to respond to that suggestion, we made a proposal that Jim Wilhelm as General Editor of Garland accepted with gratifying rapidity.

The process of extensive collaboration among the three of us has benefitted from the generous input of a number of colleagues. As is custom-ary, we affirm our responsibility for errors that may result from the choices made; nevertheless we would like to acknowledge fully how much we have learned from others and thank them as they deserve: Angelica Rieger for an edition of the trobairitz that has served as our constant guide, Margaret Switten and Fredric Cheyette for sharing unpublished work that helped situate the women troubadours textually and historically, Nat Smith for his exper-tise in Old Provençal grammar and the puzzles of translating it, Mark Stansbury and Michael Connolly for their invaluable technical assistance in computer software and typography, and Vincent Pollina for his perspec-tives on editing Provençal poetry. We would also like to acknowledge Bos-ton College's financial assistance in the form of Research Expense Grants.

Finally, we would like to thank our families for their love and support, especially our six sons to whom we dedicate this volume.

MTB

Introduction

This collection assembles twenty named women poets and a selection of anonymous *domnas*, names and voices derived from poems, rubrics, *vidas* (biographies) and *razos* (commentaries) recorded in manuscripts of the thirteenth and fourteenth centuries. If they are only twenty or so among more than four hundred named troubadours of Southern France, these women poets, active from the mid-twelfth to the mid-thirteenth centuries, nevertheless represent an exceptional and exceptionally large group of literary women within medieval tradition. As such, they deserve the attention of a modern public searching for a fuller understanding of the roles men and women have played in the formation of western culture. A modern reader, denied immediate access to the world of the Occitanic courts and their live performances of music and song, necessarily meets troubadours, male and female, in the textual world of medieval *chansonniers* in which their songs were written down in anthology form. Among the women troubadours named in the manuscripts—all noblewomen as far as their social status can be determined—only Gaudairenca, the wife of Raimon de Miraval, has left no trace in this collection, since her "coblas e dansas" have not survived (Boutière-Schutz 380). Among the anonymous *domnas* whose status as women poets remains problematic, our selection gives a wide sample of the different voices attributed to female speakers within the context of troubadour lyric. In order to understand and appreciate the accomplishments of these "trobairitz" (the feminine form of "trobador," according to the thirteenth-century romance *Flamenca*), we need to situate them and their poems in a variety of contexts, literary and historical, cultural and linguistic.

Trobairitz Interacting with the Troubadour Poetic System

The trobairitz give precious testimony of the ways aristocratic women in Southern France were able to participate fully in the game and life of poetry, not only as patrons and objects of song but as poets singing and reshaping the art of the troubadours. An art of love that is simultaneously an art of persuasion, troubadour poetry is characterized by a formalization that operates equally at the levels of form and content. If originality and creativity in the Romantic sense are not relevant categories for understanding troubadour lyric, individual invention is no less important here than in other literary forms: the poet "finds" (the normal meaning of *trobar*) within the shared materials of the poetic system new combinations and variations that continually refract the common traits of the system through a changeable lens of particular manifestations. Any trobairitz who begins to compose (the technical sense of *trobar*) enters a lyric world that may strike the modern reader as paradoxically open and confining: the choice of shape for stanza and poem—rhymes, rhyme patterns, meter, number of stanzas— is uncharted by any fixed forms like those introduced in the later Middle Ages. Yet the subject matter of a *canso* (love song) is clearly mapped out by the typical scenarios of *fin'amor*, in which the humble poet/lover begs for the love of his frequently silent and rejecting lady, describes his pain and suffering through all the ambivalent enjoyment of frustrated desire, and finally expects his service in song to be rewarded by an eventual gift of *joi*, anticipated (sometimes remembered) in the experience of the song itself. Each repetition of vocabulary, motifs, and themes enriches the power of allusion that key words and concepts infuse into the lyric voice.

Does this mean that troubadour poetry is characterized by formal freedom and thematic constraint? Yes and no, since on the one hand, troubadours frequently borrow and adapt each others' formal choices, creating a series of allusions through rhymes or stanza structures that set up, within the larger probabilities of the system as a whole, a game of recognition and play for the public of connoisseurs. On the other hand, the motifs of love that can be adequately expressed and explored in Bernart de Ventadorn's 2400-word vocabulary (Zumthor, "Recherches" 410-11) can upon occasion be interrupted by the unexpected: in the generally more free-wheeling world of the *tenso* (debate poem), Alaisina Yselda raises the uncourtly topic of sagging breasts and stretching bellies; attracted to love and marriage, she worries about the inevitable fruits and their effects on her body (no. 27). In the context of the *sirventes*, where a range of moral and political topics can be explored, the anonymous trobairitz of "Ab greu cossire" (no. 29) rails against the sumptuary laws that have robbed her and other ladies of their gold and silver chains and buttons. Her complaint is no less intensely formulated for all the humorous irony of her tone. Even within the traditional topics of love, the same motifs sung by a troubadour may have a different effect when the lady of lyric begins to sing for herself. If we would join the lyric's public of connoisseurs, it will be equally important to appreciate where the trobairitz do what troubadours do and where they do not, even if sometimes it may be difficult to tell the difference.

Although we are usually reading these poems from a written text with no melody enriching and sustaining the words, we need to keep in mind their intended life in performance and song. We have only a single stanza of one trobairitz melody transcribed in manuscript W, but there is a documented history of women as performers and composers, some professional, others amateur, that covers the whole period of the Middle Ages (Coldwell and Borroff). Until polyphonic music introduced special requirements for training, aristocratic men and women had equal access to composing monophonic music (Coldwell 42-43). How this music was actually performed, with or without musical accompaniment, has long been a subject of speculation. The musical notation of troubadour manuscripts uses notes (neumes) that indicate relative pitch with no measurement of time. However, there is general agreement among scholars and performers that the melodies must be free to adapt themselves to the rhythm of the words, especially as the same melody is repeated from stanza to stanza (Van der Werf). The music in general may be understood to serve the text without obscuring it. Vincent Pollina shows, for example, how the bipartite structure of the musical scheme in the Comtessa de Dia's "A chantar," ABABCDB, typically reinforces the standard division of the stanza into *frons* (head, i.e., the two repeated *pedes* or feet of the opening four verses: here aaaa, frequently abab or abba) and *cauda* (tail: the second half of the stanza which may be of any length, here bab). Pollina details the interplay of words and melody to demonstrate how both embody the common medieval aesthetic principle of combining continuity and discontinuity ("Melodic Continuity").

Troubadours did not always make up their own melodies and trobairitz too may have borrowed melodies. That is what Rieger suggests for Maria de Ventadorn's *tenso* with Gui d'Ussel, "Gui d'Uisel, be.m pesa de vos" (no. 12), since the initiator of the debate is assumed to be responsible for the music as well as the form of the stanza ("La *mala canso*"). Following the suggestion of a *razo* (Boutière-Schutz 212-13) that links their *tenso* to Gui's song of complaint about a "bad lady," Rieger hypothesizes that Gui's "Si be.m partetz, mala dompna, de vos" plays off against Raimbaut de Vaqueiras's "Ges, si tot ma don'et amors." Raimbaut's and Gui's songs share the same rhyme scheme and two repeated rhyme words. Since Maria uses the metric pattern, as well as the rhyme scheme of Raimbaut's song (a10 b10 b10 a10 c10 c10 d10 d10) and shares two rhyme sounds with Gui's *mala canso* (-os and -en), she may very well have borrowed Raimbaut's melody (now lost) to reinforce the pattern of interaction, playing off against the troubadours' complaints about ladies her own argument that a lady should always maintain her superior status.

These examples have already introduced some of the key elements that characterize *trobar*. Each trobairitz is as free as any troubadour to invent her own shape for the opening stanza (which will set the pattern for the entire song), as Castelloza does in "Amics s'ie.us trobes avinen" (no. 6) and "Ia de chantar" (no. 5) with their unique rhyme schemes and syllabic formulae (Frank 1: 33, 159; 2: 32, 48). That choice may overlap with patterns already used by other troubadours, as when Castelloza's "Mout avetz faich" (no. 7) shares a rhyme scheme with two other *cansos*, but repeats neither their rhymes nor their metric pattern (Frank 1: 85; 2: 85). The repetitions that result may serve as a possible allusion, whose status needs to be reinforced by other signs inscribed in the poem to permit and invite recognition.

Once the pattern is set in the first stanza, subsequent stanzas (of varying numbers) may repeat it in a variety of ways. In "A chantar," the Comtessa de Dia uses *coblas singulars*, that is, she repeats the same rhyme scheme in each strophe, but changes the *a* rhyme every time (-ia, -enssa, -uoilla, -ina, -atges). Clara d'Anduza composes "En greu esmay" (no. 9) in the more difficult form of *coblas unissonans*, where the rhyme sounds as well as the pattern must remain the same throughout the song: ababc'ddc' (-en, -or, -ia, -ar). *Coblas doblas* allow the Comtessa de Dia to associate the stanzas of "Ab ioi" (no. 1) two by two: the rhyme scheme remains constant (ab'ab'b'aab'), while the rhymes change every other stanza (except in the *tornada* which always repeats whatever portion coincides with the previous stanza). The Comtessa reinforces this pattern of two-by-two when she uses derivative rhyme to link the *a* and *b* rhymes through the play of feminine and masculine endings: -ais/-aia in I and II, -en/-ensa in III, IV, and the *tornada* (this kind of rhyme was much appreciated by the troubadours and put to excellent use by the Comtessa de Dia: see Kay, "Derivation"). The Comtessa contributes further to the play set up in the rhymes by using binomial pairs, a frequent stylistic trait of the troubadours (and of medieval writing in general), here repeated in a crisscrossing pattern that further intertwines the two opening verses of the *canso*: "Ab ioi et ab ioven m'apais / e iois e iovens m'apaia." This example notwithstanding, the trobairitz repertoire seems on the whole less marked by the fancy work of metrical variation characteristic of troubadours like Marcabru or Arnaut Daniel. Is this possibly because they arrive later in the tradition and leave fewer *cansos* behind in the manuscripts that record their compositions? We can only speculate on scant evidence.

Troubadours invented various patterns of rhyme to connect the stanzas in a fixed order, despite the general tendency of these songs to allow a good measure of *mouvance*, changeability evident in the variants across manuscripts that record the same song with different stanza orders, stylistic variations, etc. (see Van Vleck). "Per ioi que d'amor m'avegna" (no. 8), for example, consists of five *coblas unissonans capfinidas;* that is, in addition to the repetition of rhyme scheme and rhymes, each stanza is linked to the one that follows it by the reprise of its final word (sometimes in varied form) in the opening verse of the next stanza: "don per mi no.s vol partir. / Partir m'en er ..." (I/II); "de leis amar ni servir. / Leis serva ..." (II/III); "de vos amar ni grasir. / Grasisc vos ..." (III/IV); "c'autra no.m pot enriquir. / Rica soi ..." (IV/V). This technical virtuosity is reflected thematically in the opening stanza—the one stanza in the troubadour tradition most likely to remain in place—when the anonymous trobairitz insists on the problematic connections between her love and her song:

> Per ioi que d'amor m'avegna
> no.m calgra ogan esbaudir,
> qu'eu non cre qu'en grat me tegna
> cel c'anc non volc hobesir
> mos bos motz ni mas chansos;
> ni anc no fon lasaz sos
> qu'ie.m pogues de lui sofrir. (1-7)

> To delight in any joy that love might bring
> will not concern me soon,
> for I don't think he holds me dear,
> the one who never wishes to obey
> my good words or songs;
> nor was any music ever woven
> that would enable me to do without him.

Troubadours typically link the action of singing to that of loving. The two actions become synonymous, as Bernart de Ventadorn explains in "Non es maravelha s'eu chan," when he attributes his superiority in song to his superior attraction and obedience to love. The Comtessa de Dia sings likewise: "Fin ioi me dona alegranssa / per qu'eu chan plus gaiamen" (no. 4, 1-2: "Happiness brings me pure joy / which makes me sing more cheerfully"). Just as typically, a troubadour may refuse to stop singing even if his love is not returned, as Gui d'Ussel does in the *mala canso* just described. In "Per ioi" the anonymous trobairitz uses the technical vocabulary of troubadour lyric to designate the two components, words and song ("mos bos motz ni mas chanssos"), that are laced together ("lasaz") by her expertise in *trobar.* What should be produced by the "natural" congruence of joy in love and song is here produced in the negative mode as a complaint against the loved one who refuses to obey her songs and show gratitude for her singing. If he will not respond as he should, she will at least praise her own service in song ("mos bos motz") and continue to affirm her loyalty even if no joy comes to her from love.

The link between singing and loving is often expressed by troubadours, especially those of the early generations, in the topos of the "springtime opening," in which the happiness or sadness of the poet responds with particular congruence or opposition to the season and its weather. In a world dominated by the antithesis of joy and suffering (Bec, "L'antithèse"), reversals along positive and negative polarities typically channel the path of variation as much as the individual choice of particular details. In "Ar em al freg temps vengut" (no. 11), one of only two poems by trobairitz that use the springtime opening (see also "Quan vei los praz verdesir" in Rieger), Azalais de Porcairagues describes her disorientation and loss of solace (st. II), negative feelings that accord with the wintry scene she paints in the opening stanza:

> Ar em al freg temps vengut
> que.l gells e.l neus e la faingna
> e.l auçellet estan mut
> c'us de chantar non s'afraigna;
> e son sec li ram pels plais
> que flors ni foilla no.i nais
> ni rrossignols no i crida
> que l'am' en mai me rreissida.

> Now we are come to the cold time
> when there's snow and ice and sludge
> and the little birds are mute;
> not one attempts to sing,
> and the boughs are bare in hedges;
> neither flower nor leaf is sprouting there,
> nor, calling there, the nightingale
> who wakes my soul in May.

The last verse evokes the normal setting for springtime, when birdsong and new growth typically parallel the urge to sing felt by the troubadour poet. Here the birds remain silent on dried out branches, when ice and snow and mud replace flowers and leaves: Azalais's description evokes both the positive and negative images of spring, seen through the eyes of winter. She recalls a moment in the past when she has been awakened to love by the call of the nightingale, but now in the "freg temps" a new correspondence appears in the opposite mode: just as winter has reversed the movement of spring, something coming from Aurenga (14) has made her heart fall into disarray and grief.

The use of *coblas doblas* that appears in stanzas I-IV is itself disrupted by irregularities in the pairing of V and VI (the *a* and *b* rhymes do not match, while the *c* and *d* rhymes do). Aimo Sakari has speculated that the irregularities result from Azalais's effort to transform a previously written *canso* (st. III -V) into a *planh* (lament) for the death of Raimbaut d'Aurenga, with whom she exchanged poems, each designating the other by the *senhal* (secret name) Joglar ("Azalais" and "Azalais Interlocutrice"). Whether or not this furnishes a convincing motive for the poem's apparent discontinuities, Sakari's analysis does call our attention to the way Azalais establishes multiple links with fellow troubadours, Raimbaut as well as Guilhem de Saint-Leidier (see the discussion of the *ric ome* debate below), locating her poem within the places and society that enjoyed its pleasures.

In addition to the enumeration of specific places associated with Orange ("Aurenga") in st. VI, this characteristic is most noteworthy in the *tornada*, the *envoi* where troubadours and trobairitz frequently address the beloved, their patrons, other poets, and even the performer (*joglar*) who will sing their song.

> Ioglar que aves cor gai,
> ves Narbona portas lai
> ma chanson a la fenida
> lei cui iois e iovenz guida. (53-56)

> Jongleur, whose heart is gay,
> carry out toward Narbonne
> my song with these final verses
> to her whose guides are youth and joy.

Azalais asks Joglar to carry her song to Narbonne to the one guided by "iois e iovenz"—the popular binomial pair suggests again the essence of a society espousing the ethic of *fin'amor*. This allusion undoubtedly designates Ermengarde of Narbonne, given the time frame in which Azalais is placed by her *vida* and research on her literary references. Just as the lovers of troubadour lyric are frequently identified by their placement in space—the poet here (*sai*), the beloved there (*lai*)—the people in Azalais's *canso* are placed along two geographical axes that coincide with the polarization of emotions: the negative ones oriented toward Orange (and particularly valorized in the rhyme position: Belesgar, Aurenga, Proenza, ll. 41, 42, 44), the positive ones toward Velay and Narbonne. The wintry time of the "springtime opening" is thus articulated in space through the layering of stanzas that combine to form Azalais's *canso*.

Among the Comtessa de Dia's songs, she sends two to her beloved, "Ab ioi" (no. 1) and "Estat ai en greu cossirer" (no. 3). As is typical in woman's song, she addresses him as *amics* or *bels amics* (fair friend), although interestingly in some manuscripts of "Ab ioi" he appears in the *tornada* as Floris, the name of the hero from a well-known medieval romance, *Floris and Blanchaflor*. Castelloza's *tornada* in "Amics, s'ie.us trobes" (no. 6) expresses her desire not to send words, but to speak them herself: "E no.us man, q'ieu mezeussa.us o dic" (44). Here she echoes with variation Guilhem IX's fear to send a message to his lady through someone else (expressed in "Mout jauzens"). This motif not only expresses the desire for direct contact between lovers, but relates as well to the theme of secrecy, one of the key ideas of *fin'amor* as it operates in the public arena of the court. The use of a *senhal* (literally a sign, or in this context a secret code name) typically reflects this theme in troubadour lyric, as it preserves a mask of secrecy for the lover's open declarations of love and hides the name of the beloved from gossips and scandalmongers, the *lauzengier*.

In "A chantar," the Comtessa addresses her song itself as messenger and in "Fin ioi" she teasingly flouts "vos, gelos mal parlan" (no. 4, 17), the figure of the evil-speaking jealous one also frequently evoked in woman's song. The two *tornadas* of "Ia de chantar" name Castelloza's beloved—again with a *senhal*, "Bels Noms" (no. 5, 59: "beautiful name")—and another trobairitz, Almuc de Castelnou (55), recognizable in the variants of "Dompna n'Almurs (N), n'Almirs (IK), and n'Almir (d)" (Paden, ed. "Poems" 162). Both Rofin and Lady H. close their *tornadas* by calling upon Lady Agnesina to judge the opposing arguments of their *partimen* (no. 23, 65-66, 70-72), a typical gesture in the *tensos* that reminds us how real people and poetry interact in the context of Occitanic society.

To grasp further the mixture of images thus combined, we need to examine more specifically the dramatis personae placed on the stage of troubadour lyric and their incarnations in the songs of the trobairitz. In so doing, we can explore the nature of *fin'amor* as received and articulated by the women troubadours. A brief analysis of the major characters—the lyric voice of the self, its love object, and third parties—as they pass from troubadour lyric into the poems of the trobairitz, reveals an important series of shifts and reversals, even as the basic types are maintained. Marianne Shapiro has pointed out the asymmetrical polarity between courting men and courting ladies: in the troubadour's poem, the lady represents the apex of courtly values and the poet lover, though he may be a great lord, assumes the position of humble vassal. When a woman takes the position of the lover and begins to sing, the male beloved cannot simply move into her vacated position "without exciting a polemic that would attack the core of the *humilis/sublimis* paradox as it pertains to the hierarchy of courtly love" ("The Provençal *Trobairitz*" 562).

In corroboration of such a dissymmetry, Pierre Bec's analysis of the modes of address and reciprocal designations used by troubadours and trobairitz ("'Trobairitz'" 243-44) points out that in the *tensos*, for example, the trobairitz designate their male partners by their full names (with or without a title) or by a first name, more rarely by *amics* or *amics* plus a first name, while the troubadour always uses the respectful title of *domna*. Bec sees this practice as maintaining the functional distance between high-born lady and lover of lower rank, indispensable to the ideal of *fin'amor*. The *domna* imitates the troubadour (without addressing him as such) and implies that she will never love anyone but a knight or lord. Always referring to herself as *domna*, she enters the system less as a woman than as a lady, "c'est-à-dire, encore et toujours, comme protectrice et dominatrice" (244). If this is generally valid in terms of the vocabulary Bec has analyzed, we also need to explore other aspects of the trobairitz' self-representation to nuance and modify his overview for particular women poets and poems (on Castelloza's double reversal of the troubadour's stance, for example, see Bruckner, "Na Castelloza").

If the lady who begins to sing does not completely vacate her position in the asymmetrical balance of power between *domna* and lover, it should not surprise us that some of the trobairitz speak exactly as *midons* (the lady as lord) is pictured by the male troubadours in their complaints, dreams, hopes, and fears. In the *tenso* initiated by "Na donzela," "Bona domna, tan vos ay fin coratge," the lady who is asked to forgive "the one who loves you more than he's loved anyone" (no. 26, 4) corresponds exactly to the troubadours' *domna*. She knows how a lady should honorably behave when she sees her lover boasting about her and acting foolishly:

... be.m deu esser salvatge
can el gaba ni se vana de me; ...
non m'en reptetz si la foldat l'en ve,
q'aysi o aug dir que dretz es onratge. (9-10, 15-16)

... I am right to be harsh
when he mocks me and boasts about me; ...
don't scold me if I recognize his folly,
for I hear that the right way brings honor.

Concerned that his failure or betrayal may lower her own worth, she with-draws her love: "car ia per el non vuelh mon pretz dissendre" (32). The *donzela* in the meantime paints a picture of the lover that likewise recalls the troubadours' self-presentation: he is dying for love of her, a single kiss could make his heart revive, no other woman has power over him ("poder ni senhoratge," 8); his sighs should make her take pity on him. The feudal language retains the usual reversal of hierarchy: the *domna* is invested with power and a proud heart, the lover offers—through the *donzela*'s intercession—his humble heart ("sos cors humil," 36) to win her forgive-ness. The advice for future behavior the lady gives her lover, if he wants her permission to continue loving her, recalls Guilhem IX's description of an obedient lover in "Pus vezem de novel florir": he should be happy and worthy, humble and generous, courteous with all, neither evil nor too proud, but true and loving and discreet (41-48).

In general, the women poets do not respond directly to the male poets' request for love, initiating their own, parallel requests instead, as in the spirited exchange between Lombarda and Bernart Arnaut, no. 21 (see Sankovitch). If such a lady corresponds to the troubadours' expectations of difficulty, high standards, and increased worth, the idealized, but de-manding *domna* who ennobles the man who rises in merit to deserve her love, other trobairitz recall the more obliging lady of the troubadours' hopes and dreams. Some trobairitz do answer their lovers' pleas with the kind of confirmation so long desired in the troubadours' *cansos*. Consider the *tenso*, "Si.m fos graziz" (no. 24). The first part, addressed to *bella domna*, con-tains the typical complaints of the poet lover, separated from joy and en-joyment, thrown into "not-caring" (*non chaler,* 3) by his lady. But when she speaks to him in the second part, we hear just the humble voice wished for ("degues humilitatz / venir en vos," 18-19: "humility should find you"). She, too, is improved by love and, far from placing him in *non chaler* (29), she gives herself to him loyally, without deceit: "car gauz entier non puesc senz vos aver, / a cui m'autrei leialmen senz engan; / e.us lais mon cor en gauge on qu'eu m'an" (30-32: "for without you I can have no total joy. / I give myself to you with loyalty, without deception; / wherever I go, I leave you my heart as pledge").

The language of political obligation, as used here by the lady, reverses the conventionally reversed hierarchy, places the lady at the mercy of her lover—who affirmed earlier his own loss of power over his eyes and himself (13-14) in the face of the lady's power over love (22). The echoes of metaphor and language thus affirm the mutuality of their love, the mutuality of their submission to the other's power, while the obstacles to such easy reciprocity are identified by the lady as a subterfuge, a deceitful appearance that masks the lovers' reality from those cruel, troublesome people who do not like the lovers' joy (33-35).

Clara d'Anduza blames such *lauzengier* for driving away her lover, and the Comtessa de Dia laughingly dismisses them in "Fin ioi" (cf. the *domna* of no. 25, "Amics, en gran cosirier," who is less concerned than Raimbaut about the effect of *lauzengier*). They are the ubiquitous rivals and gossips in love, conventional characters among the third parties of troubadour lyric and part of its setting within the context of seigneurial courts. The husband only occasionally puts in an appearance, usually as the jealous figure represented in the popularizing lyric types, but he is evoked as well in Castelloza's "Mout avetz faich" in a less conventional role, when he is presented as grateful to her *amic* for creating his wife's suffering in love. The public of lovers is often called upon to verify or criticize a lover's conduct. Consider Azalais d'Altier's advice to a lady whose pardon she seeks for an offending lover. If she does not forgive him, she will be less esteemed ("meinz prezada," no. 32, 53) by all courtly lovers ("totz los finz amanz," 52). Castelloza fears to set a bad example for other women who love, "las autras amairitz" (no. 7, 21-22), but also maintains that her beloved is judged harshly by lovers: "qe l'amador / vos tenon per salvatge" (no. 5, 13-14). The trobairitz, like the troubadours, are aware that their songs exist in the paradox of private feelings publicly performed. Intimate emotions are directly tied to outer behavior, whether in love or in song, which inevitably connects the individual lovers to the courtly society in which they circulate.

Although we might expect the cultural model of the passive woman to make it difficult for the lady to speak out, in fact very few trobairitz mention such a constraint. Anticipating criticism from those who do not understand that courting in song does her good, Castelloza parries any possible attack in a defensively polemical way that affirms the personal benefit she feels from her singing (no. 6, st. III and IV), the same healing effect also claimed by troubadours for themselves. The Comtessa de Dia exuberantly defends a woman's right to speak openly of her love, once she has chosen an appropriately worthy lover, and expects right-thinking people ("li pro ni.ll'avinen," no. 1, 23) to have only good things to say about such a lady. In analyzing the lady's decision to court openly in song, Laurie A. Finke proposes the model of patron and client to describe what is at stake for the lady who decides to offer her love (58-59). Consider in that light Garsenda de Forcalquier's initiative in the exchange of *coblas* with Gui de Cavaillon: although she herself has just declared her love (4) and encouraged Gui to be less timid, she attributes a lady's hesitation to disclose all her desires to fear of failure (no. 16, 8-9). Hesitation to speak of their love appears elsewhere as a common motif for troubadour lovers (and is particularly developed by the trouvères of Northern France in the image of the cowardly lover). Other trobairitz remain silent on the issue of a woman speaking out, which may not in fact be perceived as a problem by ladies so closely integrated into the world of troubadour song (cf. the historical arguments offered below for the relatively favorable position of aristocratic women in Occitanian society, especially during the period when the trobairitz were singing). On the other hand, the relatively limited participation of women poets in a poetic system clearly designed from the male lover's point of view remains an important factor to consider when approaching the trobairitz corpus (cf. Gravdal's analysis of the way trobairitz grapple with the difficulty of occupying the place of the subject in troubadour lyric by changing the metaphorical stance typical of the troubadour—"I sing like a woman"—to a metonymic one—"I sing as a woman"; see also Kay, *Subjectivity* Ch. 3).

To continue the analysis of how lovers are represented by the trobairitz, we may fruitfully compare how the male and female troubadours' complaints and accusations line up against each other. F.R.P. Akehurst has summarized the male poets' list of grievances: ladies show *orgolh* (pride); they neither believe nor trust nor remember the lover, and even love other, worthless men; ladies are capricious and irrational, fail to reward proper service and cannot distinguish false lovers from true ones, who thus suffer and die. The trobairitz, too, accuse their lovers of pride and unfaithfulness. They often complain further of trust betrayed. As William Paden points out in his comments on gender difference in lyric, given a cultural context that generally calls for men to be active and women passive, trobairitz tend to speak of a love already initiated, while troubadours still hope to get theirs accepted ("Utrum" 79-80; cf. the narrative structure based on the model of the abandoned woman that Merritt Blakeslee [71-73] finds common to all the trobairitz' *cansos*, except for "Ab ioi" and "Fin ioi"). Accordingly, the trobairitz complain that their lovers are indiscreet and hurt their ladies' reputations, desert them and claim to be their equals, act cowardly and unpleasantly. The complaints of troubadours and trobairitz occasionally correspond, but they just as frequently open a gap: the trobairitz do not really respond directly to the troubadours' accusations; they insist rather on their own fidelity in love, their readiness to forgive, and the force of their desire, which makes them regret or reject any show of pride.

Both Akehurst and Kittye Delle Robbins have pointed out how important a role the theme of trust plays in the trobairitz corpus, as indicated by the vocabulary used most frequently. With a computer concordance, Akehurst has compared the twenty most frequently used nouns in the twenty-three poems of Meg Bogin's edition with the top twenty nouns of twenty troubadours (558 poems). Of the ten nouns that appear only in the women poets' list, three in particular suggest the trobairitz' concern with fidelity and infidelity between lovers: *falhimen* (offense), *drut* (lover), and *fe* (faithfulness) (see Bruckner, "Na Castelloza" 251-52 n20). The semantic field of fidelity/infidelity is richly represented among the nouns of the trobairitz corpus, including in addition to the three on the "top twenty list": *faillensa, faillida, faillir, traïr, traitor, plevir, fiansa, acordamen, acord, jurar, covinen, recrezens, recrezamen, camjar, camjairitz* (Robbins also adds *fegnedor* and *trichador*). While Akehurst relates this vocabulary group to the major complaints directed by the trobairitz against their lovers, Robbins suggests that it leads, on the one hand, to the women's desire to prove themselves worthy (while at the same time deploring the lover's unworthy betrayal) and, on the other, to the concern for reputation and the woman's particular vulnerability to the *gelos* and the *lauzengier* ("Love's Martyrdoms"; see also Kay, *Subjectivity* 107-08). These thematic avenues suggest further useful work to be done based on vocabulary studies, especially if they are expanded to include trobairitz poems left out of Bogin's edition, as well as comparisons with similar analyses of the troubadour corpus (cf. Ferrante on the use of negative constructions in the trobairitz corpus, "Notes").

The theme of trust between lovers inevitably raises the issue of sexuality. Scholars have often remarked that one of the major differences between the lady of troubadour lyric and the women troubadours is the latter's sensuous expression of desire. As the Comtessa de Dia sings:

> Estat ai en gran cossirier
> per un cavallier q'ai agut,
> e vuoil sia totz temps saubut
> cum eu l'ai amat a sobrier,
> ara vei q'ieu sui trahida
> car eu non li donei m'amor
> don ai estat en gran error
> en lieig e qand sui vestida. (no. 3: 1-8)

> I have been sorely troubled
> about a knight I had;
> I want it known for all time
> how exceedingly I loved him.
> Now I see myself betrayed
> because I didn't grant my love
> to him; I've suffered much distress
> from it, in bed and fully clothed.

In the closing stanza of her song, the Comtessa follows up on her opening remarks, suggestively situated in the context of a bed, by telling her *amic* that she would like to have him in the place of her husband ("en luoc del marit" 22), an expression whose ambiguities have been richly fueled by her previous question:

> Bels amics avinens e bos,
> cora.us tenrai en mon poder,
> e que iagues ab vos un ser,
> e qe.us des un bais amoros? (17-20)

> Fair, agreeable, good friend,
> when will I have you in my power,
> lie beside you for an evening,
> and kiss you amorously?

How does this compare to the lady envisaged by the troubadours? E. Jane Burns describes the troubadour's *domna* as a combination of "two unequal fictions: 1) an ideal desexualized lady, embodying virtues her admirer would like to attain, finds her opposite in 2) the erotic yet aloof woman who remains unattainable" (268). Many a troubadour would like to penetrate her chamber, watch her undress or place his hands under her robe, but the lady herself—as she is typically (but not universally) represented by the troubadours—does not share the lover's dream or desire. By contrast, the trobairitz' frank expression of desire has led many critics to admire or chastise their spontaneity and authenticity, while comparing them to the legendary Sappho.

Shapiro suggests that the Comtessa de Dia's persona of the passionate lady relates the trobairitz to the lady of romance ("The Provençal *Trobairitz*" 563). Of course, troubadours and trobairitz do refer to romance examples of great lovers. The Comtessa de Dia twice compares herself and her lover to such a pair, but in the crisscross pattern of the comparisons she likens herself to the male, not the female, lover. More importantly for the trobairitz, the desiring woman is abundantly available from the popularizing woman's song as well. The female speaker of the *chansons de femme* typically sings of her longings, her physical charms and desires, falls into despair without her lover to whom she offers total submission. In the face of his absence, she affirms her loyalty and pain, felt in the intensity of her desire (Bec, "'Trobairitz'" 252; Davidson 456; Earnshaw Ch. 3). The incantatory quality of Tibors' negations and repeated phrases, accumulated to suggest the power of her desire, recall with particular insistence the kind of effects achieved in the *cantigas de amigo:*

> Bels dous amics, ben vos puosc en ver dir
> qe anc non fo q'eu estes ses desir
> pos vos conuc ni.us pris per fin aman;
> ni anc no fo q'eu non agues talan,
> bels dous amics, q'eu soven no.us vezes (no. 36, 1-5)

> Fair, sweet friend, I can truly tell you
> I have never been without desire
> since I met you and took you as true lover;
> nor has it happened that I lacked the wish,
> my fair, sweet friend, to see you often.

Despite their apparent forthrightness, the trobairitz' expressions of desire remain couched in what Robbins has called "self-protective ambiguity even more multifaceted than the men's—it is always impossible to tell whether 'she does or doesn't' from their hypothetical situations, their daydreams and invitations, even their vows of (always future) surrender" ("Love's Martyrdoms"; cf. Paden, "Utrum" 81). The Comtessa de Dia would like to have her lover in (the) place of her husband, but the conditional verb suggests he hasn't been there yet. Clara d'Anduza refuses to give up her desire that only increases before others' reproaches (9-12), but the absence of her lover keeps her desire in the same state of unsatisfied longing that we associate with the typical troubadour lover himself. Indeed the expression of desire is as conventional for the male speaker of troubadour lyric, as it is for the female voice of the women's songs and offers another model the trobairitz use to their own ends. The feat of the women troubadours is to conflate two identities, male and female, in their own singing voice. As Robbins points out, the trobairitz thus reclaim and reconvert the role of love's martyr, which male troubadours first adapted from "the archetypal female figure of the virgin-martyr, the suffering saint whose death is an affirmation of love" ("Love's Martyrdoms").

This conversion and reconversion of male and female roles returns us to the issue of power, however "passively" that power may be expressed in the troubadours' "feminized" role. In troubadour lyric in general, the indissoluble link between power and love may strike us as one of the major themes of their poetry, and this is nowhere more compelling than in the *tensos* and *cansos* of the trobairitz, where the sexual balance of power often appears as the main issue debated, analyzed, and experienced. Issues of hierarchy and power are directly confronted when the trobairitz participate in the debate about the *ric ome,* the rich man (Sakari, "Thème"): should a lady love a man only if his social position is inferior to hers? Both Azalais de Porcairagues and Maria de Ventadorn take up polemical positions within that controversy and both use the language of fidelity oaths between lord and vassal to describe the relationship between lovers. In her *partimen* with Gui d'Ussel, Maria de Ventadorn herself chooses the subject for debate and places it squarely on the question of equality or hierarchy between lovers:

> vuoill qe.m digatz si deu far egalmen
> dompna per drut, qan lo qier francamen,
> cum el per lieis, tot cant taing ad amor,
> segon los dreitz que tenon l'amador. (no. 12, 5-8)

> I want you to tell me if a lady should do equally
> for her lover all that pertains to love,
> when he asks honestly, as he does for her,
> according to the laws that lovers hold.

The syntax of her question already demonstrates in its interlaced clauses how inextricably the lady and her lover are linked through the issues of desire and equality. Once Gui makes his choice for equality, Maria argues for maintaining the conventional, reversed hierarchy between *domna* and *drut*, with the lady in the position of power. She bases her argument on the troubadours' own words, their use of feudal language (which she quotes), when they offer themselves according to the ceremony of homage to the lord: on their knees, hands joined, they declare themselves the lady's vassal and offer their service freely.

> anz ditz chascus, qan vol preiar,
> mans iointas e de genolos:
> "Dompna, voillatz qe.us serva franchamen
> cum lo vostr'om," et ella enaissi.l pren. (35-40)

> instead each (lover), when he wants to court,
> says, with hands joined and on his knees;
> "Lady, permit me to serve you honestly
> as your liege man" and that's the way she takes him.

Franchamen (37), the same adverb that plays a key role in Maria's opening question—along with *egalmen* (5, 27, 28)—connotes not only the rank of a free man who participates in the reciprocal bond of fidelity and service, but also the conduct and manners appropriate to that social level. If the lady accepts that offer of service, then the servant/lover, vassal of his lady, must accept the consequences of his act: a declaration of equality in the face of such a hierarchical relationship constitutes treason: "Eu vo.l iutge per dreich a trahitor, si.s rend pariers e.is det per servidor" (39-40: "I rightly consider him a traitor if, having given himself as a servant, he makes himself an equal"), declares Maria in conclusion. Like the troubadours themselves, Maria extrapolates from the language of power relations a series of rights and obligations that limit or control the actions of the participants. Usually the lady is the target of the troubadours' complaints that she is not fulfilling her part of the feudal contract by rewarding loyal service; here the complaint falls on the man's head. He should obey her as "per amiga e per dompna eissamen" (22)—both lady and beloved—but she should honor her lover "cum ad amic, mas non cum a seignor" (24: "as a friend, but not as overlord") (N.B. the lord returns *onor*, a fief, in exchange for the vassal's service). She alone may occupy the position of authority. Appropriately, as initiator of this *tenso*, Maria has herself taken the lead, metrically and ideologically.

It is perhaps one of the great paradoxes of *fin'amor*, as elaborated by troubadours and trobairitz, to have focused on the powerful and disordering force of love, operating independently of social constraints, though not necessarily adulterous by definition, and to have elaborated that notion of love not as a malady (as in the classical conception), but as an emotion that can be channeled into a whole set of socially useful actions (courtliness in the largest sense), an emotion to be analyzed and explored with reference to principles of right and wrong. As Maria says, "segon los dreitz que tenon l'amador" (8). The parallel established between the feudal relationship of lord and vassal and the love relationship of lady and lover serves as one of the key tools for finding order within the basically disordering power of love (see Bruckner, "Fictions" 882-83; cf. Cheyette's analysis of the linguistic continuum connecting poetic and legal discourse of the period: both registers mix the languages of love and power relations).

Equally important for establishing order in disorder is the form of the *tenso* itself, the debate in which lovers argue and disagree, according to principles differently understood perhaps, but still applicable by general agreement. Hence the importance of the verb *dever* (should, ought to), invoked over and over again by both Maria (5, 19, 20, 21, 23) and Gui (14, 16, 27, 30, 32, 46, 48). The notion of a standard, rather than any particular standard, allows both for agreement and disagreement, as expressed within troubadour lyric. This agreement in disagreement is perhaps as fundamental to the *canso* as to the *tenso*, but the latter makes it more explicit, foregrounds the contest of rival views and poetic craft. If the system itself did not admit of differing points of view then there could be no *tenso*.

In order to argue for equality of the lovers, Gui d'Ussel shifts the principle by which to make such a judgment from the issue of rank to that of the quality or quantity of love shared by the lovers. If they are equally amorous, the lady should honor her lover equally (27-28). Gui repeats and elaborates the key adverb *egalmen* (cf. earlier *comunalmen* 14: in kind; *ses garda de ricor* 15: "without regard to rank"), by twice relating it to another important adverb that reflects one of the basic virtues of *fin'amor: finamen* (29; 46: "perfectly"). Just as Maria ignores in her replies Gui's attempt to redefine the nature of the argument in terms of the quality of shared love, his last stanza likewise constitutes a refusal to close the debate on her terms. Rephrasing the issue of equality in terms of the love itself, rather than the respective ranks of the lovers, Gui dictates Maria's future words as a choice *ad absurdum*: "Either you'll say (and not to your honor) / that the lover must love her more perfectly, / or you'll say that they are equals, / for he owes her nothing but what he gives for love" (45-48). A standoff in which the lady controls the opening statement, the man— inevitably by the formal principles of the *tenso* itself—the closing words, which he cleverly attributes to the lady herself.

Azalais de Porcairagues takes up her stance in this debate in stanza three of her *canso*, "Ar em al freg temps vengut":

Dompna met mout mal s'amor

> que ab ric ome plaideia,
> ab plus aut de vavasor;
> e s'ill o fai il folleia,
> car so diz om en Veillai
> que ges per ricor non vai,
> e dompna que n'es chauzida
> en tenc per envilanida. (no. 11, 17-24)

> A lady places her love poorly
> when she seeks out a man of wealth
> higher than a vavassor.
> If she does, she's acting foolish,
> for people in Velay say this:
> love does not go with riches.
> If a lady's known for that
> I consider her dishonored.

Her position in the debate requires the social rank of the lovers to correspond to a hierarchy in which the lady occupies the superior position, to
avoid the possible dishonor of attaching the lady's love to the coercions of
money and power. It may then surprise us to hear Azalais later in the same
song reverse her theoretical position by placing herself in the role of vassal, her lover in that of lord. She praises him, as the troubadour does his
lady: "Amic ai de gran valor / que sobre toz seignoreia" (25-26: "I have a
friend of utmost worth, / higher than all the others"). He has granted her
his heart and she is engaged forever in his service; to the lord's action of
granting (*autreia* 28) corresponds the vassal's promise of service (*en guatge*
34). The general issue of power phrased in terms of society's ranks for the
ric ome debate now transforms itself into a more personal mode through
the metaphorical relationship binding lover and beloved, with the twist
that in this *canso* the male and female roles are reversed, the female poet
conceding to her male beloved the power the troubadour invests in his
lady.

Sarah Kay (*Subjectivity* 104-05) points out a number of similarities
that suggest Azalais's *canso* plays off against two poems by Raimbaut d'Aurenga (probably designated in vv. 14 and 42), himself a champion of the
ric ome. In "Entre gel e vent e fanc" (no. XV in Pattison, ed.), sent to
Azalais under the *senhal* Joglar, we find a springtime opening also turned
upside down by winter's onslaught, as well as the unusual word *esglais* in
the rhyme position (Azalais 14; Raimbaut 34 and no. XXII 36, also sent to

Joglar). Equally striking is Raimbaut's invitation to the lady to put him to a test: "Mas mandatz mi per plans essais, / Per tal cobrir sol sapcha.l cais!" (47-48: "But command me to a clear trial [of my love], with such secretness that only the mouth will know it!").

In a variation produced by reversing the male/female roles, Azalais announces to her *amic* that she will soon place herself at his mercy:

> tost en veirem a l'assai,
> qu'en vostra merce.m metrai;
> vos m'aves la fe plevida,
> que no.m demandes faillida. (37-40)

> Soon we'll come to the test:
> I'll put myself at your mercy.
> You have given your word
> to ask nothing wrong of me.

These verses have kept scholars busy ever since René Nelli's theory about the *assag* as a ritual of courtly love. Whether or not they reflect such a custom (which may be too literal a reading of the game of poetry), these verses do offer a wonderful example of the concatenated, intertwined balance of power between man and woman as expressed in the political language of oaths and bonds. She will place herself in his power, yes, but according to his previous promise to ask her nothing that would constitute a failure. This is a perfect illustration of how power is conceded to the other, apparently superior, only to be ultimately controlled by the humble vassal. Azalais plays this game of disguised power as craftily as any troubadour lover, while also retaining for herself the position of open power declared in the *ric ome* stanza.

In fact, the trobairitz' way of appropriating and manipulating a linguistic and literary system created by male troubadours suggests that whoever assumes the position of speaker within that lyric system, whether male or female, will appear to attribute the power of lordship or control to the beloved other. As in Lacan's analysis of intersubjective relationships in Poe's *Purloined Letter*, what a character sees, says, or does depends more on the position occupied at a given moment than on any inherent feature that defines the character in the slot. The use of feudal language by troubadours and trobairitz may thus be keyed more to position than to gender per se, although gender shifts in the roles of subject and object may add new and changing resonances to the public's perception.

The test envisaged by Azalais recalls the Comtessa de Dia's great desire to hold her lover in the husband's place, on condition, she adds, that he promise to do all that she desires: "ab so que m'aguessetz plevit / de far tot so qu'eu volria" (no. 3, 23-24). We may wonder—and the Comtessa's expressions throughout the song encourage us to do so—if "all she would desire" calls for much or little from the lover. Among the trobairitz, the Comtessa's four *cansos* show her the most willing to try on a wide variety of self-images, as she sings (often simultaneously) from positions projected by the troubadour for himself or the *domna* or in a voice we associate more readily with the female singer in *chansons de femme*. Does she experiment here with the burlesque voice we can trace back to Guilhem IX's songs for his companions? Without going beyond the ambiguities of innuendo, she certainly enriches her verse with all the resources of suggestion.

Both Azalais's and the Comtessa's formulation of a test appears as part of a larger pattern that recurs in the trobairitz corpus: the interplay between desire and control, or rather, the desire for control over the beloved expressed in a variety of ways by women troubadours. As Maria de Ventadorn claimed in her *tenso* with Gui d'Ussel, the lover should obey his lady's commands, while she may grant his requests as coming from a friend, never obey them as commanded by a lord (no. 12, 23-24). Alamanda goes so far as to insist that a lover should believe all that his lady says—even if she declares a high mountain to be a plain (no. 13, 13-14)—and be pleased with all that she gives him, whether good or bad (15). Indeed it is precisely this kind of desire for control over all the lover's actions that Lanfranc Cigala laments in his *partimen* with Guilielma de Rosers: "qu'oimais vei zo qe de donas crezia: / qe no vos platz q'autre pelegrinatge / fassan li drut, mas ves vos tota via" (no. 22, 34-36: "now I see confirmed my belief about ladies: / for you, there's no other pilgrimage / lovers should make except, by all roads, to you"). Lovers, like horses, should be trained with good sense and measure, "car lo drutz cochatz tan malamen / lur faill poders" (39-40: "but you spur your lovers so harshly / that their powers fail"). Lanfranc's comparison introduces all sorts of innuendoes that Guilielma is quick to pick up and play with in her response (47-48).

Their witty repartee is typical of the kind of humorous attacks that characterize many of the debate poems and recalls another *partimen* in the trobairitz repertoire, that between Rofin and Domna H., which is based on a question whose form echoes Azalais's test: a lady invites her two lovers to swear an oath, before entering her bed, that they will do no more than hug and kiss her. The one who cares little about oaths swears immediately, the other does not. Rofin chooses the side of strict obedience and argues according to the conventional image of the humble lover who obeys his lady and wants only to please her. Since the lady has given Rofin the choice of which side to defend, she is obliged to argue on behalf of the lover who would break his oath under the effect of his passion for the lady, and she does so with great gusto, insisting that the lover's lack of restraint is an appropriate indication of his love. As in Lanfranc and Guilielma's *partimen*, the debate itself shifts from general question to personal confrontation, as the notion of the test reverberates between sexual and verbal contest. When Aimeric de Peguilhan and Elias d'Ussel debate a variation of the same question ("N'Elias, conselh vos deman")—phrased by Elias as a test offered to him by his lady—the public which recognizes the recurrent motif will be able to savor the ingenuities of each poet who reinvents situations and arguments within a common scenario (whose misogynistic overtones have been signalled by Kay, *Subjectivity* 99).

In each of these examples we see trobairitz and their male counterparts interacting not only within the poetic system as a whole, but more specifically listening and singing to each other, responding to and reinventing each other's songs, as they refashion the common materials of troubadour lyric. The trobairitz explore that system from a woman's point of view, without reducing women's points of view to unanimity. For readers who are attentive to their play, these female voices, whether invented by women poets or male troubadours, enrich and enlarge the scope of troubadour tradition.

Finding the Trobairitz

The twenty names of women troubadours supplied by manuscripts often pose as many questions as they seem to resolve. Can we attach a specific identity to an unqualified first name or a simple initial, as in the case of "Lombarda" or "Domna H."? Can we be confident that a real woman poet is designated by the name or is she a fiction invented by a male troubadour, as scholars have frequently speculated regarding not only the anonymous *domnas* but also named poets like Alamanda and Ysabella?

Margaret Switten's research suggests that trobairitz are identified by manuscript attributions about as reliably as troubadours (which is to say sometimes we can believe the manuscripts and sometimes not). Their distribution across *chansonniers* from different regions demonstrates a certain scarcity in the north (they appear in only one trouvère collection, W) and not much better representation in their home territory (C, E, and R, the important Provençal or Occitan collections have few of their songs). Their more hospitable reception in the Italian *chansonniers* (where the troubadours in general are better represented than anywhere else, but usually with no transmission of their melodies) may account for the fact that only one trobairitz song comes to us accompanied by its music ("A chantar" in W). While most manuscripts mix together songs of male and female poets, Pierre Bec and others have noted that some Catalan and Italian *chansonniers* of the 13th and 14th c. group them all together, as if recognizing at that point the anomaly of their appearance as female poets singing in a male-dominated tradition ("'Trobairitz'" 262; Paden, ed. "Poems" 163; Rieger, "'Ins e.l cor'" 389-91). These tend to be the same manuscripts whose authors, editors, or scribes feel the need to write biographies and commentaries that introduce the songs to an audience separated by time and geography from the Occitanian society in which they were originally composed and performed.

What do the *vidas* and *razos*, our first examples of vernacular literary history and interpretation, teach us about the trobairitz? Only five have *vidas*, all of them quite short: Tibors, Comtessa de Dia, Azalais de Porcairagues, Castelloza, and Lombarda. Lombarda's *vida* quickly becomes a more elaborate *razo* that sets into a narrative explanation the *coblas* she exchanges with Bernart Arnaut. In similar fashion, *razos* allegedly explain the *tensos* between Almuc de Castelnau and Iseut de Capio, Maria de Ventadorn and Gui d'Ussel, Guillelma de Rosers and Lanfranc Cigala, Alamanda and Giraut de Bornelh. Garsenda, the Countess of Provence, is mentioned as the object of love and song in the *vidas* of Elias de Barjols and Gui de Cavaillon. Clara d'Anduza appears in a *razo* to one of Uc de Saint Circ's songs. If we include Gaudairenca from Raimon de Miraval's *razo*, this brings to thirteen the total number of trobairitz named in *vidas* and *razos* (one hundred and one names are listed in the Table of Contents of the *Biographies des troubadours*).

More importantly, Bec's brief analysis of the length and contents of these *vidas* and *razos* points out that biographers seem to have made no fundamental distinction between male and female poets in their use of commonplaces or style in general ("'Trobairitz'" 238-39). Ladies—and they are all *domnas*—whether loved by troubadours, loving in turn, or only protecting the poets who sing their praises (multiple roles frequently combined), are described with the same adjectives, the same set of qualities, taken for the most part from the lyrics themselves. The trobairitz are *gentil*, *bella, avinens, enseignada* (noble, beautiful, charming, educated). Maria de Ventadorn is "la plus preziada dompna qe anc fos en Lemozin" (Boutière-Schutz 213: "the most prized lady ever found in Limousin"). The women are frequently described as having composed or knowing how to compose songs (*trobar*). As Tibors' biographer says: "cortesa fo et enseignada, avinens e fort maïstra; e saup trobar" (Boutière-Schutz 498: "she was courteous/courtly and educated, charming and very learned, and she knew how to compose songs").

Each biography locates the lady in a place, gives her a lover (often named) and sometimes a husband. The Comtessa de Dia, for example, is described as the wife of "En Guillem de Peitius," but she loves and sings about Raimbaut d'Aurenga (Boutière-Schutz 445). Despite her highly unusual name (Paden, ed. "Poems" 158-59), Castelloza is firmly situated in Auvergne as the wife of Turc de Mairona; her beloved and the subject of her songs is identified as Arman de Breon (Boutière-Schutz 333). Love and desire for fame frequently go hand in hand in this world, as we see in the rest of Tibors' *vida* where she is described as both loving and loved ("enamorada" and "fort amada per amor"), honored by all the good men, feared and obeyed by all the worthy ladies of the region (Boutière-Schutz 498). Clara d'Anduza's desire for worth and praise inspires first Uc de St. Circ's songs and then their mutual love, according to the *razo* (Boutière-Schutz 244), and in similar fashion we are told how Azalais loved Gui Guerrejat and "fez de lui maintas bonas cansos" (Boutière-Schutz 342: "she made many good songs about him"). The gender of the pronouns may change, but the kinds of relationships illustrated remain the same. What we see represented in the *vidas* and *razos*, as well as in the songs, is a network of crisscrossed ties linking men and women, loved and loving, troubadours and trobairitz, patrons and patronesses, husbands and wives, rivals, friends, and relatives. The legendary level—the stories invented around the poems—parallels and elaborates the intertextual allusions of the songs themselves, in which trobairitz poems respond to those of the troubadours (Robbins, "Love's Martyrdoms").

To what extent can we believe the information so gleaned? Scholarly research suggests that a good deal of historical information lies buried in these *vidas*, but sometimes it eludes our grasp or seems to be garbled with an overlay of romance generated by the situations implied in the lyrics (and therefore repeated from one *vida* or *razo* to another). Turc de Mairona, for example, is named independently of Castelloza in a *sirventes* by Dalfin d'Alvernha, but no other historical documentation can verify the three figures mentioned in her *vida* or their relationships (Paden, ed. "Poems" 159-

62). Tibors, located by her *vida* in Provence at the castle of Lord Blacatz (Boutière-Schutz 498) is also named as the judge in a *tenso* between Bertran de Saint-Felix and Uc de la Bacalaria and may appear as "Na Tibortz de Proensa" in a *dansa* by Guiraut d'Espanha (Boutière-Schutz 499 n2; Bec, ed. 66-67). With these clues, research on Raimbaut d'Aurenga has yielded enough to suggest that Tibors (a common name at that time) was either Raimbaut's mother or, more likely, his sister, the wife of Bertrand des Baux, a major patron of the troubadours (Pattison 10-27; Bogin 162-63). The Comtessa de Dia might be Beatrice, wife of William II of Poitiers, count of Valentinois, a contemporary of Raimbaut d'Aurenga (her name is often given to the Comtessa de Dia in anthologies), or Isoarde, the daughter of the Count of Die and wife of Raimon d'Agout who lived at the time of Raimbaut IV, a generation later (Pattison 27-30). Jean-Charles Huchet suggests the *vida* simply invents a literary fiction that brings the Comtessa into the presence of two great troubadours, the founder Guilhem IX and Raimbaut d'Aurenga, one of the masters of twelfth-century *trobar* (62-63). Based on the extant documents, no definitive identification seems possible, although Rieger's formal analysis of the Comtessa de Dia's songs locates them in the second half of the twelfth century and associates her through intertextual evidence with the circle of poets that includes Raimbaut d'Aurenga, Bernart de Ventadorn, and Azalais de Porcairagues (614, 621).

With other trobairitz archival research yields more positive identification and information. Take the example of "la contesa de Proensa," as she is named in Ms. F, or Garsenda, as she appears in two troubadour *vidas*. Stanislaw Stronski identifies her as the daughter of Raines de Claustral de Forcalquier, Garsenda, granddaughter of Guilhem IV, last particular count of Forcalquier ("Notes" 22-23). She brought Forcalquier as a dowry upon her marriage in 1193 to Alphonse II, count of Provence, brother of Pedro II of Aragon. According to Elias de Barjol's *vida*, she served as his literary patron after her husband's death. This occurred in 1209, after which her role at the court in Aix can be divided into two periods. Between 1209 and 1216, while her son Raimon-Berangar lived with the father's family in Aragon, she had neither title nor official authority at Aix, since these were usurped by her brother-in-law, Pedro II. In 1216 when her son returned, Garsenda successfully reclaimed her guardianship and exercised full authority in Aix until her son's majority and marriage to Beatrice of Savoy in 1219/20. As this new Countess of Provence claimed all the troubadours' attention, Garsenda retired to a nearby monastery, the abbey of La Celle, where she took her vows in 1225, with the proviso that she would retire completely only after she settled some outstanding affairs (Stronski 23-26). During her life, Garsenda thus played a key role in the power struggle between the Forcalquier family and the Counts of Provence, two of the most powerful and important noble families of southern France (Bogin 172), not only through her marriage but also through the guardianship she exercised during her son's minority, when she acted directly in the games of feudal power politics.

Maria de Ventadorn, daughter of Helis de Castelnau and Raimon II, Viscount of Turenne (1143-1191) in the Limousin, became the second wife (ca. 1190?) of Eble V, the great-grandson of one of the founding troubadours, Eble II (ca. 1106-47), and the grandson of Eble III, patron and rival of Bernart de Ventadorn (Rieger, "La *mala canso*" 1072-73). Bertran de Born praised the beauty of Maria and her two sisters ("las tres de Torena," Rieger 1072), and Maria herself became an important patron of troubadours. She frequently appears in that role in dedicatory closing stanzas (*tornadas*), as well as in a number of *razos*, where she may be evoked as beloved, intercessor (e.g. in a *razo* for Pons de Capdoill, Boutière-Schutz 314-15), or inspiration to song. In a long *razo* linking several of Gaucelm Faidit's songs, for example, Maria is presented as the object of his love and songs, whose praise she enjoys without returning his love (Boutière-Schutz 170-76). Maria served as patroness for an impressive list of troubadours—who dedicate their songs to her or ask her to adjudicate their poetic debates—including Gaucelm, Gui de Puycibot, Giraut Rostanh de Merguas, the four Ussel poets, the Monk of Montaudon, Pons de Capdoill, Uc de Saint-Circ, Savaric de Mauleon, and Guiraut de Calanson (Bogin 169; Rieger, "La *mala canso*" 1073).

While none of these facts can tell us exactly why Maria or Garsenda themselves became trobairitz, they do reveal something about the kind of society in which troubadour lyric flourished and about the roles women could play in it. It is a commonplace of troubadour scholarship to explore the mysterious origins of courtly love in an effort to explain a poetic world that turns upside down our notions of patriarchal medieval society, in which women are necessarily and clearly subordinated to men, according to the combined ideologies of Christianity and feudalism. Sociological and historical approaches like Erich Köhler's and Georges Duby's seek, in some sense, to rectify the scandal of making a *domna* the ruling party in a feudal relationship and having her served by the humble poet vassal. If we understand, according to these theories, that the lady is really a stand-in for her husband (the *dominus*) in the struggle of landless knights or young bachelors to gain fiefs, then the lady is cleverly removed once again from a position of real power and restored to the subordinate status that befits her. Although it would be foolhardy to argue for matriarchy in Southern France or to read troubadour poetry as a direct mirror of society, historical research suggests that Occitanic society, in comparison with Northern France, did offer women wider scope for exercising power and participating in economic and political life. Codes of law persisted there allowing women a more privileged status, especially in relation to inheriting property, and the crusades left noble women at home with great administrative responsibilities (Bogin 20-36; Herlihy "Land" 89-120). Southern France was remarkable both for the extent of women's lands and the use of matronymics, despite feudalism's theoretical exclusion of women from seigniory (Herlihy "Land" 108).

By analyzing the language of legal charters, lists of witnesses, and the men and women designated as taking and receiving oaths, social historian Fredric Cheyette suggests that a disjuncture between powerful women in lyric and powerless women in patriarchal society simply does not apply to the Occitan society of this period. The rich, urbanized Occitania of the twelfth century did not make it difficult for the petty nobility or younger brothers to establish themselves economically, nor did it exclude women from all power relations. Ermengarde of Narbonne, for example, exercised military and political power in her own name, regardless of her marital status. As well documented as any lay lord of her time and place, the childless Ermengarde acted in relation to her sister's sons, their property rights and rights of succession, with what Cheyette calls "a powerful sense of dynasty, patrilineal, to be sure, yet not transportable by marriage into another patriline. In the absence of a male heir, it was women who were expected to maintain dynastic continuity, to train their sons or nephews or daughters in the traditions and rights of their *maternal* line" (11; italics in original).

Ermengarde has usually been viewed as exceptional, yet Cheyette describes her as typical within the larger pattern of relationships in Occitania, which were based primarily on *covinens*, personal ties and pledges of faithfulness. The language of oaths, as well as that of contracts of sale and gift, indicate that women and men were frequently in relations of power, fidelity, and service: at certain places and times men swore oaths of fidelity to women, to whom they were expected to give the same loyalty and service as to male lords; some charters show women giving such oaths to men as well. Legal documents of the period do not simply generalize in the masculine form, but specify the possible actions of men or women ("si homo aut femina"), either of whom might break their contracts and agreements (Cheyette 13).

As frequently happens, our preconceptions about the Middle Ages need to be modified, or at the very least nuanced by more detailed knowledge of specific times and places. What Duby finds to be true for the "juvenes" in Northwestern France does not necessarily apply to the South. Women's choices may be severely restricted in medieval society, as we are reminded by alternatives set up in Alaisina's *tenso* with Carenza (no. 27) or in "Coindeta sui" (no. 33), where the female speaker has no desire for her husband and would like him to be as young and gay as her lover. But we can also glimpse how troubadour songs may allude (however indirectly) to moments and places where women do exercise some power. Consider in this light the study of Martí Aurell i Cardona which begins by describing through a number of specific examples the privileged status of women in tenth-century Provence. From this highpoint, he then demonstrates an over-all deterioration in the position of aristocratic women in Southern France from the tenth to the thirteenth centuries, linked to a shift from "hypergamy" (men marrying women above them in the social scale) to "hypogamy" (men marrying their social inferiors). Despite this general trend, however, the Catalan historian identifies a kind of renaissance in women's status in the period between 1180 and 1230, which corresponds approximately to the period when the trobairitz were singing (see also Paden, *Voice* 1-19; cf. Courtemanche, who analyzes the position of women in fourteenth-century Provence).

Both literary and historical analysis lead us to understand troubadour lyric and the *fin'amor* it proclaims as manifestations of an elaborate social game, enjoyed, practiced, and performed in song by both men and women of the Occitanic courts. While the poetic system of the troubadours spread widely across the European continent and enjoyed tremendous success for hundreds of years, only in Southern France did it produce a substantial number of women poets. As far as we can determine, they were active from around 1170 until about 1260: they began singing after the first two generations of troubadours brought their poetic system to its classical stage and ceased before the last generation of the troubadours themselves fell silent (Paden, *Voice* 14). Although we may never be able to explain just why they existed, clues lie in the characteristics of the society in which troubadour lyric originated and in the roles associated with singing, com-posing, and patronizing troubadour song in the life of the Occitan courts.

The Trobairitz Corpus

Measured against the approximately 2500 troubadour songs in manuscript, the corpus of the trobairitz presents a sample in miniature of the major and some of the minor lyric genres cultivated by the troubadours: *cansos* (love songs, the most prestigious and cultivated form among the troubadours), *tensos* (debate poems), *sirventes* (political poems), *planh* (lament), *salut d'amor* (a love letter not in strophic form), and several of the popularizing genres with refrains, *alba* (dawn song) and *balada* (dance song). Only part of one stanza from Tibors's *canso* reaches us; "Dieus sal" also appears in manuscript as a fragment (from a *canso* or a *chanson d'ami*). All the other trobairitz are represented by a single poem, except the Comtessa de Dia (four *cansos*) and Castelloza (three *cansos* or four, if one accepts Paden's and Rieger's arguments for assigning to her the anonymous *canso*, "Per ioi"). We might compare this with the typical extant output of the troubadours in general, which is calculated at about three or four poems apiece (Tavera 146).

The smallness of the corpus is, however, no great advantage for overcoming a number of uncertainties that make its delineation as problematic as counting the number of identifiable trobairitz. Recent editions have varied from twenty-three poems (Bogin) to forty-six (Rieger). Paden's checklist of poems by named and anonymous trobairitz, whether believed to be historical or fictional women, tallies forty-nine poems (*Voice* 227-37). The thirty-six selected for this edition include two (no. 33 and no. 34) of the three listed by Paden but not published by Rieger, whose "maximal corpus" does not include popularizing songs in which the woman's voice is not, in her view, an independent one. The difference in numbers and much of the scholarly discussion about what should be included in the trobairitz corpus involves recognizing that, within the troubadour corpus as a whole, we need to distinguish between real women poets composing songs and women's voices singing in lyric, whether invented by male or female poets (Bruckner, "Fictions"). The distinction is easy enough to grasp, but we cannot always be sure where and exactly how it applies in particular cases, especially (but not only) when a song appears anonymously in the *chansonniers*.

This question of gender and authorship involves a number of issues, first among them the role and character of woman's song and its links with troubadour lyric. The existence of the trobairitz themselves suggests a tradition of woman's song in the south of France, even if it was not often set down in manuscript (Bec, "'Trobairitz'" 254). As Pierre Bec has indicated, the lady who decides to compose in the aristocratic style of the troubadour has at her disposal a range of female voices from the popularizing genres: *chansons d'ami*, *albas*, *chansons de mal mariées*, and *chansons de toile* (252-59).

Doris Earnshaw hypothesizes that the energetic and outspoken female persona invented by troubadours (like the feisty shepherdess in Marcabru's *pastorela*) helps explain both the presence of women poets in the troubadour tradition and their almost complete absence elsewhere in medieval lyric (155-59). Although female personae that appear in *chansons de femme* composed in different Romance vernaculars generally share the same basic characteristics, the female character who speaks through the Old Provençal poets has to a certain extent been influenced by the characteristics of the male voice. Whereas female speech is typically marked in woman's songs by an incantatory or archaic style, the female voice in Marcabru, for example, is more rationalizing: she is witty and forthright. In Earnshaw's view, it is just such a female persona that invites real women poets to compose troubadour songs, to speak out in their medium.

What we can know with certainty is that men and women were borrowing each others' voices as formalized by different poetic traditions, each combining characteristics of the aristocratic troubadour style with the popularizing woman's song—characteristics that may contrast or overlap in particular instances (cf. Mölk's typology for two perspectives within the popular register, *chanson de femme* and *chanson d'homme*, both opposed to the elevated style of troubadour lyric). Bec distinguishes between *fémininité génétique*, where the poet is a woman, and *textualité féminine*, where the voice is female but the poet is not necessarily ("'Trobairitz'" 258). This is a useful and necessary distinction for working with this corpus, but it does not guarantee that a given poem whose attribution is in dispute can be pronounced with certainty the work of a trobairitz or a troubadour. The personae created by identifiable male poets through the autobiographical claims of the first person are constructed as a game that revels in fictional role-playing, however tantalizingly the fictions cross over and play with a reality that can sometimes be historically documented. Even in the *sirventes*, a genre that frequently alludes to specific circumstances and real people, the poet creates a fiction of himself that does not quite coincide with his historical reality, as the most recent editors of Bertran de Born's poetry have so masterfully demonstrated (Paden, Sankovitch, Stäblein, eds.).

Women poets, no less than their male counterparts, may avail themselves of the possibilities of fiction, whether they speak in a voice identified with their proper name, with their title as lady, or in the typically anonymous voice of the popularizing genres (cf. Zink, "Remarques"). In a corpus like the troubadours', where a not inconsiderable group of women poets can be documented, it does not seem unreasonable to suppose that some of the unknown ladies or the anonymous female voices are invented by women. Where there is no specific reason to disqualify "anonymous" as a woman, we have admitted her poems to the trobairitz repertoire, in order to give readers the full range of female voices singing in the context of troubadour lyric. Thus, the *alba,* "En un vergier" (no. 34), and the *balada,* "Coindeta sui" (no. 33, also a kind of *chanson de mal mariée*), give readers access to two examples of this popularizing, anonymous female voice, which may also be observed elsewhere in the *balada,* "Quan lo gilos er fora" (cf. the *canso* with refrain, "Quan vei les praz verdesir").

A second issue raised by the question of gender and authorship involves the way scholars deal with manuscript attributions. As suggested above, these attributions are not always reliable: when do we decide to put them into question for the trobairitz? Ms. T attributes "Na Maria" (no. 10) to "nabietris deroman," easily recognizable as Lady Bietris de Roman (Zufferey 32). ("Bietris" has also been read as "Bieris.") Nevertheless, this attribution has frequently been discussed and rejected, because the poem in question is addressed to a lady in a language and style identical to those of the troubadour addressing his beloved. The resulting speculations that ensue include allegorical interpretations of Maria as the Virgin, discussions of possible lesbianism (rejected by Rieger, "Was Bieris?"), and the transformation of the poet's sex. Most recently, for example, Elizabeth Wilson Poe has reanimated Schultz-Gora's suggestion and argued for reading the attribution as a reference to Alberico da Romano. She has, at the same time, elaborated an argument for putting into question the attributions of poems by Azalais d'Altier, Clara d'Anduza, Iseut de Capion and Almuc de Castelnou, based on her reading of the poems themselves and Uc de Saint-Circ's authorship of many *vidas* and *razos.* Poe claims that Uc himself, the promotor of trobairitz, would be the poet behind all of these compositions—an argument that William Paden finds unconvincing ("Recent Studies" 111-12).

A *sirventes* (no. 28) against the defamation of women by *antic trobador* (old time troubadours), spoken by a woman's voice, is attributed to Raimon Jordan in ms. C. Although a number of scholars have noticed the possible discrepancy, Rieger is the first to include it in an anthology of trobairitz, along with two other *sirventes*, "Ab greu cossire" (here no. 29, attributed by its unique manuscript R to an unidentified P. Basc and not included in Paden's checklist or Zufferey), and Gormonda de Monpeslier's "Greu m'es a durar" (no. 30). Gormonda's poem, a passionate and angry response to Guilhem Figueira's attack against Rome, "D'un sirventes far" (which furnishes the model stanza by stanza for Gormonda's defense of Rome: see Städtler, "The *Sirventes*"), was left out of Schulz-Gora and Bogin's anthologies and thus overlooked by Bec in his response to Bogin's edition ("'Trobairitz'" 237). Although women poets may not have been frequent participants in the political and moral arena of the *sirventes*, these few examples are precious reminders that medieval women and female voices can be heard even in discourses dominated by men.

The most disputed territory in the trobairitz repertoire concerns the *tensos* between male and female speakers. When Maria de Ventadorn invites Gui d'Ussel to participate in a *partimen* (a type of debate poem in which the two parties take up opposing sides on a question proposed by the initiator, also known as *joc partit*), scholars have no trouble recognizing that the female speaker in her *tenso* has been invented by a woman poet (though we have yet to determine what may be at stake in that identification). But the list of twenty-six *tensos* brought together in Angelica Rieger's edition of the trobairitz (twenty-three of which involve male and female speakers) includes many named and anonymous ladies where we cannot always be sure if we are dealing with historical women poets or *textualité féminine* created by male troubadours. Elias Cairel's historical existence is attested by his *vida*, but who is Ysabella, named only by the troubadour in their shared *tenso* (no. 18)? Who are the anonymous ladies debating with named poets like Bertran del Pojet (no. 15), Pistoleta (no. 17), and Raimon de las Salas (no. 24)? Medievalists have frequently pronounced such trobairitz to be fictions.

Ladies who debate with celebrated poets are especially vulnerable to speculations that they are simply literary fictions. Despite her named presence in "Si.us quier conseil" (no. 13) and the *razo* that accompanies it, Alamanda is frequently declared the creation of Giraut de Bornelh, since only his name appears in the fourteen manuscript attributions that identify the poem with the work of the "maestre dels trobadors" (Boutière-Schutz 39). Rieger has recently argued, on the basis of intertextual allusions and historical clues, that Alamanda, whose name also appears in poems by Bertran de Born and Bernart Arnaut, was a real woman, Alamanda de

Castelnau, whose tombstone can be seen at the Musée des Augustins in Toulouse ("Alamanda de Castelnau" 47-57). Rieger's demonstration may or may not convince (see Chambers and Paden, "Recent Studies" 109). The three manuscripts that contain "Amics, en gran cossirier" (no. 25) name only Raimbaut, but many modern scholars have followed the suggestion of the Comtessa de Dia's *vida* and named her as the female speaker addressed only as *domna* in the *tenso*. Judging by the power of her poetic accomplishments, Alfred Jeanroy (2: 257) even wonders if she might be the sole author of both voices. Using situational and verbal similarities between this *tenso* and the Comtessa de Dia's poems (especially the opening line of "Estat ai en greu cossirier"), Walter Pattison (27-30) suggests the process whereby her biographer may have invented the *vida*. He then uses the same kind of stylistic argument to link the *tenso* to Raimbaut d'Aurenga's corpus, since both speakers express ideas typical of that troubadour. Judging the lady's wit to be "more in keeping with Raimbaut's other works than those of the Countess" (157), Pattison concludes by giving sole authorship to Raimbaut, although none of his arguments excludes the possibility of a female poet debating the troubadour, whether or not she may be identified with the Comtessa de Dia (cf. Sakari's argument for identifying the *domna* as Azalais de Porcairagues, "Azalais Interlocutrice").

It does seem likely that some *tensos* between troubadours and anonymous ladies were fictional dialogues. When Raimbaut de Vaqueiras debates with a lady, whose Genoese language and earthy style contrast with the poet's elegant Provençal, the resulting parodic *tenso* reflects most probably the linguistic pyrotechnics of Raimbaut's own art, elsewhere displayed in his multilingual *descort* (but see Gaunt for a reading that credits the independence of the female speaker). When male and female speakers alternate phrases within the same line, as in Arnaut Plagues and Felipa's "Ben volgra midons saubes" (no. 20), we may find it difficult to believe that two poets have really invented the dialogue for two voices, even though the lady is named in the first of two *tornadas*. On the other hand, when a *tenso* between two male poets is recorded with one of them unidentified, scholars rarely raise the issue of fictionality (Gaunt 302).

In the corpus of nine or ten fictional *tensos* between male and female speakers discussed by Marianne Shapiro ("'Tenson'" 292-93, 293 n10, 299 n10), most of the designations regarding their fictionality are based on stylistic evaluations, rather than textual or historical evidence: the popular language and humor (e.g. Guillem Rainol d'Apt's "Quant aug chantar lo gal sus en l'erbos"), the obscenity of the speakers (e.g. Montan's "Eu veing vas vos, seigner"), or perhaps the frame supplied by the male poet's open-ing or closing stanza (e.g. Pistoleta's "Bona Domna, un conseill" [no. 17] and Guillem Rainol d'Apt's "Quant aug"). In a more recent evaluation of debate poems between men and women, Frank Chambers opts for fictional *tensos* composed by a male poet in sixteen out of twenty-two cases. When names in manuscript rubrics or poems cannot be substantiated with his-torical information, these evaluations tend to reflect subjective and cultur-ally-determined assumptions about how "ladies" speak or what kind of humor they indulge in. In our concern to explore the gender question in the trobairitz corpus, it is particularly important to avoid falling once again into the trap of characterizing "woman," whether she is the poet outside the poem or a character within it, as an essence that can be neatly defined and delimited.

Witty insults and sexual innuendoes characteristic of the humor fa-vored in many *tensos* remind us how the courtly register of lyric poetry plays implicitly—and sometimes explicitly—with the uncourtly. The reg-ister of the burlesque has often been excluded from the canon of trouba-dour lyric, whether in medieval manuscripts or in modern anthologies, and much has probably been lost. Yet, as elsewhere in medieval literary tradi-tions (cf. the Goliards in Latin lyric), the uncourtly functions in a kind of creative tension with the courtly model, defining and sometimes penetrat-ing its shifting borders. If we judge by the scant manuscript evidence, fe-male voices operating in the burlesque mode speak no less aggressively than male ones, as we see in the *tenso* between a *domna* and Peire Duran (no. 19). Must we assume that all these female speakers are fictions?

Given that, in a significant number of cases, we cannot determine with any certitude if the female speaker is created by a troubadour or a trobairitz, we may at times have no choice but to put aside the question of the poet's gender and the effect it might have on the kind of fiction created for the female voice. Perhaps our reading of the *tenso* between Raimbaut and an unidentified *domna* would not change in any significant way, whether we think it was composed by one poet or two. On the other hand, it may not always be so simple to put aside the sex of the poet, even if we cannot determine which it is. Sometimes it does matter if the author behind the fiction of a female speaker is really a man or a woman. We may read or react differently if we think a piece is written by a man or a woman.

For example, in an exchange between Raimon de las Salas and an anony-mous *domna*, "Si.m fos grazis," the male poet's three stanzas begin like a *canso*, with two stanzas describing his lady's indifference and his pain.

The third stanza addresses her directly and asks for a favorable glance (no. 24, 19-20: "humil semblaz / vas mi"). In the following two stanzas, the lady herself assures him of her love and puts the blame for her feigned indifference on the shoulders of *lauzengier*, "una genz enoiosa e fera" (33: "troublesome and savage people"). If we agree with Chambers, who believes this lady is a fiction (since she says exactly what the troubadour wants to hear), we interpret the last two stanzas as a fantasy: troubadour lyric's most intense joys are frequently those of dream and poetry. Raimon may project the lady of his wishes into the "reality" of his song, but that reality remains hypothetical, limited to the confines of art. But what if a real woman poet responded to Raimon de las Salas and played the role of his beloved? Then seeing a lady, too, declaring her love, giving herself loyally and leaving her heart as pledge ("en gauge," 32), we might interpret the song as proof that *fin'amor* is not limited to Narcissistic projection by the male lover: mutual love can be declared within the realm of possibilities expressed in lyric (even if that does not happen often). The silent *domna* may occasionally speak for herself. Of course, this interpretation does not escape the confines and conventions of art; it simply includes more possibilities within it. Do we need to posit a woman poet in order to explore that second reading? What if the song's two voices were both composed by the male poet, but a woman performed the song with Raimon or another man? What if a man or a woman sings both roles?

The possibilities for speculation are endless, and this is precisely the game of fiction and illusion invited by troubadour lyric in general: any one of us can try on the song's expression of love; our own first person will each time move into the place of the singer, make the feelings our own, at least for the space of the song. With this song the stakes of assigning authorship may not seem very high, but elsewhere, especially in controversial areas that involve the balance of power between the sexes, our choices are not innocuous (Bruckner, "Debatable Fictions").

The high percentage of *tensos* in the trobairitz repertoire contrasts with the troubadour corpus as a whole, dominated by the large proportion of *cansos* (only 194 *tensos* are listed in István Frank's inventory of 2548 troubadour songs). The balance within the trobairitz corpus—however accidental it may be, given the likelihood that many poems have been lost—draws our attention to the way women's voices take an active role in dialogue with men's (in *"En Conselh"* Rieger gives an overview of the twenty-six *tensos* included in her edition). It also reflects the degree to which the question of hierarchy and the balance of power between lovers and ladies functions as a major issue of troubadour lyric and a matter of dispute between its male and female interpreters. Where the troubadour's *canso* enacts through a single voice the reversed hierarchy of *fin'amor*—though with the power still ultimately held by the speaking poet/lover—the *tenso* asks questions about that balance of power within the more equal contest of the debate form. Jean-Charles Huchet has argued that the feminine Other (to which he reduces the trobairitz by denying their historical existence) puts into question the fundamental givens of the troubadours' poetic system. We might see this contestation rather as already inscribed in the *tenso*, one of the major lyric genres, even when it occurs between two male poets. The *tensos* remind us repeatedly that disagreement, different points of view, and different ideals, are as much a part of troubadour lyric as the shared motifs, vocabulary, and themes that, to an uninitiated public, make so many of the songs seem like the same song. But the introduction of a woman's point of view does make that *mise en question* more striking—and, especially important, introduces it not only in the male/female *tensos*, but in the *canso* as well.

The eleven *cansos* composed by women include some of the finest lyrics in the troubadour repertoire. In them we can see most vividly how the trobairitz are able to renew the troubadour's poetic system from within by combining in a variety of ways the different personae of women generally separated and fragmented by the male poets—the images of the desiring woman from *chansons de femme*, the *domna* of troubadour lyric, as well as the "feminized" "I" of the male poet/lover himself, reclaimed for the trobairitz' own female voice. Through the kaleidoscope of her songs, the trobairitz becomes at once woman, lady, and poet (for detailed analysis and comparison of the Comtessa de Dia's and Castelloza's strategies, for example, see Bruckner, "Fictions"). Whether in the *canso*, the *tenso*, or other lyric genres represented in this corpus, we can see the women poets interacting with their male counterparts, setting up a dialogue that demonstrates their mastery and manipulation of a poetic system shaped by the troubadours (cf. Paterson's argument for individuality among the troubadours).

In the context of such a tradition, even when we listen to historical women poets speaking in the first person, we may never hear the direct, spontaneous expression of a "real" woman's voice. The trobairitz, like the troubadours, operate in a lyric whose fiction would have us believe its claims to speak truthfully from the heart. If the song succeeds, we may indeed believe—for the space of a performance. But the initiated public, who appreciates the game of *trobar* as it was played in the courts of Occitania, cannot forget that each of the trobairitz' songs (re)invents, within the varied parameters of the highly formalized lyric system, an individual voice whose difference can be heard only in interaction with other voices, male and female, from the brilliant and varied chorus of troubadour lyric.

MTB

Manuscripts Consulted

The following manuscripts were consulted for the preparation of this edition:

A   Rome, Biblioteca vaticana, lat. 5232; parchment; 13th century; Italy

B   Paris, Bibliothèque Nationale, fr. 1592; parchment; 13th century; Italy

C   Paris, Bibliothèque Nationale, fr. 856; parchment; 14th century; Narbonne

D   Modena, Biblioteca Estense, α.R.4.4; parchment; 13th century; Italy

F   Rome, Biblioteca vaticana, Chigi L. IV,106; parchment; 14th century; Italy

H   Rome, Biblioteca vaticana, lat. 3207; parchment; 13th century; Italy

I   Paris, Bibliothèque Nationale, fr. 854; parchment; 13th century; Italy

K   Paris, Bibliothèque Nationale, fr. 12473; parchment; 13th century; Italy

L   Rome, Biblioteca vaticana, lat. 3206; parchment; 14th century; Italy

M   Paris, Bibliothèque Nationale, fr. 12474; parchment; 14th century; Italy

N   New York, Pierpont Morgan Library, 819; parchment; 14th century; Italy

O   Rome, Biblioteca vaticana, lat. 3208; parchment; 14th century;

Italy

Q   Florence, Biblioteca Riccardiana, 2909; parchment; 14th century; Italy

R   Paris, Bibliothèque Nationale, fr. 22543; parchment; 14th century; Languedoc

T   Paris, Bibliothèque Nationale, fr. 15211; parchment; 15th century; Italy

V   Venice, Biblioteca Marciana, fr. App. cod. XI; parchment; 1268; Catalonia

W   Paris, Bibliothèque Nationale, fr. 844; parchment; 13th century; France

a   Florence, Biblioteca Riccardiana, 2814 and Modena, Biblioteca Estense, Campori g. N.8.4, 11, 12, 13; the two parts of a 16th-century copy from Tarascona of an anthology compiled in the late 13th or early 14th century by Bernart Amoros of Auvergne, a cleric and student of troubadour poetics

"G"   Barcelona, Biblioteca de Catalunya; late 14th century; Catalonia

Bibliography

Dictionaries and Grammars:

Anglade, Joseph. *Grammaire de l'ancien provençal ou ancienne langue d'oc.* Paris: Klincksieck, 1977.

Crescini, Vincenzo. *Manuale per l'avviamento agli studi proenzali.* Milan: Hoepli, 1926.

Grandgent, C. H. *An Outline of the Phonology and Morphology of Old Provençal.* Boston: Heath, 1905.

Hamlin, Frank R. et al. *Introduction à l'étude de l'ancien provençal.* Geneva: Droz, 1967.

Jensen, Frede. *The Syntax of Medieval Occitan.* Tübingen: Niemeyer, 1986.

Levy, Emil and Carl Appel. *Provenzalisches Supplement-Wörterbuch.* 8 vols. Leipzig: Reisland, 1894-1924.

Levy, Emil. *Petit dictionnaire provençal-français.* Heidelberg: Winter, 1973.

Raynouard, François-Just-Marie. *Lexique roman ou Dictionnaire de la langue des troubadours.* 6 vols. Paris: Silvestre, 1836-44.

Roncaglia, Aurelio. *La lingua dei trovatori.* Rome: Ateneo, 1965.

Smith, Nathaniel and Thomas G. Bergin. *An Old Provençal Primer.* New York: Garland, 1984.

—. "Usual Pronunciation of Late 12th-Century Old Occitan as Spelled in Modern Editions." *Tenso* 6.2 (1981): 51-56.

Von Wartburg, W. *Französisches etymologisches Wörterbuch.* Bonn: Klopp, 1928.

Editions, Anthologies and Translations:

Action Poétique, 1978.

Albert-Birot, Arlette. "Du côté de Clara d'Anduze." In *Mélanges de littérature du moyen âge et du XXe siècle offerts à Mademoiselle Jeanne Lods.* 2 vols. Paris: Ecole Normale Supérieure de Jeunes Filles, 1978; I, 19-26.

Anglade, Joseph. *Anthologie des troubadours.* Paris: E. de Boccard, 1927.

—. *Les troubadours de Toulouse.* Paris: Didier, 1928-29 (rpt. Geneva: Slatkine, 1973).

Appel, Carl. *Das Leben und die Lieder des Trobadors Peire Rogier.* Berlin: Reimer, 1882.

—. *Provenzalische Chrestomathie mit Abriss der Formenlehre und Glossar.* Leipzig: Reisland, 1895.

—. *Provenzalische Inedita aus pariser Handschriften.* Leipzig: Reisland,

1890.

Audiau, Jean. *Les poésies des quatre troubadours d'Ussel.* Paris: Delagrave, 1922 (rpt. Geneva: Slatkine, 1973).

Azaïs, Gabriel. *Les Troubadours de Béziers.* Béziers: Malinas, 1869 (rpt. Geneva: Slatkine, 1973).

Balaguer, Victor. *Historia política y literaria de los trovadores.* 5 vols. Madrid: de Fortanet, 1878-79.

Barbieri, Giammaria. *Dell'origine della poesia rimata,* ed. G. Tiraboschi. Modena: Società tipografica, 1790.

Bartsch, Karl. *Chrestomathie provençale.* Elberfeld: Friderichs, 1875.

—. *Provenzalisches Lesebuch.* Elberfeld: Friderichs, 1855 (rpt. Geneva: Slatkine, 1974).

Bec, Pierre. *Anthologie des troubadours.* Paris: 10/18, 1979.

—. "Avoir des enfants ou rester vierge? Une tenson occitane du XIIIe siècle entre femmes." In *Mittelalterstudien: Erich Köhler zum Gedenken,* eds. Henning Krauss and Dietmar Rieger. Heidelberg: Carl Winter Universitätsverlag, 1984. 21-30.

—. *Burlesque et obscénité chez les troubadours: Le contre-texte au Moyen Age.* Paris: Stock, 1984.

—. *Petite anthologie de la lyrique occitane du Moyen Age: Initiation à la langue et à la poésie des troubadours.* Paris: Aubanel, 1954.

Berry, André. *Florilège des troubadours.* Paris: Firmin-Didot, 1930.

Bertoni, Giulio. *Antiche poesie provenzali.* Modena: Società Tipografica, 1937.

—. *Il canzoniere provenzale di Bernart Amoros (Complemento Cámpori), Edizione diplomatica preceduta da un'introduzione.* Freiburg: Libreria dell'Università O. Gschwend, 1911.

—. *Il canzoniere provenzale della Riccardiana No. 2909, Edizione diplomatica preceduta da un'introduzione.* Dresden: Gesellschaft für romanische Literatur, 1905.

—. *I trovatori d'Italia.* Modena: Orlandini, 1915 (rpt. Geneva: Slatkine, 1974).

Bogin, Meg. *The Women Troubadours.* New York and London: W.W. Norton & Co., 1980 (Paddington Press Ltd., 1976).

Bonnarel, Bernard. *Las 194 cançons dialogadas dels trobadors.* Paris: Bonnarel, 1981.

Boutière, Jean and Alexander Herman Schutz, eds. *Biographies des troubadours: Textes provençaux des XIIIe et XIVe siècles.* Paris: Nizet, 1964.

Branciforti, Francisco. *Il canzoniere di Lanfranco Cigala.* Florence:

Olschki, 1954.

Brunel, Clovis. *Les plus anciennes chartes en langue provençale. Recueil des pièces originales antérieures au XIIIe siècle.* 2 vols. Paris: Picard, 1926.

Brunel-Lobrichon, Geneviève. "Images of Women and Imagined Trobairitz in Béziers Chansonnier." In Paden, ed. *The Voice of the Trobairitz.* 157-73.

Burgwinkle, William E. *Razos and Troubadour Songs.* New York: Garland, 1990.

Carstens, Henry. *Die Tensonen aus dem Kreise der Trobadors Gui, Eble, Elias und Peire d'Uisel.* Königsberg: Leupold, 1914.

Cavaliere, Alfredo. *Cento liriche provenzali.* Bologna: Zanichelli, 1938.

Chabaneau, Camille. *Les biographies des troubadours en langue provençale.* Toulouse: Privat, 1885 (rpt. Geneva: Slatkine, 1975).

—. "Chanson inédite de Raimon de las Salas et d'une Dame." *Revue des Langues Romanes* 33 (1889): 107-08.

—. "Die beiden ältesten provenzalischen Grammatiken. *Lo Donatz proensals* und *Las Rasos de trobar* herausgeben von Edmund Stengel (Review). *Revue des Langues Romanes* 13 (1878), 138-46.

—. "Plainte de la Sainte Vierge au pied de la croix." *Revue des Langues Romanes* 32 (1888): 578-80.

—. "Un planh catalan." *Revue des Langues Romanes* 18 (1880): 18-19.

Chambers, Frank. "Raimon de las Salas." In *Essays in Honor of L. F. Solano.* Chapel Hill: University of North Carolina, 1970. 29-51.

Charvet, Gratien. "Les troubadours d'Alais aux XIIe et XIIIe siècles: Azalaïs de Porcairages, Clara d'Anduze et Pierre de Barjac." *Mémoires et comptes-rendus de la Société Scientifique et Littéraire d'Alais* 12 (1880): 129-51.

Chaytor, Henry John. *The Troubadours of Dante.* Oxford: Clarendon Press, 1902.

Crescini, Vincenzo. "Azalais d'Altier." *Zeitschrift für romanische Philologie* 14 (1890): 128-32.

—. *Per gli studi romanzi: Saggi ed Appunti.* Padua: Draghi, 1892.

de Bartholomaeis, Vincenzo. *Poesie provenzale storiche relative all'Italia.* 2 vols. Rome: Istituto Storico Italiano, 1931.

de Caluwé, Jacques. *Le moyen âge littéraire occitan dans l'œuvre de Frédéric Mistral. Utilisation éthique et esthétique.* Paris: Nizet, 1974.

de Casas, Felicia and Jesús Cantera. "La Condesa de Dia y las convenciones sociales." *Filologia moderna* 16 (1975-76): 5-19.

Dejeanne, Jean-Marie-Lucien. "Les *coblas* de Bernaut-Arnaut d'Armagnac et de Dame Lombarda." *Annales du Midi* 18 (1906): 63-68.

De Lollis, Cesare. "Bertran del Pojet." In *Miscellanea di studi critici in onore di Arturo Graf.* Bergamo: Istituto Italiano d'Atti Grafiche, 1903. 708-10.

—. "Appunti dei manuscritti provenzali Vaticani." *Revue des Langues Romanes* 33 (1889): 157-93.

de Riquer, Martin. *Los Trovadores: Historia literaria y textos.* 3 vols. Barcelona: Editorial Planeta, 1975.

Desazars de Montgailhard, Marie-Louis. "Les premières femmes lettrées à Toulouse." *Revue des Pyrénées* 23 (1910): 56-91.

Dronke, Peter. "The Provençal *Trobairitz* Castelloza in K." In *Medieval Women Writers,* ed. K. M. Wilson. Athens: The University of Georgia Press, 1984. 131-52.

—. *Women Writers of the Middle Ages: Critical Texts From Perpetua (†203) to Marguerite Porete (†1310).* Cambridge: Cambridge University Press, 1983.

Fabre d'Olivet, Antoine. *Le Troubadour, Poésies occitaniques du XIIIe siècle.* 2 vols. Paris: Henrichs, 1803-1804.

Farrayre, Jean-René. *Les chansons de Béatrix Comtesse de Die.* Rochemaure: Curandera, 1982.

Faucheux, Christian."Etude sémantique et syntaxique de l'œuvre de la Comtesse de Die." *Signum* 1.1 (1974): 1-17.

Faure-Cousin, Jeanne. *Les Femmes troubadours.* Paris: Denoël/Gonthier, 1978.

Frings, Theodor. "Frauenstrophe und Frauenlied in der frühen deutschen Lyrik." In *Festschrift H. A. Korff.* Leipzig, 1957. 13-28.

Gaubert, Ernest-Augustin and Jules Véran. *Anthologie de l'Amour Provençale.* Paris: Mercure de France, 1909.

Gauchat, Louis and Heinrich Kehrli. "Il canzoniere provenzale H." *Studi di filologia romanza* 5 (1891): 341-568.

Gentile, Galileo. *Antichi testi provenzali con grammatica e glossario.* Genova, 1947.

Goldin, Frederick, tr. *Lyrics of the Troubadours and Trouvères.* New York: Anchor Books, 1983.

Goût, Raoul. *Le miroir des dames chrétiennes. Pages féminines du Moyen Age.* Paris: Société Commerciale d'Edition et de Librairie, 1935.

Hagan, P. *The Medieval Provençal "Tenson": Contribution for the Study of the Dialogue Genre.* Diss. Yale University, 1975.

Hamlin, Frank R., Peter T. Ricketts and John Hathaway. *Introduction à l'étude de l'ancien provençal.* Geneva: Droz, 1967.

Hill, Raymond T. and Thomas G. Bergin. *Anthology of the Provençal Troubadours.* 2nd edition. 2 vols. New Haven: Yale University Press, 1973. 1941.

Hueffer, Francis. *The Troubadours: A History of Provençal Life and Literature in the Middle Ages.* London: Chatto & Windus, 1878 (rpt. New York: AMS, 1977).

Jaeschke, Hilde. *Der Troubadour Elias Cairel.* Berlin: Ebering, 1921 (rpt. Liechtenstein, 1967).

Jeanroy, Alfred. *Anthologie des troubadours,* ed. J. Boelcke. Paris, Nizet, 1974.

—. *Jongleurs et troubadours gascons.* Paris: Champion, 1957.

Kasten, Ingrid. *Frauenlieder des Mittelalters.* Stuttgart: Reclam, 1990.

Kay, Sarah. "Derivation, Derived Rhyme, and the Trobairitz." In Paden, ed. *The Voice of the Trobairitz.* 157-73.

Kjellman, Hilding. *Le troubadour Raimon-Jordan vicomte de Saint-Antonin.* Uppsala: Almqvist & Wiksell, 1922.

Kolsen, Adolf. "25 bisher unedierte provenzalische Anonyma." *Zeitschrift für romanische Philologie* 38 (1917): 281-310.

—. "Giraut de Bornelh, der Meister der Trobadors." *Berliner Beiträge, Roman.* I, Berlin, 1894.

Kussler-Ratyé, Gabrielle. "Les chansons de la comtesse Béatrice de Die." *Archivum Romanicum* 1(1917): 161-82.

La Curne de Sainte-Palaye, Jean-Baptiste. *Histoire littéraire des Troubadours, concernant leurs vies, les extraits de leurs pièces et plusieurs particularités sur les mœurs, les usages et l'histoire du 12me et 13me siècle.* 3 vols. Paris, 1774.

Lafont, Robert. *Trobar. XIIe-XIIIe siècles: Soixante chansons de troubadours situées et annotées avec une étude sur la langue et le texte du 'trobar' et un lexique.* Montpellier: Centre d'Etudes Occitanes de l'Université de Montpellier, 1972.

La Salle de Rochemaure, Félix de and René Lavaud. *Les Troubadours cantaliens: XII-XXe siècles.* 3 vols. Aurillac: Imprimerie Moderne, 1910.

Lavaud, René. *Les trois troubadours de Sarlat: Aimeric, Guiraut de Salignac, Elias Cairel.* Périgueux, 1912.

Lewent, Kurt. "Das Scherzgedicht des Peire Duran." *Neuphilologische Mitteilungen* 39 (1938): 237-60.

Levy, Emil. *Guilhem Figueira, ein provenzalischer Troubadour.* Berlin: Liebrecht, 1880.

Liborio, Mariantonia. *Storie di dame e di trovatori di Provenza.* Milan: Bompiani, 1982.

Mahn, Carl. *Die Werke der Troubadours in provenzalischer Sprache.* 4 vols. Berlin: Duemmler, 1846-53. (rpt. Geneva: Slatkine, 1977).

Marfany, Joan-Lluís. *Poesia catalana medieval.* Barcelona: Ediciones 62, 1966.

Milá y Fontanals, Manuel. *De los trovadores en Espana.* Barcelona: Verdaguer, 1861.

Mamino, Alberto. *La poesia e la musica dei trovatori.* Genoa: Tolozzi, 1986.

Marone, Gherardo. *Trovadores y juglares.* Buenos Aires: Facultad de Filosofía y Letras, Instituto de Literatura, 1948.

Massó Torrents, Jaime. *Repertorio de l'antiga literatura catalana: La poesia.* Barcelona: Alpha, 1932.

—. "Raimbau de Vaqueres en els cançoners catalans." In *Institut d'Estudis Catalans, Anuari.* Barcelona (1907): 414-62.

Meyer, Paul. *Le roman de Flamenca.* Paris: Franck, 1865.

Mistral, Frédéric. "Claro d'Anduzo." *Aióli* 167 (1895): 1.

Mölk, Ulrich. *Romanische Frauenlieder.* Munich: Fink, 1989.

Monaci, Ernesto. *Crestomazia italiana dei primi secoli.* Castello: Lapi, 1889.

Nelli, René. *Ecrivains anticonformistes du moyen-âge occitan. Anthologie bilingue.* 2 vols. Paris: Phébus, 1977.

Neumeister, Sebastian. *Das Spiel mit der höfischen Liebe. Das Altprovenzalische Partimen.* Munich: Fink, 1969.

Niestroy, Erich. "Der Trobador Pistoleta." *Zeitschrift für romanische Philologie* 52 (1914): 65-70.

Paden, William D., Jr., et al. "The Poems of the *Trobairitz* Na Castelloza." *Romance Philology* 35.1 (1981): 158-82.

Paden, William D., Jr., Tilde Sankovitch and Patricia Stäblein. *The Poems of the Troubadour Bertran de Born.* Berkeley: University of California Press, 1985.

Pasero, Nicolo. *Guglielmo IX d'Aquitania. Poesia.* Modena: Mucchi, 1973.

Pattison, Walter T. *The Life and Works of the Troubadour Raimbaut d'Orange.* Minneapolis: University of Minnesota Press, 1952.

Perkal-Balinsky, Deborah. *The Minor Trobairitz: An Edition with Translation and Commentary.* DAI 47 (1987): 2577A Northwestern University, 1986.

Piccolo, Francesco. *Primavera e fiore della lirica provenzale.* Florence:

Olschki, 1948.

Poe, Elizabeth Wilson. "Another *salut d'amor*? Another *trobairitz*? In Defense of *Tanz salutz et tantas amors*." *Zeitschrift für romanische Philologie* 106 (1990): 425-42.

Portal, Emmanuel. "Azalaïs d'Altier et Clara d'Anduze. Poétesses Cécenoles." *Mémoires et comptes-rendus de la Société Scientifique et Littéraire d'Alais* 27 (1898): 265-81.

Raynouard, François-Just-Marie. *Choix des poésies originales des troubadours.* 6 vols. Paris: Didot, 1816-21 (rpt. Geneva: Slatkine, 1982).

—. *Lexique roman ou Dictionnaire de la langue des troubadours.* Paris: Silvestre, 6: 1836-44.

Restori, Antonio. *Letteratura provenzale.* Milan: Hoepli, 1891.

Richter, Reinhilt. *Die Troubadourzitate im* Breviari d'Amor. *Studi, testi e manuali.* Modena: Mucchi, 1976.

Ricketts, Peter T. *Le Breviari d'Amor de Matfre Ermengaud.* Leiden: Brill, 1976.

Rieger, Angelica. "Un *sirventes* féminin—la *trobairitz* Gormonda de Monpeslier." In *Actes du Premier Congrès International de l'Association Internationale d'Etudes Occitanes,* ed. Peter T. Ricketts. Westfield College, London: AIEO, 1987. 423-55.

—. *Trobairitz: Der Beitrag der Frau in der altokzitanischen höfischen Lyrik; Edition des Gesamtkorpus.* Tübingen: Niemeyer, 1991.

—. "Was Bieris de Romans Lesbian? Women's Relations with Each Other in the World of the Troubadours." In Paden, ed. *Voice of the Trobairitz.* 73-94.

Rieger, Dietmar. *Mittelalterliche Lyrik Frankreichs: Lieder der Trobadors, Provenzalisch/Deutsch.* Stuttgart: Reclam, 1980.

Rochegude, Henri-Pascal. *Le parnasse occitanien.* Toulouse: Benichet Cadet, 1819 (rpt. Geneva: Slatkine, 1977).

Roubaud, Jacques. *Les Troubadours: Anthologie bilingue.* Paris: Seghers, 1971.

Sakari, Aimo. "Azalais de Porcairagues interlocutrice de Raimbaut d'Orange dans la tenson *Amics, en gran cossirier*?" *Neophilologica Fennica* 45 (1987): 429-40.

—. "Azalais de Porcairagues, le Joglar de Raimbaut d'Orange." *Neuphilologische Mitteilungen* 50 (1949): 23-43, 56-87, 174-98.

Sankovitch, Tilde. "Lombarda's Reluctant Mirror: Speculum of Another Poet." In Paden, ed. *The Voice of the Trobairitz.* 183-93.

Sansone, Giuseppe. *La poesia dell'Antica Provenza: Testi e storia dei trovatori.* 2 vols. Milan: Guanda, 1984.

Santy, Sernin. *La Comtesse de Die: Sa vie, ses œuvres complètes, les fêtes données en son honneur, avec tous les documents.* Paris: Picard, 1893.

Schultz-Gora, Oskar. *Die provenzalischen Dichterinnen.* Leipzig: Gustav Foch, 1888.

Selbach, Ludwig. *Das Streitgedicht in der altprovenzalischen Lyrik und sein Verhältnis zu ähnlichen Dichtungen anderer Litteraturen.* Marburg: Elwert, 1886.

Serra-Baldó, Alfons. *Els Trobadors: Text provençal i versió catalana.* Barcelona, 1934.

Sharman, Ruth Verity. *The Cansos and Sirventes of the Troubadour Guiraut de Borneil: A Critical Edition.* Cambridge: Cambridge University Press, 1989.

Shepard, William P. and Frank Chambers. *The Poems of Aimeric de Peguilhan.* Evanston, Ill.: Northwestern Univ. Press, 1950.

Simonelli, Maria. *Lirica moralistica nell'Occitania del XII secolo: Bernart de Venzac.* Studi, testi e manuali, Istituto di Filologia Romanza dell'Università di Roma. Modena: Mucchi, 1974.

Städtler, Katharina. "The *Sirventes* by Gormonda de Monpeslier." In Paden, ed. *The Voice of the Trobairitz.* 129-55.

—. *Altprovenzalische Frauendichtung (1150-1250): Historische-soziologische Untersuchungen und Interpretationen.* Heidelberg: Carl Winter, 1990.

Stengel, Edmund. *Die provenzalische Blumenlese der Biblioteca Chigiana.* Marburg: Friedrich, 1877.

Stronski, Stanislaw. *Le troubadour Elias de Barjols.* Toulouse: Privat, 1906.

—. "Recherches historiques sur quelques protecteurs des troubadours: les douze preux nommés dans le *Cavalier soisseubut* d'Elias de Barjols." *Annales du Midi* 19 (1907): 40-57.

Suchier, Hermann. *"Raimon Jordan." Jahrbuch für romanische und englische Literatur* 14 (1873): 284.

Toja, Gianluigi. *Lanfranc Cigala, Liriche.* Florence: Olschki, 1952.

Torres Amat, Félix. *Memorias para ayudar a formar un diccionario crítico de los escritores catalanes y dar alguna idea de la antigua y moderna literatura de Cataluña.* Barcelona: Verdaguer, 1836.

Véran, Jules. *Les Poétesses provençales du Moyen Age.* Paris: Quillet, 1946.

Vidal Alcover, Jaume. "El plaint amorós *Ab lo cor trist:* Assaig de restauració d'un text corrupte." In *Miscellània Pere Bohigas.* 2 vols. Barcelona: Abadia de Montserrat, 1982. 85-95.

Zufferey, François. "Toward a Delimitation of the Trobairitz Corpus." In Paden, ed., *The Voice of the Trobairitz.* 31-43.

Literary, Historical and Textual Studies:

Akehurst, F.R.P. "The Paragram AMOR in the Troubadours." *Romanic Review* 69 (1978): 15-21.

Anderson, Patricia. *"Na Carenza al bel cors avinen*: A Test Case for Recovering the Fictive Element in the Poetry of the Women Troubadours." *Tenso: Bulletin of the Société Guilhem IX* 2 (1987): 55-64.

Anglade, Joseph. *Les Troubadours: Leurs vies, leurs œuvres, leur influence.* Paris: Colin, 1929 (rpt. Geneva: Slatkine, 1977).

Aurell, Martin. *La vielle et l'épée: Troubadours et politique en Provence au XIIIᵉ siècle.* Paris: Aubier, 1989.

Aurell i Cardona, Martí. "La détérioration du statut de la femme aristocratique en Provence (Xᵉ-XIIIᵉ siècles)." *Le Moyen Age* 40 (1985): 5-32.

Avalle, D'Arco Silvio. *La letteratura medievale in lingua d'oc nella sua tradizione manoscritta: Problemi di critica testuale.* Turin: Einaudi, 1961.

Avalle, D'Arco Silvio and Emanuele Cassamassima. "Introduzione." In *Il canzoniere provenzale estense.* 2 vols. Modena: Mucchi, 1979. 1: 17-28.

Bec, Pierre. "L'antithèse poétique chez Bernard de Ventadour." *Mélanges Jean Boutière.* Liège: Soledi, 1971. 1: 107-37.

—. *Burlesque et obscénité chez les troubadours: Le contre-texte au Moyen Age.* Paris: Stock, 1984.

—. *La Lyrique française au moyen âge (XIIᵉ-XIIIᵉs).* 2 vols. Paris: Picard, 1977.

—. "Pour une typologie de la *balada* occitane: A propos de la pièce 'Quant lo gilos er fora.'" In *Hommage à Jean-Charles Payen: "Farai chansoneta novele." Essais sur la liberté créatrice au Moyen Age.* Caen: Université de Caen, 1989. 53-65.

—. "'Trobairitz' et chansons de femme: Contribution à la connaissance du lyrisme féminin au moyen âge." *Cahiers de Civilisation Médiévale* 22.3 (1979): 235-62.

Benton, John F. "Clio and Venus: An Historical View of Medieval Love." In *The Meaning of Courtly Love,* ed. F.X. Newman. Albany: State University of New York Press, 1972. 19-42.

Blakeslee, Merritt R. "Apostrophe, Dialogue and the Generic Conventions of the Troubadour *Canso." The Spirit of the Court: Selected Proceedings of the Fourth Congress of the International Courtly Literature Society (Toronto 1983),* ed. Glyn Burgess et al. Dover, NH: D. S. Brewer,

1985. 41-51.

—. "La chanson de femme, les *Hérïodes*, et la *canso* occitane à voix de femme: Considérations sur l'originalité des *trobairitz*." In *Hommage à Jean-Charles Payen: "Farai chansoneta novele."* *Essais sur la liberté créatrice au Moyen Age.* Caen: Université de Caen, 1989. 67-75.

Boroff, Edith. "Women and Music in Medieval Europe." *Mediævalia* 14 (1988): 1-21.

Bruckner, Matilda Tomaryn. "Debatable Fictions: The *Tensos* of the *Trobairitz*." In *Literary Aspects of Courtly Culture: Selected Papers from the Seventh Triennial Congress of the International Courtly Literature Society,* ed. Donald Maddox and Sara Strum-Maddox. Cambridge: D. S. Brewer, 1994. 19-28.

—. "Fictions of the Female Voice: The Women Troubadours." *Speculum* 67 (1992): 865-91.

—. "Jaufré Rudel and Lyric Reception: The Problem of Abusive Generalization." *Style* 20.2 (1986): 203-19.

—. "Na Castelloza, *Trobairitz*, and Troubadour Lyric." *Romance Notes* 25.3 (1985): 239-53.

Brunel, Clovis."Almois de Châteauneuf et Iseut de Chapieu." *Annales du Midi* 28 (1915-16): 262-68.

Burns, E. Jane. "The Man Behind the Lady in Troubadour Lyric." *Romance Notes* 25.3 (1985): 254-70.

Camproux, Charles. "On the Subject of an Argument Between Elias and his Cousin." In *The Interpretation of Medieval Lyric Poetry,* ed. W.T.H. Jackson. New York: Columbia University Press, 1980. 61-90.

Careri, Anna. "Sul canzoniere provenzale H (Vat. Lat . 3207)." In *Actes du XVIIIe Congrès International de Linguistique et de Philologie Romanes,* ed. D. Kremer. Tübingen: Niemeyer, 1988. 6: 100-07.

Chambers, Frank. *An Introduction to Old Provençal Versification.* Philadelphia: American Philosophical Society, 1985.

—. *Proper Names in the Lyrics of the Troubadours.* University of North Carolina Studies in the Romance Languages and Literatures 113. Chapel Hill: The University of North Carolina Press, 1971.

—. *"Las trobairitz soiseubudas."* In Paden, ed. *The Voice of the Trobairitz.* 45-60.

Cheyette, Fredric. "Troubadour Poetry and the Politics of Twelfth-Century Languedocian Courts," presented at the Seminar on Medieval Literature and Culture, Harvard University, March 15, 1993.

Cnyrim, Eugen. *Sprichwörter, sprichwörtliche Redensarten und Sentenzen bei den provenzalischen Lyrikern.* Marburg: Elwert, 1888.

Coldwell, Maria V. "*Jougleresses* and *Trobairitz*: Secular Musicians in Medieval France." In *Women Making Music: The Western Art Tradition, 1150-1950*, ed. Jane Bowers and Judith Tick. Urbana: University of Illinois Press, 1986. 39-61.

Courtemanche, Andrée. "Femmes et accès au patrimoine en Provence: Manosque au XIVe siècle." *Le Moyen Age* 96 (1990): 479-501.

Davidson, Clifford. "Erotic 'Women's Songs' in Anglo-Saxon England." *Neophilologus* 59 (1975): 451-462.

Di Girolamo, Costanzo. *Elementi di versificazione provenzale*. Naples: Liguori, 1979.

—. *I trovatori*. Turin: Bollati Boringhieri, 1989.

Dragonetti, Roger. "*Aizi* et *aizimen* chez les plus anciens troubadours." In *Mélanges de linguistique romane et de philologie médiévale offerts à M. Maurice Delbouille*, eds. J. Renson and M. Tyssens. Gembloux: Duculot, 1964. 2: 127-53.

Dronke, Peter. *Medieval Latin and the Rise of European Love-Lyric*. 2 vols. Oxford: Clarendon Press, 1968.

Duby, Georges. "Dans la France du nordouest au XIIe siècle: les 'jeunes' dans la société aristocratique." *Annales: Economies, Sociétés, Civilisations* 19 (1964): 835-46.

Earnshaw, Doris. *The Female Voice in Medieval Romance Lyric*. Romance Languages and Literature 68. New York: Peter Lang, 1988.

Ferrante, Joan. "Notes Toward the Study of a Female Rhetoric in the Trobairitz." In Paden, ed. *The Voice of the Trobairitz*. 63-72.

—. *Woman as Image in Medieval Literature: From the Twelfth Century to Dante*. New York: Columbia University Press, 1975.

Finke, Laurie A. "The Rhetoric of Desire." In *Feminist Theory, Women's Writing*. Ithaca: Cornell University Press, 1992. 29-74.

Frank, István. *Répertoire métrique de la poésie des troubadours*. 2 vols. Paris: Champion, 1953.

—. "De l'Art d'éditer les textes lyriques." In *Recueil de travaux offerts à Clovis Brunel, par ses amis, collègues et élèves*. 2 vols. Paris: Société de l'Ecole de Chartes. 2: 465-75. Translated in *Medieval Manuscripts and Textual Criticism*, ed. Christopher Kleinhenz. 123-38.

Gaunt, Simon. "Sexual Difference and the Metaphor of Language in a Troubadour Poem." *Modern Language Review* 83 (1988): 297-313.

Gégou, Fabienne. "*Trobairitz* et amorces romanesques dans les 'Biographies' des troubadours." In *Studia occitanica in memoriam Paul Remy*, eds. Hans-Erich Keller et al. Kalamazoo, Mich.: Medieval Institute Publications, 1986. 2: 43-51.

Goldin, Frederick. *The Mirror of Narcissus in the Courtly Love Lyric.* Ithaca: Cornell University Press, 1967.

Gravdal, Kathryn. "Metaphor, Metonymy, and the Medieval Women Trobairitz." *Romanic Review* 83.4 (1992): 411-26.

Haidu, Peter. "Text and History: The semiosis of twelfth-century lyric as sociohistorical phenomenon (Chrétien de Troyes: 'D'Amor qui m'a tolu')." *Semiotica* 33.1-2 (1981): 1-62.

Herlihy, David. "Did Women Have a Renaissance? A Reconsideration." *Mediaevalia et Humanistica: Studies in Medieval and Renaissance Culture* 13 (1985): 1-22.

—. "Land, family and women in Continental Europe, 701-1200." *Traditio* 18 (1962): 89-120.

Huchet, Jean-Charles. "Les femmes troubadours ou la voix critique." *Littérature* 51 (1983): 59-90.

Huot, Sylvia. *From Song to Book: The Poetics of Writing in Old French Lyric and Lyrical Narrative Poetry.* Ithaca, N.Y.: Cornell University Press, 1987.

Jeanroy, Alfred. *La Poésie Lyrique des troubadours.* 2 vols. Paris: Privat, 1934.

Kay, Sarah. *Subjectivity in Troubadour Poetry.* Cambridge: Cambridge University Press, 1990.

Kelly, Joan. "Did Women Have a Renaissance?" In *Becoming Visible: Women in European History,* ed. Renate Bridenthal and Claudia Koonz. Boston: Houghton Mifflin, 1977. Rpt. in *Women, History and Theory: The Essays of Joan Kelly.* Chicago: University of Chicago Press, 1984. 19-50.

King, Margaret. "The Renaissance of the Renaissance Woman." *Medievalia et Humanistica* 16 (1988): 165-75.

Kleinhenz, Christopher, ed. *Medieval Manuscripts and Textual Criticism.* University of North Carolina Studies in the Romance Languages and Literatures Symposia 4. Chapel Hill: University of North Carolina Press, 1976.

Köhler, Erich. "Observations historiques et sociologiques sur la poésie des troubadours." *Cahiers de Civilisation Médiévale* 7 (1964): 27-51.

Lejeune, Rita. "La femme dans les littératures française et occitane du XIe au XIIIe siècle." *Cahiers de Civilisation Médiévale* 20 (1977): 201-216.

Marshall, John H. *The Transmission of Troubadour Poetry.* An Inaugural Lecture delivered at Westford College, 5th March, 1975. Watford: Watford Printers, 1975.

—. Trois fragments du chansonnier provençal H." *Romania* 97 (1976):

400-05.

Meneghetti, Maria Luisa. *Il pubblico dei trovatori*. Modena: Mucchi, 1984.

Mölk, Ulrich. "Chansons de femme, trobairitz et la théorie romantique de la genèse de la poésie lyrique romane." *Lingua e stile* 25 (1990): 135-46.

Monfrin, J. "Notes sur le chansonnier provençal." In *Recueil de travaux offerts à Clovis Brunel, par ses amis, collègues et élèves*. Paris: Société de l'Ecole de Chartes. 2: 292-312.

Monson, Don A. "Lyrisme et sincérité: Sur une chanson de Bernart de Ventadorn." In *Studia Occitanica in Memoriam Paul Remy*, ed. Hans-Erich Keller et al. Kalamazoo, Mich.: Medieval Institute Publications, 1986. 2: 143-59.

Napholz, Carol. "(Re)locating Lost Trobairitz: The Anonymous Female Voice in Provençal Debate Poems." *Tenso: Bulletin of the Société Guilhem IX* 7.2 (1992): 125-41.

Nelli, René. *L'Erotique des troubadours*. Toulouse: Privat, 1963.

Nichols, Stephen G. "Medieval Women Writers: *Aisthesis* and the Powers of Marginality." *Yale French Studies* 75 (1988): 77-94.

Ourliac, Paul. "Troubadours et juristes." *Cahiers de Civilisation Médiévale* 8 (1965): 159-177.

Paden, William D., Jr. "Some Recent Studies of Women in the Middle Ages, Especially in Southern France." *Tenso: Bulletin of the Société Guilhem IX* 7.2 (Spring 1992): 94-124.

—. "Utrum copularentur: of *Cors*." *L'Esprit Créateur* 19.4 (1979): 70-83.

— ed. *The Voice of the Trobairitz: Perspectives on the Women Troubadours*. Philadelphia: University of Pennsylvania Press, 1989.

Parkes, M. B. *Pause and Effect: An Introduction to the History of Punctuation in the West*. Cambridge: Cambridge University Press, 1992.

Paterson, Linda M. *Troubadours and Eloquence*. Oxford: Clarendon Press, 1975.

—. *The World of the Troubadours: Medieval Occitan Society, c. 1000-c. 1300*. Cambridge: Cambridge University Press, 1993.

Pillet, Alfred and Henry Carstens. *Bibliographie der Troubadours*. NY: Burt Franklin, 1968 (rpt.).

Poe, Elizabeth Wilson. *From Poetry to Prose in Old Provençal: The Emergence of the* Vidas, *the* Razos, *and the* Razos de trobar. Birmingham, Alabama: Summa Publications, 1984.

—. "A Dispassionate Look at the Trobairitz." *Tenso: Bulletin of the Société Guilhem IX* 7.2 (1992): 142-64.

Pollina, Vincent. "Melodic Continuity and Discontinuity in *A chantar m'er* of the Comtessa de Dia." In *Miscellanea di Studi Romanzi offerta a*

Giuliano Gasca Queirazza, eds. Anna Cornagliotti et al. Turin: Edizioni Dell'Orso, 1988. 887-96.

—. "Troubadours dans le nord: Observations sur la transmission des mélodies occitanes dans les manuscrits septentrionaux." *Romanistische Zeitschrift für literaturgeschichte* 3.4 (1985): 263-78.

Power, Eileen. "The Position of Women." In *The Legacy of the Middle Ages*, eds. G. G. Cramp and E. F. Jacob. Oxford: Clarendon Press, 1926. 401-33.

Rieger, Angelica. "Alamanda de Castelnau—Une *trobairitz* dans l'entourage des comtes de Toulouse?" *Zeitschrift für romanische Philologie* 107 (1991): 47-57.

—. "*En conselh no deu hom voler femna:* Les dialogues mixtes dans la lyrique troubadouresque." *Perspectives Médiévales* 16 (1990): 47-57.

—. "'Ins e.l cor port, dona, vostra faisso:' Image et imaginaire de la femme à travers l'enluminure dans les chansonniers de troubadours." *Cahiers de Civilisation Médiévale* 28 (1985): 385-415.

—. "La *mala canso* de Gui d'Ussel, un exemple d'intertextualité de pointe.'" In *Contacts de langues, de civilisations et intertextualité: Actes du IIIème Congrès International de l'Association Internationale d'Etudes Occitanes, Montpellier, 20-26 septembre 1990*, ed. Gérard Gouiran. Montpellier: Centre d'Etudes Occitanes de l'Université de Montpellier, 1993. 2: 1071-88.

Rieger, Dietmar. "Die *trobairitz* in Italien: Zu den altprovenzalischen Dichterinnen." *Cultura Neolatina* 31 (1971): 205-23.

Robbins, Kittye Delle. "Love's Martyrdoms Revised: Conversion, Inversion and Subversion of *Trobador* Style in *Trobairitz* Poetry." Troubadour Symposium, UCLA. March, 1979.

—. "Woman/Poet: Problem and Promise in Studying the *Trobairitz* and their friends." *Encomia* 1.3 (1977): 12-14.

Sakari, Aimo. "A propos d'Azalais de Porcairagues." In *Mélanges Jean Boutière*, eds. Irénée Cluzel et François Pirot. 2 vols. Liège: Soledi, 1971. 1: 517-28.

—. "Le thème de l'amor du 'Ric Ome' au début de la poésie provençale." In *Actes et mémoires du IIIe Congrès International de langue et littérature d'oc.* (Bordeau, 3-8 Sept. 1961). Bordeau: Université de Bordeau, Faculté des Lettres, 1965. 2: 88-94.

—. "Un vers embarrassant d'Azalais de Porcairagues." *Cultura Neolatina* 38 (1978): 215-21.

Segouffin, Nanette Paradis. "Trobairitz." *Vent Terral* 8 (1982): 35-46.

Shapiro, Marianne. "The Provençal *Trobairitz* and the Limits of Courtly

Love." *Signs* 3.2 (1978): 560-71.

—. "'Tenson' et 'partimen': La 'tenson' fictive." In *XIV Congresso internazionale di linguistica e filologia romanza: Atti*, ed. Alberto Várvaro. Naples: Macchiaroli, 1981. 5: 287-01.

Simonelli, Maria Picchio. "Il *grande canto cortese* dai provenzali ai siciliani." *Cultura Neolatina* 47.3-4 (1982): 201-39.

Spampinato, Margherita Beretta. "Le *trobairitz:* La *fin'amors* al femminile." *Le Forme e la Storia* 1 (1980): 51-70.

Speer, Mary B. "Editing Old French Texts in the Eighties: Theory and Practice." *Romance Philology* 45.1 (1991): 7-43.

Sponsler, Lucy A. *Women in the Medieval Spanish Epic and Lyric Traditions*. Lexington, KY: University Press of Kentucky, 1975.

Stronski, Stanislaw. "Notes sur quelques troubadours et protecteurs des troubadours." *Revue des langues romanes* 50 (1907): 5-44.

Switten, Margaret. "Does the manuscript tradition of the *trobairitz* allow us to sing their songs?" (unpublished manuscript).

Tavera, Antoine. "A la recherche des troubadours maudits." *Senefiance* 5 (1978): 135-62.

Thiolier-Méjean, Suzanne. *Les Poésies satiriques et morales des troubadours du XIIᵉ siècle à la fin du XIIIᵉ siècle*. Paris: Nizet, 1978.

Thomas, Antoine. Review of *Die provenzalischen Dichterinnen*, by O. Schultz-Gora. *Annales du Midi* 1 (1889): 407-10.

van der Werf, Hendrik. *The Chansons of the Troubadours and Trouvères: A Study of the Melodies and Their Relations to the Poems*. Utrecht: Oosthoek, 1972.

Van Vleck, Amelia E. *Memory and Re-creation in Troubadour Lyric*. Berkeley: University of California Press, 1991.

Warning, Rainer. "Moi lyrique et société chez les troubadours." Tr. Werner Kügler. In *Archéologie du signe*, ed. Lucie Brind'Amour and Eugène Vance. Papers in Medieval Studies 3. Toronto: Pontifical Institute of Medieval Studies, 1982. 63-100.

Zink, Michel. *La Pastourelle: Poésie et folklore au moyen âge*. Paris: Bordas, 1972.

Zufferey, François. *Recherches linguistiques sur les chansonniers provençaux*. Geneva: Droz, 1987.

Zumthor, Paul. *Langue et techniques poétiques à l'époque romane*. Paris: Presses Universitaires de France, 1984.

—. *La Poésie et la voix dans la civilisation médiévale*. Paris: Klincksieck, 1963.

—. "Recherches sur les topiques dans la poésie lyrique des XIIe et XIIIe siècles." *Cahier de Civilisation Médiévale* 2 (1959): 409-27.

Note on the Texts

We have conceived of this edition as the script for a performance: a printed version of the script written six hundred years ago for performances in great halls, chambers and gardens, and a script for performance by our readers, in the imagination, in the classroom or among friends. As the editor of the Occitanic texts, I have tried to mediate between the demands of past and present. On the one hand, the version of a poem or song that is found in a single manuscript is presented as faithfully as possible. On the other, we have printed texts in the Occitanic language that are grammatically correct (which is not always the case in the manuscripts) and that can be read and performed in a fair approximation of the medieval song. Alas, we are not able to convey the musical tradition that must have been part of a medieval performer's education.

Troubadour poetry has many characteristics associated with oral poetry (see, for example, Zumthor, *La poésie* 80-82). In fact, the surviving manuscripts of troubadour verse, some deluxe, comprehensive anthologies, some the notebooks of enthusiastic amateurs, were mostly compiled about a century after the flowering of troubadour culture, in the late thirteenth and fourteenth centuries in different regions of Mediterranean Europe. Nonetheless, evidence that the poetry had circulated both orally and in writing in the previous century is not scarce. A late thirteenth-century Italian illumination of a poet at work at his desk, pen in hand, tells us that early consumers took it for granted that troubadour song was generated in written form (Avalle 47-48; Rieger, "'Ins e.l cor'" 399). Poets and performers recorded their verse on parchment sheaves or scrolls, and at least two poets, Peire Vidal in the beginning of the thirteenth century and Guiraut Riquier at the end, edited their own poems for distribution. Sometimes it was the *joglar*, secretary, or protector who collected the poet's materials and prepared them for dissemination.

The extant manuscripts preserve different versions of the poems and there are many ways to explain this variation. Songs were transformed by the dynamic of performance and reception. For aesthetic or practical purposes troubadours reworked poems after they had been performed in public: with only minor changes to the *tornada* a *canso* could be recycled as a troubadour moved from court to court. Parchment is perishable and scribes fallible. The language of the troubadours was usually a foreign language to the scribe who was frequently separated in time and space from Occitania. Often the director of a scriptorium and sometimes a scribe would act as editor of the material he was copying. But it is important to note that while some poems do have significantly diverse manuscript traditions, in general the frequency of variants in the troubadour corpus is not higher than that of any literary tradition that was not transmitted mechanically (Avalle 56-57).

The historical development of poetic anthologies can be reconstructed from the composition of extant manuscripts. Ordered series of poems by a single author like those prepared by Peire Vidal and Guiraut Riquier are preserved intact. We also catch a glimpse in surviving manuscripts of the earliest anthologies of Provençal poetry, which may date back to the twelfth century. These anthologies were personal lyric collections, and poems by different authors tend to be jumbled together, attribution of authorship is often erroneous and variant readings are frequent. One such "personal" anthology, the source for the last part of manuscript H (Vat. lat. 3207), may have consisted entirely of works by trobairitz (Marshall, "Trois fragments" 403). Rieger suggests it could have been composed by or for a woman ("'Ins e.l cor'" 390). H probably dates from the mid-thirteenth century and it contains trobairitz works not found elsewhere, including the exchange between Lombarda and Bernart Arnaut (no. 21), the *cobla* of Tibors (no. 36), "Dieus sal la terra e.l pais" (no. 35), and the *tenso* between Almuc and Iseut (no. 14). At least ten folios are missing from the section devoted to trobairitz and it seems plausible that some poems have been lost (see Avalle 89-92; 107-09; Marshall, "Trois fragments" 400-03; Rieger, "'Ins e.l cor'" 389-92; Careri). The second half of the thirteenth century marked the invention of the modern anthology: poems are grouped by author and organized by genre; the entire anthology is structured with consideration to chronological, aesthetic, or spiritual criteria (Avalle 84-91).

Examination of the manuscripts reveals that groups of them had common but evolving sources. There is no single "best" manuscript in which one finds the "best" version of every poem; when editing troubadour verse, every version of a poem must be analyzed for its own merits. A comparison of two manuscript renderings of the first poem of this anthology will serve to explain the kind of variation that is commonly found, and permit us to illustrate our editorial policy of preserving the reading of our base manuscript as long as it is valid and grammatically and phonetically correct. Manuscripts A (Vat. lat. 5232) and B (Paris, Bibl. Nat. fr. 1592) were compiled from the same source material in the late thirteenth century by natives of the Midi. In spite of the similarity of their origins, differences exist at every level because the source material was constantly evolving, because of different principles of organization and editing adhered to by the two scribes, because of scribes' dissimilar orthographic habits and because of the subsequent history of the manuscripts (Zufferey, *Recherches* 35-38). In the case of "Ab ioi et ab ioven m'apais," there are about a half dozen variant readings in AB. Some are purely orthographic, as in verse 24:

> A *no.n dirant mas avinenssa*
> B *no.n diran mas avinenssa*
> AB (they say only pleasing things).

Variants may alter the text, but not meaning, as in verse 22:

> A *que domna, pois ama a presen*
> B *e domna, pois ama a presen*
> A (for a lady, since she loves openly)
> B (and a lady, since she loves openly).

Some change the message, as in line 13-14:

> A *e qui que mal l'en retraia / no.l creza*
> B *e qui que mal l'en retraia / non creza*
> A (and whoever speaks ill of him / let him
>   not believe him)
> B (and whoever speaks ill of him / let him
>   not believe it).

In these three cases we have not emended the base manuscript B. In line 36 where B is clearly erroneous, we emend the text in accordance with A:

> A *si.us plai, vostra mantenensa*
> B *si us platz, vostra mantenensa*
> AB (if you please, [lend me] your protection).

Both manuscripts contain an error in line 23 that violates the scheme of derivative rhyme operative throughout the poem:

> AB *ia pois li pro ni li valen*
> AB (since the worthy and valiant people),

A correction is made in our edition on the basis of D (Modena, Bibl. Estense α.R.4.4), a late thirteenth- or early fourteenth-century manuscript produced in Veneto, which is generally very close to AB in its rendering of this poem. Either the editor/scribe of D intervened independently and restored the only reading justified by the rhyme scheme,

> D *ia pois li pro ni.ll avinen*
> D (since the worthy and pleasant people),

or else he relied on another manuscript to correct the reading. Two other manuscripts contain an important reading of the poem that is not found in AB. Like D, I (Paris, Bibl. Nat. fr. 854) and K (Paris, Bibl. Nat. fr. 12473) are thirteenth- or early fourteenth-century parchment manuscripts produced at professional scriptoria in Veneto from the same constantly evolving source material of ABD. DIK differ significantly from AB when naming the addressee in the *tornada*. The first line of the *tornada* in AB reads

> AB <u>*Amics*</u>, *la vostra valensa*
> AB (Friend, your valor).

In DIK the line reads

> DIK <u>Floris</u>, la vostra valensa
> DIK (Floris, your valor).

The reading in DIK is a *lectio difficilior* (a more specific, or literally, a more difficult reading), here the *senhal* that may perhaps be associated with Raimbaut d'Aurenga (Rieger 621). Textual critics attribute greater authority to a *lectio difficilior* than to a generic reading like *amics.* Perhaps a personal collection like the one that was the source for the last part of H (which reads *Floris*) fell into the hands of the director of the Veneto scriptorium and he emended the source material on that basis. But *amics*, the reading found in our base manuscript B, is valid and has been preserved in our edition of the poem; the *lectio difficilior* is in the End Notes.

Our goals in editing the poems are to present texts that are faithful to the base manuscript, texts that are grammatically correct and metrically regular, texts that makes sense and can be performed as an Occitanic work. These goals are to some extent incompatible: only a diplomatic or facsimile edition is faithful to a manuscript and the other goals preclude these possibilities. We have selected base manuscripts containing versions of the poems that could be printed with as little emendation as possible. The grammar has been corrected where it is erroneous, but the many variant forms and structures that characterize the Medieval Occitanic poetic language are admitted. There are a few verses where the authority of the voice must have conveyed meaning that the essentially correct syntax does not quite manage to do, and at those points we have resisted emendation. The declension system, not always observed in the base manuscripts, is restored to all common nouns (see the discussion of Paden, Sankovitch, Stäblein, eds., 97). When the graphemes of a base manuscript cannot be read in a way that will reproduce a Medieval Occitanic word, the orthography is emended. (We make the single generalized exception of printing the voiced dentolabial fricative as *v* in our texts, although it occurs as *u* in the manuscripts.) We have normalized the orthography of place names within the texts, rhymes are regularized, and metrical anomalies are treated as errors. In the case of metrical anomalies and passages where the text makes no sense, emendations are based on the reading of a manuscript closely related to the base manuscript. When this is not possible, minor emendations to the text have been admitted, more substantial emendations relegated to the End Notes. Pertinent rubrics from the base manuscript are included in bold lettering. The standard form of poets' names is used in notes and headings that are not drawn directly from the manuscripts. Sixteen of the works contained in this book have been preserved in a single manuscript. Again we edited these texts as conservatively as possible, regularizing rhymes, correcting solecisms and admitting a number of textual emendations of other sorts, especially when they are justified by the rhyme scheme.

All emendations to the readings contained in the base manuscripts are italicized. In the interest of economy the critical apparatus is limited and focused on the points where our edition diverges from the base manuscript. The variants of other manuscripts that significantly alter meaning are also noted. Orthographic variants, readings that make no sense or are obviously erroneous, and variants that do not alter the sense of the verse are excluded. We have combined the critical apparatus with some interpretive notes and identified this material as "End Notes."

Manuscript punctuation consists, at most, of a point to mark the end of a line. Except where punctuation is necessary to clarify semantic, syntactic and rhetorical structures that are otherwise obscure, the use of syntactic punctuation in our edition is minimal.

Although modern editors usually normalize orthography, we prefer to alert readers to the different aesthetic and conditions of transmission operative in medieval vernacular writing, and for that reason have kept the manuscript spellings. In the manuscripts, *cors* also occurs as *kors, qors* and *quors*, *voill* as *volh*. A poem from a single folio offers diverse graphic forms because scribes ignored the concept of orthography. Furthermore, Occitania covered a vast and dialectically rich region that stretched from the Pyrenees in the south, to the Loire in the north. Scribes varied *canso* with *chanso*, *pois* with *puois*. Although it is commonly assumed that the troubadours used a *koine*, a common language that embraced generalized linguistic characteristics and avoided those most closely associated with a specific region, Marshall and Zufferey warn against minimizing the dialectal diversity that is intrinsic to troubadour poetics (Marshall, "Transmission"; Zufferey, *Recherches* 312). Of course, the manuscripts do not present the trobairitz' own texts; they are the products of scribes who were separated from the auctorial moment in space and time. Older written forms are embedded in the more recent manuscripts and at the same time Italian, French and Catalan forms encroach on the Occitanic.

Angelica Rieger's excellent edition of forty-six trobairitz lyrics, *Der Beitrag der Frau in der altokzitanischen höfischen Lyrik: Edition des Gesamptkorpus,* has been an invaluable tool. I have acknowledged our debt to Rieger at every point, and especially in the notes and brief discussions of evidence pertaining to the historical identities of the trobairitz. We urge readers to consult Rieger's critical apparatus for a more complete knowledge of the manuscript tradition of the trobairitz. We refer to Rieger's edition as "Rieger" throughout the book.

Numerous differences between this volume and Rieger's edition arise principally because we have reedited the texts from base manuscripts, and whenever an element that is not found in a base manuscript is interpolated into our edition, it is identified with italics. Rieger has, in most cases, edited poems on the basis of previous editions and accepted the manuscript emendations made by previous editors, signaling these emendations in the End Notes and not in the text of the poems. Our approach offers the advantage of greater consistency at several levels: italics in the text of a poem always indicate deviation from the manuscript source, and not, at some points, deviation from another printed source, as in Rieger's edition. Orthographic normalization is consistent in our text: it occurs in rhyme words. Although Rieger claims that only rhyme words are regularized in her text (xi-xii), the orthographic, morphological and grammatical normalizations by previous editors are admitted in the poem texts and not signaled except in the End Notes. The reevaluation of the manuscript texts has permitted us to retrieve, at several points, readings that had been transformed beyond recognition by a century or more of editorial intervention. We have also depended on the editions of Rieger and many generations of scholars in our effort to establish the text, and we acknowledge their contribution to our understanding throughout.

Finally, I want to thank my colleagues for the many happy and instructive hours that we spent together. I would like to express my special gratitude to Mark Stansbury who guided me in the formatting of this book with great patience and expertise, and Professor Michael Connolly and the Boston College Faculty Microcomputer Resource Center for support in the printing of the text. Our thanks to Enric Bou for assisting in the quest for a photocopy of "G", and to the Biblioteca Riccardiana in Florence, Italy.

LAS

Note on the Translations

Amicx, tan ai d'ira e de feunia
quar no vos vey, que quant eu cug chantar
planh e sospir, per qu'ieu no puesc so far
a mas coblas que.l cors complir volria.

Clara d'Anduza

Friend, I'm in such rage and torment
because you're out of sight, that when I try to sing,
I complain and sigh, for I cannot, with my verses,
accomplish what I wish.

In the final lines of her *canso,* Clara d'Anduza laments an absence that has affected her process of composition. Here, her translator notes several absences that loom over the work of translating the poem. The lack most keenly felt is that of the music that would have accompanied her song. Then there is the loss of Clara's "unisounding" rhymes, mnemonic end notes that shape her stanzas, binding them together on the page and in listeners' minds. Virtuosic rhyming was the essence of any claim to practice the art of *trobar,* but attempts to reproduce that rhyme in modern English entail unacceptable losses and distortions. In addition, I sigh for the absence of a Romance system in which common nouns and adjectives have gender, so that abstractions like *dol* (sorrow, m.) and *ira* (anger, f.) join with *amicx* and *amiga,* with proper nouns and pronouns, to perform a dance of masculine and feminine. Most of all, the contemporary translator misses a shared cultural lexicon that allowed Clara d'Anduza's public to sense the sparks of anger in a phrase like *abaissador de joi e de joven* "bringers down of joy and youth" and savor juxtaposed opposites like *amicx/enemicx* (friend/enemy), *amador/ trichador* (lover, traitor), *veser/departir* (to see/to part), and *remirar/lonhar* (to gaze/to separate).

My co-authors and I present our translations as guides to the workings of the Old Occitan texts. Accordingly, I have arranged lines and expressions in an order as parallel to the originals as possible without writing garbled, archaic, or arhythmic English. I have not supplied English words to account for every single Occitan lexeme: equivalents for *que* (the ubiquitous relative pronoun, conjunction, and filler-syllable) and for hard-working *en, ni,* and *ne* have been omitted at times, though not always. In fact,

I do represent such function-words more frequently than I would if I were conforming to the poetic practice of any other language or era. To modern readers, an extensive apparatus of *because's, so that's, provided that's* and *although's* seems disastrously prosaic. But in this case, indices, subordinators and qualifiers are neither incidental nor superfluous. Rather, they lay out with obsessive exactitude the lover's logic of each song. Clara d'Anduza, for instance, chooses precise phraseology to damn her slanderers, inviting reader-listeners to calibrate the doubled negatives, measured intensifiers, explicit conditions and results by which she articulates her threat: "There's no man, *however much my enemy, /* that I *won't* love *if* I hear him approve of this /* and *if* he disapproves, he *can't do or say anything* that pleases me *at all.*" The trobairitz of "Per ioi que d'amor m'avegna" pleads cautiously and hypothetically: "Let him obey me *in this small way [d'aitant],* that by some agreeable responses he may keep my heart in joy." Ezra Pound may have prized the Occitan lyric for its limpid imagery and vigorous sounds, but an unbesotted look at the corpus shows that painstaking, often tortuous, argumentation and cajolery are equally crucial in the work of men and women troubadours, whose songs present a strange amalgam of Play, Performance and Persuasion. In discourse as in punctuation, I have tried to balance two concerns: on the one hand, a loyalty to the trobairitz' non-modern wit; on the other hand, an awareness that contemporary readers prefer poetry weighted with fewer explanatory strategies and bound by fewer logical connectors.

In the interest of readability, I have slighted the complexity of numerous polysemic terms. A glossary may give eleven valid equivalents of a term such as *ric,* a list including *rich, noble, precious, happy, pleased, fortunate, abundant,* and *vain,* but I have in each occurrence narrowed the choice to only one. Throughout the 36 poems, however, I have varied English equivalents for a single Occitan word: *franc* is *honest* in one poem, *open* in another; *semblansa* is *opinion* in one instance, *expression* in another; *razo* and its derivatives become *argument, defense, reason,* and *thing.* These shifts should convey some sense of the wide semantic fields in which key terms play. Similarly, in several instances (notably, the controversial Alaisina Yselda *tenso*), identical Occitan words and phrases can be read in either sacred or secular contexts. We have sometimes privileged one frame of reference over another, while indicating the polyvalence in a note.

As principal translator, I take responsibility for the English versions of our texts and for their moments of awkwardness and imprecision. I am grateful that such moments are far less frequent than they would have been if the

36 translations had not passed through the sensitive, skillful hands of my co-authors. Each poem, before undergoing the last "planings and filings" (to borrow a troubadour image), was exhaustively discussed among the three of us. Many pleasurable, instructive hours were spent together poring over problems, weighing alternatives, choosing those imperfect solutions that best satisfied the team.

I would like to add that my participation in the project would have been much more arduous without help and encouragement from a colleague whose *lungo studio e grande amore* have greatly enriched the field of troubadour studies. Nathaniel Smith's kind tutelage, his broad knowledge of Occitan tradition, and his keen interest in its feminine exponents were invaluable to me, especially during months spent at a distance from my Boston collaborators. Thanks to him and other friends, the absences, imperfections, sighs and complaints have contributed to something present: a new group of songs awaiting their music.

SW

POEMS

1. La Comtessa de Dia, "Ab ioi et ab ioven m'apais"

I. *A*b ioi et ab ioven m'apais
  e iois e iovens m'apaia,
  que mos amics es lo plus gais
  per qu'eu sui coindeta e gaia,
 5 e pois eu li sui veraia
  be.is taing q'el me sia verais,
  c'anc de lui amar no m'estrais
  ni ai cor que m'en estraia.

II. Mout mi plai car sai que val mais
 10 cel q'ieu plus desir que m'aia,
  e cel que primiers lo m'atrais
  Dieu prec que gran ioi l'atraia,
  e qui que mal l'en retraia,
  non creza, fors qu'ie.l retrais,
 15 c'om cuoill maintas vetz los balais
  ab q'el mezeis se balaia.

III. Dompna que en bon pretz s'enten
  deu ben pausar s'entendenssa
  en un pro cavallier valen
 20 pos ill conois sa valenssa
  que l'aus amar a presenssa,
  e dompna, pois ama a presen,
  ia pois li pro ni.ll'*avin*en
  no.n diran mas avinenssa.

IV. 25 Q'ieu n'ai chausit un pro e gen
  per cui pretz meillura e genssa,
  larc et adreig e conoissen,
  on es sens e conoissenssa;
  prec li non aia *cre*z*e*nssa,
 30 ni hom no.il puosca far crezen
  q'ieu fassa vas lui faillimen,
  sol non trob en lui faillensa.

1. La Comtessa de Dia, "Ab ioi et ab ioven m'apais"

I.   I feed on joy and youthfulness
        and joy and youthfulness content me;
        since my friend is the most cheerful
        I am cheered and charmed by him,
  5 and because I'm true to him,
        it's well that he be true
        to me; I never stray from loving him
        nor does my heart lead me astray.

II.   I'm pleased to know there's so much worth
  10 in him, the one that I most wish would have me;
        I pray that God may bring great joy
        to the man who brought him to me.
        May he disbelieve whoever speaks
        false words to him, and believe what I say,
  15 for many people bind brooms
        and with those brooms are swept away.

III.   The lady who has faith in virtue
        surely ought to put her faith
        in a knight of heart and worth;
  20 when she knows how worthy he is,
        let her dare reveal she loves him;
        a lady who reveals her love
        hears virtuous, pleasant people
        say only pleasing things about her.

IV. 25 For I've chosen one who's brave and noble
        in whom worth becomes ennobled:
        openhanded, agile, knowing,
        full of knowledge and good sense.
        I pray that he believe in me
  30 and that none make him believe
        I'm failing him, always provided
        that I find no fault in him.

V.   Amics, la vostra valenssa
      sabon li pro e li valen,
   35 per q'ieu vos qier de mantenen
      si.us pla*i* vostra mantenenssa.

V.   My friend, brave, worthy persons
         know your worth,
     35 and so I ask you presently:
         please lend me your protecting presence.

2. La Comtessa de Dia, "A chantar m'er de so q'ieu no volria"

La Comtessa de Dia

I.   A chantar m'er de so q'ieu no volria,
tant me rancur de lui cui sui amia,
car eu l'am mais que nuilla ren que sia;
vas lui no.m val merces ni cortesia
5 ni ma beltatz ni mos pretz ni mos sens,
c'atressi.m sui enganada e trah*i*a
com degr'esser s'ieu fos desavinens.

II.   D'aisso.m conort car anc non fis faillenssa,
amics, vas vos per nuilla captenenssa,
10 anz vos am mais non fetz Seguis Valenssa,
e platz mi mout que eu d'amar vos venssa,
lo mieus amics, car etz lo plus valens;
mi faitz orgoil en digz et en parvenssa
e si etz francs vas totas autras gens.

III 15 Meraveill me cum vostre cors s'orgoilla,
amics, vas me per q'ai razon qe.m doilla;
non es ies dreitz c'autr'amors vos mi toilla
per nuilla ren qe.us diga ni.us *a*coilla,
e membre vos cals fo.l comenssamens
20 de nostr'amor, ia Dompnedieus non vuoilla
q'en ma colpa sia.l departimens.

IV.   Proessa grans q'el vostre cors s'aizina
e lo rics pretz q'avetz m'en ataina,
c'una non sai loindana ni vezina
25 si vol amar vas vos no si aclina;
mas vos, amics, e*z* ben tant conoissens
que ben devetz conoisser la plus fina,
e membre vos de nostres covinens.

V.   Valer mi deu mos pretz e mos paratges
30 e ma beutatz e plus mos fins coratges,
per q'ieu vos man lai on es vostre estatges

2. La Comtessa de Dia, "A chantar m'er de so q'ieu no volria"

I.   I must sing of what I'd rather not,
          I'm so angry about him whose friend I am,
          for I love him more than anything;
          mercy and courtliness don't help me
    5 with him, nor does my beauty, or my rank, or my mind;
          for I am every bit as betrayed and wronged
          as I'd deserve to be if I were ugly.

II.   It comforts me that I have done no wrong
          to you, my friend, through any action;
    10 indeed, I love you more than Seguis loved Valenssa;
          it pleases me to outdo you in loving,
          friend, for you are the most valiant;
          you offer prideful words and looks to me
          but are gracious to every other person.

III. 15 It amazes me how prideful your heart is
          toward me, friend, for which I'm right to grieve;
          it isn't fair that another love take you away
          because of any word or welcome I might give you.
          And remember how it was at the beginning
    20 of our love; may the Lord God not allow
          our parting to be any fault of mine.

IV.   The great valor that dwells in your person,
          and the high rank you have, these trouble me,
          for I don't know a woman, far or near,
    25 who, if she wished to love, would not turn to you;
          but you, friend, are so knowing,
          you surely ought to know the truest one,
          and remember what our agreement was.

V.   My rank and lineage should be of help
    30 to me, and my beauty and, still more, my true heart;
          this song, let it be my messenger;

   esta chansson que me sia messatges,
   e voill saber, lo mieus bels amics gens,
   per que m'etz vos tant fers ni tant salvatges,
35 no sai si s'es orgoills ni mals talens.

VI.   Mas aitan plus vuoill li digas, messatges,
    q'en trop orgoill ant gran dan maintas gens.

therefore, I send it to you, out in your estate,
and I would like to know, my fine, fair friend,
why you are so fierce and cruel to me.
35 I can't tell if it's from pride or malice.

VI.   I especially want you, messenger, to tell him
that too much pride brings harm to many persons.

3. La Comtessa de Dia, "Estat ai en greu cossirier"

La Comtessa de Dia

I.   Estat ai en greu cossirier
per un cavallier q'ai agut,
e vuoil sia totz temps saubut
cum eu l'ai amat a sobrier.
5 Ara vei q'ieu sui trahida
car eu non li donei m'amor
don ai estat en gran error
en lieig e qand sui vestida.

II.   Ben volria mon cavallier
10 tener un ser *en* mos bratz nut,
q'el s'en tengra per ereubut
sol q'a lui fezes cosseillier;
car plus m'en sui abellida
no fetz Floris de Blanchaflor;
15 eu l'autrei mon cor e m'amor,
mon sen, mos huoills *e* ma vida.

III.   Bels amics, avinens e bos,
cora.us tenrai *en* mon poder,
e que iagues ab vos un ser,
20 e qe.us des un bais amoros?
Sapchatz gran talan n'auria
qe.us tengues en luoc del marit
ab so que m'aguessetz plevit
de far tot so qu'eu volria.

3. La Comtessa de Dia, "Estat ai en greu cossirier"

I.   I have been sorely troubled
          about a knight I had;
          I want it known for all time
          how exceedingly I loved him.
    5 Now I see myself betrayed
          because I didn't grant my love
          to him; I've suffered much distress
          from it, in bed and fully clothed.

II.   I'd like to hold my knight
   10 in my arms one evening, naked,
          for he'd be overjoyed
          were I only serving as his pillow,
          and he makes me more radiant
          than Floris his Blanchaflor.
   15 To him I grant my heart, my love,
          my mind, my eyes, my life.

III.   Fair, agreeable, good friend,
          when will I have you in my power,
          lie beside you for an evening,
   20 and kiss you amorously?
          Be sure I'd feel a strong desire
          to have you in my husband's place
          provided you had promised me
          to do everything I wished.

12

4. La Comtessa de Dia, "Fin ioi me dona alegranssa"

La Contessa de Dia

I.   Fin ioi me dona alegranssa
    per qu'eu chan plus gaiamen,
    e no m'o teing a pensanssa
    ni a negun penssamen,
    5 car sai que son a mon dan
    li fals lausengier truan
    e lor mals diz non *m*'esglaia,
    anz en son dos tanz plus gaia.

II.   En mi non a*n* ges fianssa
    10 li lausengier mal dizen,
    c'om non pot aver honranssa
    qu'*a* ab els acordamen,
    qu'ist son d'altrestal semblan
    com la nivol que s'espan
    15 qe.l sole*lh*s en pert sa raia,
    per qu'eu non am gent savaia.

III.   E vos, gelos mal parlan,
    no.*u*s cuges qu'eu mon tarçan (?)
    que iois e iovenz no.m plaia
    20 per tal que dols vos deschaia.

4. La Comtessa de Dia, "Fin ioi me dona alegranssa"

I.   Happiness brings me pure joy
which makes me sing more cheerfully,
and I have no heavy thought
nor any heaviness at all
5 from knowing that my harm
is sought by those mean, lying gossips;
their false words don't frighten me
but only make me twice as cheerful.

II.   In me the false-speaking gossips
10 find no ally,
for no one can be honored
who conspires with them;
they're exactly like
the fog that spreads
15 and makes the sun lose brightness;
for that I love no wicked people.

III.   And you, foul-tongued, jealous man,
don't think that I'll be slow
to please myself with joy and youth
20 just because it may upset you.

5. Castelloza, "Ia de chantar non degra aver talan"

Na Castelloza

I.   Ia de chantar non degra aver tal*an*
      car on mais cha*n*
      e pieitz me vai d'amor,
      que plaing e plor
5   fant en mi lor estatge,
      car en mala merce
      ai mes mon cor e me,
      e s'*e*n breu no.m rete,
      trop ai faich lonc badatge.

II.   10 Ai! bels amics, sivals un bel semblan
      mi faitz enan
      q'ieu muoira de dolor,
      q*e* l'amador
      vos tenon per salvatge,
15   car ioia no.m ave
      de vos, don no.m recre
      d'amar per bona fe
      totz temps ses cor volatge.

III.   Mas ia vas vos non aurai cor truan
20   ni plen d'engan,
      si tot vos n'ai peior,
      c'a grand honor
      m'o teing e*n* mon coratge,
      anz pens qan mi sove
25   del ric pretz qe.us mante
      e sai ben qe.us cove
      dompna d'aussor paratge.

IV.   Despois vos vi fui al vostre coman
      et anc per ta*n*,
30   amics, no.us n'aic meillor,
      que preiador
      no.m mandetz ni messatge

5. Castelloza, "Ia de chantar non degra aver talan"

I. I should never have the wish to sing
 because the more I sing
 the worse it goes for me in love;
 laments and tears
 5 find their home in me,
 for I have placed my heart, my self
 where there's no mercy;
 if he does not accept my service soon,
 I will have stayed too long.

II. 10 Ah! Fair friend, show at least one
 gracious look
 to me before I die of grief;
 all lovers
 consider you a beast
 15 for no joy comes to me
 from you whom I don't fail
 to love most faithfully
 at all times, with no change of heart.

III. My heart will never betray you
 20 nor seek to trick you,
 though I have the worst from you;
 for in my heart
 I take it as an honor;
 indeed, I'm sure, when I remember
 25 the high rank you enjoy,
 that you deserve
 a lady of higher lineage than mine.

IV. Since I saw you, I've been at your command,
 and for my pains,
 30 friend, I've had nothing better from you:
 you send no plea-bearer or messenger;

que ia.m viretz lo fre,
amics, non fassatz re.
35 Car iois no mi soste
a pauc de dol non ratge.

V.   Si pro.i agues, be.us membri'en chantan
q'aic vostre gan
q'enbliei ab gran temor,
40 puois aic paor
qe i aguessetz dampnatge
d'aicella qe.us rete,
amics, per q'ieu desse
l*o* tornei, car ben cre
45 q'eu non ai poderatge.

VI.   Dels cavalliers conosc que *i* fant *lor dan,*
car ia prei*a*n
dompnas plus q'ellas lor,
c'autra ricor
50 no.i ant ni seignoratge,
que pois dompna s'ave
d'amar, preiar deu be
cavallier, s'en lui ve
proeza e vassalatge.

VII. 55 Dompna Na Mieils, ancse
am so don ma*l* mi ve,
car cel qui pretz mante
a vas mi cor volatge.

VIII.   Bels Noms, ges no.m recre
60 de vos amar iasse
car viu en bona fe,
bontatz e ferm coratge.

as for turning in my direction,
friend, you do no such thing!
Because no joy sustains me,
35 I'm all but mad with grief.

V.   If it helped me, I'd remind you, singing,
that I had your glove,
the one I stole in fear and trembling;
then I feared
40 you would be harmed
by the lady who has your service;
so, friend, at once
I gave it back, because I know
I have no rightful claim.

VI.   45 I know knights who harm themselves
when they plead
with ladies more than ladies plead with them,
for no further rank
or power is gained by it;
50 so when it happens that a lady
loves, she ought to court
the knight if she sees
prowess and knightly worth in him.

VII.   Lady-the-Best, I always
55 love what brings me harm,
for he who upholds honor
has an inconstant heart towards me.

VIII.   Fair Name, I never fail
to love you at all times,
60 for I dwell where there's good faith,
good will and constant heart.

6. Castelloza, "Amics, s'ie.us trobes avinen"

Na Castelloza

I.   Amics, s'ie.us trobes avinen,
humil e franc e de bona merce,
be.us amera, quand era m'en sove
q'us trob vas mi mal e fellon e tric,
5 e fauc chanssos per tal q'eu fassa auzir
vostre bon pretz, dond eu non puosc sofrir
que no.us fassa lauzar a tota gen,
on plus mi faitz mal et adiramen.

II.   Iamais no.us tenrai per valen
10 ni.us amarai de bon cor e de fe
tro que veirai si ia.m valria re
si.us mostrava cor fellon ni enic;
non farai ia, car no vuoil puscatz dir
q'ieu anc vas vos agues cor de faillir,
15 c'auriatz pois calque razonamen
s'ieu fazia vas vos nuill falimen.

III.   Eu sai ben c'a mi est*a* gen,
si be.is dizon tuich que mout descove
que dompna prei a cavallier de se
20 ni que.l teigna totz temps *tan lonc pressic*,
mas cel q'o ditz non sap ges ben gauzir
q'ieu vuoill proar enans qe.m lais morir
qe.l preiar ai un gran revenimen
qan prec cellui don ai greu pessamen.

IV. 25 Assatz es fols qui m'en repren
de vos amar, pois tant gen mi cove,
e cel q'o ditz non sap cum s'es de me,
ni no.us vei ges aras si cum vos vic,
qan me dissetz que non agues cossir
30 que calc'ora poiria endevenir
que n'auria enqueras gauzimen,
de sol lo dich n'ai eu lo cor gauzen.

6. Castelloza, "Amics, s'ie.us trobes avinen"

I.   Friend, if I had found you kind,
        humble, frank and merciful,
        I'd love you well; but now I recall
        that I find you evil, harsh and false to me.
    5 I sing in order to make known
        your great worth and therefore cannot stand
        not to have you praised by everyone
        at the point when you harm and rile me most.

II.   I will never hold you worthy
   10 nor will I love you with good, faithful heart
        until I see if it would help me
        to have a harsh or evil heart toward you.
        But no, not that! I don't want to enable you
        to say my heart was ever false
   15 to you for then you'd have an argument
        against me if I failed in any way.

III.   I know this is a fitting thing for me,
        though everybody says it isn't proper
        for a lady to plead her case with a knight,
   20 or to make such long speeches to him;
        he who says this has no knowledge of true joy.
        I'd like to prove, before I let death come,
        that in pleading I find great renewal
        when I court the one who gives me heavy pain.

IV.   25 He's a great fool who blames me
        for loving you, because it suits me well,
        and one who says this knows not how it is
        with me. Nor do I see you now as I saw you
        when you told me not to worry
   30 because at any moment it might happen
        that I would have joy again;
        just these words fill my heart with joy.

V.   Tot'autr'amor teing a nien,
            e sapchatz ben que mais iois no.m soste
     35   mas lo vostre que m'alegra e.m reve
            on mais en sent d'afan e de destric,
            e.m cuig ades alegrar e gauzir
            de vos, amics, q'ieu non puosc convenir,
            ni ioi non ai, ni socors non aten
     40   mas sol aitant qan n'aurai en dormen.

VI.   Oimais non sai qe.us mi presen,
            que cercat ai et ab mal et ab be
            vostre dur cor don lo mieus no.is recre,
            e no.us o man q'ieu mezeussa.us o dic
     45   qu'enoia me si no.m voletz gauzir
            de calque ioi, e si.m laissatz morir
            faretz pechat e serai n'en tormen
            e seretz ne blasmatz vilanamen.

V.   I count all other love as nothing;
       you can be sure no joy sustains me
 35   except yours, which cheers and revives me
       when I most feel the anguish and distress
       of it; and now I think I'll take pleasure and joy
       in you, friend whom I cannot summon;
       I have no joy, nor do I expect help
 40   except as much as I will have in sleeping.

VI.   From now on, I don't know how to act
       with you: I've studied, with good and bad intent,
       your hard heart, from which mine does not shrink;
       and I'm not sending this, I'm telling you myself:
 45   I'm angry if you refuse me
       any joy, and if you let me die
       you'll commit a sin. I'll be in torment,
       and you'll be vilely blamed.

7. Castelloza, "Mout avetz faich lonc estatge"

Na Castelloza

I.   Mout avetz faich lonc estatge,
amics, pois de mi.us partitz,
et es mi greu e salvatge
car me iuretz e.m plevitz
5 que als iorns de vostra vida
non acsetz dompna mas me,
e si d'autra vos perte
mi avetz morta e trahida,
c'avia en vos m'esperanssa
10 que m'amassetz ses doptanssa.

II.   Bels amics, de fin coratge
*v*us am*ei* puois m'abellitz,
e sai que fatz hi follatge
que plus m'en etz escaritz
15 c'anc non fis vas vos ganchi*d*a,
e si.m fasetz mal per be
be.us am e no m'en recre,
mas tant m'a amors sazida
qu'eu non cre que benananssa
20 puosca aver ses vostr'amanssa.

III.   Mout aurai mes mal usatge
a las autras amairitz,
c'om sol trametre messatge
e motz triatz e chausitz,
25 et eu tenc me per garida,
amics, a la mia fe,
qan vos prec, c'aissi.m cove,
qe.ill plus pros n'es enriquida
s'a de vos cal*c'aon*danssa
30 de baisar o d'acoindanssa.

7. Castelloza, "Mout avetz faich lonc estatge"

I.   You've stayed a very long time away
           from me, my friend, since you departed,
           and I find it harsh and grim,
           because you pledged and swore
       5 that all your days
           you'd have no lady besides me;
           and if you're attending to another,
           you have murdered and betrayed me,
           for in you I had my hope
      10 that you would love me without wavering.

II.   Fair friend, with true heart
           I loved you because you pleased me;
           I know it's foolish of me,
           for you've abandoned me more often
      15 than I've wronged you;
           and though you do me harm for good,
           I truly love you and do not shrink
           from it; but love has seized me so
           that I don't think any blessing
      20 can be mine without your love.

III.   I'll set a very poor example
           to other loving ladies:
           usually a man sends messages,
           well-chosen and selected words,
      25 while I consider myself healed,
           friend, truthfully,
           when I court you, for that suits me;
           the noblest lady is exalted
           to obtain the gift
      30 of your kisses or embraces.

IV.   Mal ai'eu s'anc cor volatge
         vos aic, ni.us fui camiairitz,
         ni drutz de negun paratge
         per mi non fo encobitz,
    35   anz sui pensiva e marrida
         car de m'amor no.us sove
         e si de vos iois no.m ve,
         tost mi trobaretz fenida,
         car per pauc de malananssa
    40   mor dompna s'om tot no.il lanssa.

V.   Tot lo maltraich e.l dampnatge
         que per vos m'es escaritz
         vos grazir fan mos lignatge
         e sobre totz mos maritz,
    45   e s'anc fetz vas mi faillida
         perdon l'a.us per bona fe,
         e prec ...
         ... qand auretz auzida
         ma chansson qe.us fai fianssa,
    50   sai trobetz bella semblanssa.

IV.   May evil take me if my heart was ever fickle
        toward you, or if I was untrue,
        nor have I ever desired
        another lover of any lineage;
35   rather I'm pensive and dismayed,
        for you forget my love;
        if I don't have some joy from you,
        you will soon find me dead;
        for a lady all but dies of her sickness
40   if no man treats it.

V.   For all the damage and the harm
        that come to me from you
        my family thanks you,
        especially my husband.
45   If ever you have failed me,
        I pardon you in all good faith
        and pray [that you will come to me]
        as soon as you have heard
        my song, for I promise
50   that you'll find warm welcome.

8. Anonymous, "Per ioi que d'amor m'avegna"

I.   *P*er ioi que d'amor m'avegna
        no.m calgra ogan esbaudir,
        qu'eu non cre qu'en grat me tegna
        cel c'anc non volc hobesir
    5 mos bos motz ni mas chansos,
        ni anc no fon lasaz *sos*
        qu'ie.m pogues de lui sofrir,
        ans tem que.m n'er a morir
        ... c'ab tal autra regna
   10 don per mi no.s vol partir.

II.   *P*artir m'en er, mas no.m degna,
        que morta m'an li conssir,
        e pos no.ill platz que.m retegna
        vueilla.m d'aitant hobesir
   15 c'ab sos avinenz respos
        me tegna mon cor ioios,
        e ia a sidonz non tir
        s'ie.l fas d'aitan enardir
        qu'ieu no.l prec per mi que.s tegna
   20 de leis amar ni servir.

III.   *L*eis serva mas mi.n revegna
        que no.m lais del tot morir
        ... que m'estegna
        s'amors don me fa languir.
   25 Hai! amics, valenz e bos,
        car es lo meiller c'anc fos
        non vuillaz c'aillors me vir,
        mas no.m volez far ni dir
        con eu ia iorn me captegna
   30 de vos amar ni grasir.

IV.   *G*rasisc vos con que m'en pregna
        tot lo maltrag e.l consir,
        e ia cavaliers no.s fegna
        de mi, c'u*n* sol non desir;

8. Anonymous, "Per ioi que d'amor m'avegna"

I.   To delight in any joy that love might bring
         will not concern me soon,
         for I don't think he holds me dear,
         the one who never wishes to obey
   5 my good words or songs;
         nor was any music ever woven
         that would enable me to do without him;
         so I fear it will be mine to die
         ... for he dwells with another
  10 and won't part from her for my sake.

II.   I must depart; he no longer prizes me,
         for I've been killed by painful thoughts,
         and since it doesn't please him to retain me,
         let him obey me in this small way:
  15 that by some agreeable responses
         he may keep my heart in joy.
         And let it not distress his lady
         that I make him just this bold,
         for I don't ask him, for my sake, to cease
  20 loving or serving her.

III.   Let him serve her but return to me
         in order not to let me die entirely.
         ... that his love
         ruins me and makes me languish.
  25 Ah, worthy and good friend,
         for you're the best that ever was,
         don't wish me to turn away;
         you still don't want to do or say
         what might one day help me keep myself
  30 from loving or praising you.

IV.   I praise you, whatever may befall me
         from all the ill use and painful thought,
         and let no knight ever make claims
         on me, for I don't want a single one,

35 bels amics, si faz fort vos
   on tenc los oilz ambedos;
   e plaz me can vos remir,
   c'anc tan bel non sai chausir.
   Dieus prec c'ab mos bratz vos segna
40 c'autre no.m pot enriquir.

V.   Rica soi ab que.us suvegna
        com pogues en luec venir
        on eu vos bais e.us estregna
        c'ab aitan pot revenir
45   mos cors, ques es enveios
        de vos mout e cobeitos;
        amics, no.m laissatz morir,
        pueis de vos no.m puesc gandir
        un bel semblan que.m revegna
50   faiz que m'ausiza.l consir.

35 fair friend, so great is my desire for you
on whom I train both eyes;
it truly pleases me to gaze at you
for I couldn't find another one as fair.
God, I pray that I may press you in my arms
40 for no one else can so enrich me.

V.   I am rich as long as you remember
how I might come to a place
where I could embrace and kiss you,
for just from that my heart
45 can recover—it's so desirous
of you and full of wishes.
Friend, don't let me die;
since I can't leave you,
keep a kind look that may revive me
50 and kill the painful thought.

9. Clara d'Anduza, "En greu esmay et en greu pessamen"

Clara d'Anduza

I.   En greu esmay et en greu pessamen
an mes mon cor et en granda error
li lauzengier e.lh fals devinador,
abayssador de ioy e de ioven,
5 qar vos q'eu am mais que res qu'el mon sia
an fait de me departir e lonhar
si q'ieu no.us puesc vezer ni remirar,
don muer de dol, d'ira e de feunia.

II.   Selh que.m blasma vostr'amor ni.m defen
10 no podon far en re mon cor mellor
ni.l dous dezir qu'ieu ai de vos maior
ni l'enveya ni.l dezir ni.l talen,
e non es hom, tan mos enemicx sia,
si.l n'aug dir ben, que no.l tenha en car,
15 e si.n ditz mal, mais no.m pot *dir* ni far
neguna re que a plazer me sia.

III.   Ia no.us donetz, belhs amicx, espaven
que ia ves vos aia cor trichador,
ni qu'ie.us camge per nul autr'amador
20 si.m pregavon d'autras donas un cen,
qu'amors que.m te per vos en sa bailia
vol que mon cor vos estuy e vos gar
e farai o, e s'ieu pogues emblar
mon cors, tals l'a que iamais non l'auria.

IV. 25 Amicx, tan ai d'ira e de feunia
quar no vos vey, que quant yeu cug chantar,
planh e sospir per qu'ieu no puesc so far
a mas coblas que.l cor*s* complir volria.

9. Clara d'Anduza, "En greu esmay et en greu pessamen"

I.   In grave distress, grave trouble,
          and great confusion my heart is thrown
          by slanderers and treacherous spies,
          bringers down of joy and youth,
          5 for you whom I love best in all the world
          they've stolen and sent away from me
          so I can't see or gaze at you
          and I'm dying of grief, torment, and anger.

II.   He who blames or forbids my loving you
          10 cannot in any way amend my heart
          nor increase the sweet desire I have for you
          nor the wish, nor the desiring, nor the yearning;
          and there's no man, however much my enemy,
          that I won't love if he speaks well of my friend;
          15 if he speaks ill, he cannot say or do
          anything at all that pleases me.

III.   Have no fear, fair friend,
          that my heart will ever be false to you,
          or that I'll exchange you for another
          20 even if a hundred other ladies beg me.
          Love that has me in its power because of you
          commands my heart to enclose and keep you,
          which I will do; yet someone has my body
          who never would, if I could steal it back.

IV.   25 Friend, I'm in such rage and torment
          because you're out of sight, that when I try to sing,
          I complain and sigh, for I cannot, with my verses,
          accomplish what I wish.

10. Bietris de Roman, "Na Maria, pretz e fina valors"

Na Bietris de Roman

I.   Na Maria, pretz *e* fina valors
e.l gioi e.l sen e la fina beutatz
e l'acuglir e.l pretz e las onors
e.l gent parlar e l'avinen sola*tz*
5 e la do*uz* cara e la gaia cu*e*ndansa
e.l ducz esgart e l'amoros se*m*blan,
*q*e son e*n* vos, don non avetz egansa,
me fan traire vas vos s*e*s cor truan.

II.   Per *q*e vos prec, si.*us* platz, *q*e fin'amors
10 e gausiment et doutz umilitatz
me puosca far ab vos tan de socors,
*q*e mi donetz, bella do*m*pna, si.*us* platz,
so don plus ai d'aver gioi esperansa,
*c*ar en vos ai mon cor e mon tal*a*n
15 e per vos ai tut so c'ai d'alegransa
e per vos vauc mantas ves sospiran.

III   E car beutas e valor*s* vos enansa
sobra tutas, c'una no.*us es* denan,
vos prec, se.*us* plas, per so *q*e.*us* es onransa,
20 *q*e non ametz entendidor truan.

IV.   Bella dompna, cui pretz e gioi enan*s*a,
e gient parlar, a vos m*a*s coblas man,
car e*n* vos es *gauss'*et alegransa
et tut lo ben c'om e*n* dona deman.

10. Bietris de Roman, "Na Maria, pretz e fina valors"

I.   Lady Maria, the virtue and pure worth
        and joy and wisdom and pure beauty
        and graciousness and virtue and honor
        and noble speech and lovely company
     5 and sweet face and cheerful manner
        and sweet gaze and amorous expression,
        these things, in which no one equals you,
        draw me to you with no deceitful heart.

II.   For this I beg you, please, to let pure love,
    10 delight, and sweet humility
        give me the help I need with you
        so you will grant me, lovely lady, please,
        what I most hope to enjoy;
        for in you lie my heart and my desire:
    15 I have all my happiness because of you,
        I'm sighing many sighs because of you.

III.   As beauty and worth exalt you
        above all other women (none surpass you)
        I pray you, please (for this will bring you honor)
    20 not to love any deceitful admirer.

IV.   Lovely lady, exalted in virtue, joy
        and noble speech, I send my song to you,
        because in you live gaiety and happiness
        and every quality one looks for in a lady.

11. Azalais de Porcairagues, "Ar em al freg temps vengut"

N'Alasais de Porcaragues

I.   Ar em al freg temps vengut
que.l gells e.l neus e la faingna,
e.*l* auçellet estan mut
c'us de chantar non s'afraigna,
5 e son sec li ram pels plais
que flors ni foilla no.i nais
ni rrossignols no i crida
que l'am'e*n* mai me rreissida.

II.   Tant ai lo co*r* deseubut
10 per qu'eu soi a toz estraigna,
e sai que l'om a perdut
molt plus tost que non gasaingna,
e s'ieu faill ab motz verais
d'Aurenga me moc l'esglais,
15 per qu'eu m'estauc esbaida
e.n pert solatz en partida.

III.   Dompna met mot mal s'amor
que ab ric ome pla*i*deia,
ab plus aut de vavasor,
20 e s'ill o fai il folleia,
car so diz om en Veillai
que ges per ricor non vai,
e dompna que n'es chauzida
en tenc per envilanida.

IV. 25 Amic ai de gran valor
que sobre toz seignoreia,
e non a cor trichador
vas me que amor m'autreia.
Eu dic que m'amors l'eschai
30 e cel que dis que non fai,
Dieus li don mal'esgarida,
qu'eu m'en teing fort per guerida.

11. Azalais de Porcairagues, "Ar em al freg temps vengut"

I.   Now we are come to the cold time
          when there's snow and ice and sludge
          and the little birds are mute,
          not one attempts to sing,
     5 and the boughs are bare in hedges;
          neither flower nor leaf is sprouting there,
          nor, calling there, the nightingale
          who wakes my soul in May.

II.   My heart's in such disarray
     10 that I am estranged from everyone;
          I know that we have lost
          in less time than it took to gain.
          And if truthful words fail me,
          it's that my grief comes from Aurenga,
     15 and leaves me confounded,
          so I've nearly lost my comfort.

III.   A lady places her love poorly
          when she seeks out a man of wealth
          higher than a vavassor.
     20 If she does, she's acting foolish,
          for people in Velay say this:
          love does not go with riches.
          If a lady's known for that
          I consider her dishonored.

IV.   25 I have a friend of utmost worth,
          higher than all the others.
          He doesn't have a treacherous heart
          towards me, for he grants me love.
          I say that my love falls to him,
     30 and God send evil luck
          to the one who says it is not so,
          for I consider myself safe.

V.   Bels amics, de bon talan,
            son ab vos toz iorz en gua*t*ge,
       35   corteza *e* de bel semblan,
            sol no.m demandes outra*t*ge;
            tost en veirem a l'assai
            qu'en vostra merce.m metrai;
            vos m'aves la fe plevida
       40   que no.m demandes faillida.

VI.   A Dieu coman Belesgar
            e plus la siutat d'Aurenga
            e Gloriet'e.l caslar
            e lo seignor de Proenza,
       45   e tot cant vol mon ben lai
            e l'arc on son fag l'assai;
            cellui perdiei c'a ma vida
            en serai toz iorz marrida.

VII.   Ioglar que aves cor gai
       50   ves Narbona portas lai
            ma chanson a la fenida
            lei cui iois e iovenz guida.

V.   Fair friend, with good intent
        I am at all times promised to you,
35 courteous and smiling
        as long as you ask of me no outrage.
        Soon we'll come to the test:
        I'll put myself at your mercy.
        You have given your word
40 to ask nothing wrong of me.

VI.   I commend Belesgar to God
        also the city of Aurenga
        and Glorieta and the castle
        and the lord of Provence,
45 and all those who wish me well
        and the arch where deeds are carved.
        I have lost him who has my life
        and will always grieve about it.

VII.   Jongleur, whose heart is gay,
50 carry out toward Narbonne
        my song with these final verses
        to her whose guides are youth and joy.

12. Maria de Ventadorn and Gui d'Ussel, "Gui d'Ussel be.m pesa"

Na Maria de Ventedorn e'N Gui d'Uissel

I.   Gui d'Ussel be.m pesa de vos
        car vos etz laissatz de chantar,
        e car vos i volgra tornar
        per que sabetz d'aitals razos,
    5 vuoill qe.m digatz si deu far egalmen
        dompna per drut, qan lo qier francamen,
        cum el per lieis, tot cant taing ad amor,
        segon los dreitz que tenon l'amador.

II.   Dompna Na Maria, tenssos
   10 e tot cant cuiava laissar,
        mas aoras non puosc estar
        q'ieu non chant als vostres somos.
        E respond eu a la dompna breumen
        que per son drut deu far comunalmen
   15 cum el per lieis ses garda de ricor,
        q'en dos amics non deu aver maior.

III.   Gui, tot so don es cobeitos
        deu drutz ab merce demandar,
        e.il dompna pot *o* comandar,
   20 ...
        E.l drutz deu far precs e comandamen
        cum per amiga e per dompna eissamen,
        e.il dompna deu a son drut far honor
        cum ad amic, mas non cum a seignor.

IV. 25 Dompna, sai dizon demest nos
        que, pois que dompna vol amar,
        engalmen deu son drut onrar,
        pois engalmen son amoros.
        E s'esdeven que l'am plus finamen,
   30 e.l faich e.l dich en deu far aparen,
        e si ell'a fals cor ni trichador,
        ab bel semblan deu cobrir sa follor.

12. Maria de Ventadorn and Gui d'Ussel, "Gui d'Ussel be.m pesa "

I.   Gui d'Ussel, I'm troubled about you
           because you've left off singing;
           so, as I wish to bring you back to it,
           and because you know so much about such things,
     5 I want you to tell me if a lady should do equally
           for her lover all that pertains to love,
           when he asks honestly, as he does for her,
           according to the laws that lovers hold.

II.   Lady Maria, I thought I was done
    10 with *tensos* and with all songs,
           but now it isn't possible
           for me not to sing at your command.
           So I answer the lady in few words:
           She should return in kind to her lover
    15 what he gives her, without regard to rank,
           for between two friends neither should be greater.

III.   Gui, a lover must ask for all he wants
           as for a favor,
           and the lady may command,
    20 ...
           And the lover should fulfill pleas and commands
           for her who is both his friend and his lady,
           and the lady must honor her lover
           as a friend, but not as overlord.

IV.   25 Lady, among us they say
           that when a lady wants to love
           she should honor her lover on equal terms
           because they are equally in love.
           And if she happens to love him more perfectly
    30 she should let it show in deeds and words;
           and if she has a false or treacherous heart
           she should hide her folly with pleasant looks.

V.   Gui d'Uissel, ges d'aitals razos
        non son li drut al comenssar,
35 anz ditz chascus, qan vol preiar,
        mans iointas e de genolos:
        "Dompna voillatz qe.us serva franchamen
        cum lo vostr'om," et ella enaissi.l pren.
        Eu vo.l iutge per dreich a trahitor
40 si.s rend pariers e.is det per servidor.

VI.   Dompna, so es plaitz vergoignos
        ad ops de dompna a razonar
        que cellui non teigna per par
        a cui a faich un cor de dos.
45 O vos diretz, e no.us estara gen,
        que.l drutz la deu amar plus finamen
        o vos diretz q'il son par entre lor,
        que ren no.il deu drutz mas qant per amor.

V.   Gui d'Ussel, at the beginning, lovers
        say no such thing;
   35   instead, each one, when he wants to court,
        says, with hands joined and on his knees:
        "Lady, permit me to serve you honestly
        as your liege man" and that's the way she takes him.
        I rightly consider him a traitor if, having given
   40   himself as servant, he makes himself an equal.

VI.   Lady, it's a shameful claim
        on a lady's part to argue
        that she should not consider equal
        the man with whom she's made two hearts into one.
   45   Either you'll say (and not to your own honor)
        that the lover must love her more perfectly,
        or you'll say that they are equals,
        for he owes her nothing but what he gives for love.

13. Alamanda and Giraut de Bornelh, "S'ie.us qier conseill,
bella amia Alamanda"

Girautz de Borneill

I.   S'ie.us qier conseill, bella amia Alamanda,
no.l mi vedetz, c'om cochatz lo.us demanda,
que so m'a dich vostra dompna truanda
que loing sui fors issitz de sa comanda,
5 que so qe.m det m'estrai er e.m desmanda.
Qe.m cosseillatz?
c'a pauc lo cors totz d'ira no m'abranda,
tant fort en sui iratz.

II.   Per Dieu, Giraut, ies aissi tot a randa
10 volers d'amics no.is fai ni no.is garanda,
que si l'uns faill, l'autre coven que blanda
que lor destrics no.is creisca ni s'espanda,
e s'ela.us ditz d'aut puoig que sia landa,
vos l'an crezatz,
15 e plassa vos lo bes e.l mals q'il manda,
c'aissi seretz amatz.

III.   Non puosc mudar que contr'orguoill non gronda;
ia siatz vos, donzella, bella e blonda,
pauc d'ira.us notz e paucs iois vos aonda,
20 mas ies non etz primieira ni segonda.
Eu, qe.m tem fort d'est ira qe.m confonda,
vos me lauzatz,
si.m sent perir, qe.m tenga plus vas l'onda;
mal cre qe.m capdellatz.

IV.   25 Si m'enqeretz d'aital razon prionda,
Per Dieu, Giraut, non sai cum vos responda;
vos m'apellatz de leu cor iauzionda,
mais vuoill pelar mon prat c'autre.l mi tonda,
que s'ie.us era del plaich far desironda,
30 vos escercatz
cum son bel cors vos esduia e.us resconda.
Ben par cum n'etz coitatz.

13. Alamanda and Giraut de Bornelh, "S'ie.us qier conseill,
    bella amia Alamanda"

I.   If I ask your advice, lovely friend Alamanda,
        don't refuse me; it's a tortured man who asks it,
        for your treacherous lady has informed me
        that I have strayed from her command,
      5 and what she gave me she now takes back, withdraws.
        What's your advice?
        For rage has all but set me on fire,
        this angers me so much.

II.   For God's sake, Giraut, in no such haste
     10 is a lover's wish ever fulfilled or carried out;
        for if one friend fails, he must indulge the other
        so that their trouble's not increased or spread around;
        and if she tells you a high mountain is a plain,
        agree with her,
     15 and be content with both the good and ill she sends;
        that way you'll be loved.

III.   I can't help grumbling about pride.
        You may be a beautiful blond maiden,
        drowned by the least anger, overwhelmed by the least joy,
     20 but you are neither first nor second-best,
        and to me, who fear my anger may confound me,
        you suggest,
        when I think I'm drowning, that I head into the waves;
        I think you misguide me badly.

IV. 25 If you ask me about such deep things,
        by God, Giraut, I don't know how to respond;
        you claim my heart is easily made joyful;
        I just want to trim my field before another person mows it.
        For if I wished to make the plea that you request,
     30 I'd say seek out
        the reason she locks up and hides her lovely self from you.
        It's clear how much you're tortured.

V.   Donzella oimais non siatz tant parlieira,
        qu'il m'a mentit mais de cinc vetz prim*i*eira.
    35 Cuiatz vos doncs q'ieu totz temps lo sofieira?
        Semblaria c'o fezes per nescieira,
        d'autr'amistat ai talan q'ie.us enqieira,
        si no.us callatz,
        meillor cosseil dava Na Berengieira
    40 que vos no m'en donatz.

VI.   Lora vei ieu, Giraut, q'ella.*u*s o m*i*eira,
        car l'apelletz camiairitz ni leugieira,
        pero cuiatz que del plaich vos enqieira?
        Ieu non cuig ies qu'il sia tant main*i*eira;
    45 anz er oimais sa promessa derrieira,
        que qe.us digatz,
        s*i*.s destreing tant que contra vos sof*i*eira
        trega ni fi ni patz.

VII.   Bella, per Dieu, non perda vostr'aiuda,
    50 ja sabetz vos cum mi fo covenguda.
        S'ieu ai faillit per l'ira c'ai aguda
        no.m tenga dan, s'anc sentitz cum leu muda
        cors d'amador, bella, e s'anc foz druda
        del plaich penssatz.
    55 Q'ieu sui be mortz s'*e*naissi l'ai perduda,
        mas no.ill o descobratz.

VIII.   Seign'En Giraut, ia n'agr'ieu fin volguda,
        mas ella ditz q'a dreich s'es irascuda
        c'autra.n preietz cum fols tot a saubuda
    60 qe non la val ni vestida ni nuda.
        No.i fara doncs si no.us gic, que vencuda
        n'er? So sapchatz,
        be.us en valrai et ai la.us mantenguda
        si mais no.us hi mesclatz.

IX. 65 Bella, per Dieu, si de lai n'etz crezuda
        per mi l'o affiatz.

V.   Maiden, from now on don't be so talkative,
        for she has lied to me at least five times before.
   35 Do you think I'll endure it forever?
        If I did I would look feeble-brained.
        I have a mind to ask about a different friendship,
        if it's all the same to you,
        for Lady Berengeira gave me better counsel
   40 than you are giving.

VI.   Now I see, Giraut, she's giving you what you deserve
        for calling her inconstant and vain,
        but do you think she seeks accord with you?
        I just don't think she's that forgiving.
   45 From now on, her promise will be slow in coming,
        whatever you may tell yourself,
        even if she constrains herself to tolerate
        truce, faith, or peace with you.

VII.   Beauty, by God, don't let me lose your help.
   50 You know quite well what the agreement was with me.
        If I have failed, it was because of my angry feelings;
        don't hold it against me; if you've ever known how fast
        a lover's heart shifts, if you've ever been a lover,
        beauty, think of my cause;
   55 for I'm quite dead if I have lost her in this way.
        But don't tell her that.

VIII. Lord Giraut, I would have wished an end to it,
        but she says she has a right to her anger,
        because you, like a madman, court
   60 another, in the open,
        one who, clothed or naked, is not her equal.
        If my lady doesn't leave you, won't she cause her own defeat?
        Know this: I'll be helpful to you, though I've defended her,
        if you'll make no more mischief.

IX.   65 Beauty, by God, if she trusts you in these things,
        give her my word.

X.   Ben o farai, mas qan vos er renduda
          s'amors, no la.us toillatz.

X.   I'll do that, certainly. But when her love's returned
             to you, don't let it go.

14. Almuc de Castelnou and Iseut de Capion, "Dompna N'Almulcs,
    si.us plages"

I.   Dompna N'Almulcs, *si*.us plages,
        be.us volgra preiar d'aitan
        qe l'ira e.l mal talan
        vos fezes fenir merces
     5 de lui qe sospir'e plaing
        e muor lang*uen* e.s complaing
        e qier perdon humilmen,
        qe.us fatz per lui sagramen
        si tot li voletz fenir
    10 q'el si gart meils de faillir.

II.   Dompna N'Iseuz s'ieu saubes
        q'el se pentis de l'engan
        q'el a fait vas mi tan gran,
        ben fora dreichz q'eu n'agues
    15 merc*e*, mas a mi no.s taing
        pos qe del tort no s'afraing
        ni.s pentis del faillimen,
        qe n'aia mais chausimen,
        mas si vos faitz lui pentir
    20 leu podes mi convertir.

14. Almuc de Castelnou and Iseut de Capion, "Dompna N'Almulcs, si.us plages"

I.   Lady Almuc, if you please,
          I'd like to ask this much:
          may you mercifully put an end
          to anger and ill will
    5 toward one who sighs, laments,
          dies fainting, complains,
          and humbly begs your pardon;
          for I would swear an oath on his behalf
          that if you're willing to end all this
  10 he'll better keep himself from failing you.

II.   Lady Iseut, if I were sure
          that he repented the grave wrong
          he has done me,
          it would be entirely right for me
  15 to show him mercy; but it isn't proper
          that I be more forgiving,
          for he does not restrain his wickedness,
          but if you make him repent
          you'll find it easy to convert me.

15. Domna and Bertran del Pojet, "Bona dona d'una re que.us deman"

Bertran del Poget

I.   Bona dona, d'una re que.us deman
mi digaz ver, segon vostre semblan,
si.us vostre fis amics vos ama tan
c'altra ves vos non razona ni.n blan,
5 ar mi digaz segon vostre veiaire
si l'amerez o sofrirez son dan,
q'eu sui aqel que lo.ill sabrai retraire.

II.   E vos digaz, fei que.m devez, Bertran,
cals es l'amics qe.l vol saber enan,
10 qu'eu tem de vos, per que vau plus doptan,
que vos siaz messagiers per engan,
donc sabrez greu que n'ai *en* cor a faire
qu'eu no voill di*r* tan sopte mon talan,
que ses menti*r* no m'en pogues estraire.

III. 15 Domna, s'eu fos aqel que vos cuiaz
que.us enqueses, ben i for'enganaz
        ...
per amor cel qu'es vostre [e*n*do*meniaz*]
e.us ama tan que non tem nuill ma*ltr*ai*r*e
20 per vostr'amor, e vos, donna, si.us plaz,
voillaz c'ab ioi lo seus tristz cors s'esclaire.

IV.   Per vostr'amor, Ber*tran,* car m'en pregaz,
l'amarai eu, mas el er pauc amaz,
qu'eu no.ill promet ni nuill respeit no.ill fa*z*
25 que.ill do m'amor, car s'es ves mi celaz,
ni eu non cre c'amors l'apoder gaire,
que s'ill ames ni.l forces voluntaz,
calque semblan feir*a* que fos amaire.

V.   Donna, eu sui lo vost*r*'amics aitals,
30 fis e fecels, vers e dreiç e leials,
e serai vos de servir ta*n* venals
que ia no*n* er affanz a soffrir mals,

15. Domna and Bertran del Pojet, "Bona dona d'una re que.us deman"

I.   Good Lady, on the point I'm consulting you about
tell me the truth as you see it:
if your true lover loves you so much
that he neither courts nor flatters anyone but you,
5 then tell me, according to your thinking,
if you'll love him or allow him to suffer,
for I'm the one who can convey your answer to him.

II.   And tell me, Bertran, by the truth you owe me,
who is this friend, for I want to know that first,
10 for I'm afraid (this is why I grow more hesitant)
that you may be a devious messenger;
you'll have a hard time finding out what I want;
I don't want to reveal my wishes so readily
for I couldn't save myself without lying.

III.   15 Lady, if I were the man you take me for,
making inquiries of you, you would be much deceived,
...
who is, for love, your utter servant
and loves you so much that he fears no mistreatment
20 from your love; and you, lady, if it pleases you,
kindly brighten his sad heart with joy.

IV.   For love of you, Bertran, because you ask me,
I will love him, but he'll be little loved
for I promise I'll neither grant him hope
25 nor give my love, because he's hidden himself from me;
nor do I think he really feels love's power,
for if he loved and if desire compelled him
he would give some sign that he was a lover.

V.   Lady, I am that lover of yours,
30 perfect and faithful, true and just and loyal;
and I will be so humbly your servant
that to endure pain will be no burden.

e vos, donna, si cum es de bon aire,
retenez mi, que ben es vostre sals
35 ab tan que ia de re vas vos no vaire.

VI.   Amics Ber*tran*, ben es iocs cumunals
          q'eu am celui qu'es m*os* amics corals,
          e l'amics voill que *sia*, sabez cals?
          fis e ficels, vertadiers e no fals
40 ni trop parliers ni iangl*os* ni gabaire
          mas de bon prez a son poder sivals
          c'aissi cove fors e dinz son repaire.

VII.   Donna, cel sui que non enten en als
          ni ves altra mos cors no pot at*r*aire.

VIII. 45 Amics Ber*tran*, ben deu a*n*ar cabals
          druz, cant es francs, fiçels e non trichaire.

> And you, lady, as gracious as you are,
> accept my service, for it's much to your advantage
> 35 as long as I never stray from you in any way.

VI.   Friend Bertran, this is a game we share
> for I love the one who is my heartfelt lover,
> and do you know how I want that friend to be?
> Perfect and faithful, truthful and undeceiving,
> 40 not too talkative, or indiscreet, or boastful,
> but very worthy at least as far as he can be,
> because it's fitting at his home or away from it.

VII.   Lady, I am he who thinks of no one else,
> nor can my heart be drawn to any other.

VIII. 45 Friend Bertran, a lover must act nobly
> if he is honest, faithful, and no deceiver.

16. La Comtessa de Proensa (Garsenda de Forcalquier) and Gui de Cavaillon, "Vos qe.m semblatz dels corals amadors"

La Contesa de Proensa

I.   *Vos* qe.m semblatz dels corals amadors,
ja non volgra qe fossez tan doptanz,
e plaz mi molt qar vos destreing m'amors,
q'autressi sui eu per vos malananz,
5 ez avez dan en vostre vulpillage
qar no.us ausaz de preiar enardir,
e faitz a vos ez a mi gran dampnage
qe ges dompna non ausa descobrir
tot so q'il vol per paor de faill*ir*.

En Gui de Cavaillon

II. 10 *Bona* dompna, vostr'onrada valors
mi fai estar temeros, tan es granz,
e no.m o tol negun'autra paors
q'eu non vos prec, qe.us volria enanz
tan gen servir qe non fezes oltra*g*e,
15 q'aissi.m sai eu de preiar enardir,
e volria q'il faich fosson message,
e presessez en loc de precs servir
q'us honratz faitz deu be valer un dir.

16. La Comtessa de Proensa (Garsenda de Forcalquier) and Gui
de Cavaillon, "Vos qe.m semblatz dels corals amadors"

The Countess of Provence

I.   You who seem to me a true-hearted lover,
I wish you wouldn't be so hesitant;
I'm very pleased that you're beset by love for me,
for I am likewise forlorn on your account;
5 and you are hurt by your timidity,
for you dare not take the risk of courting;
you do yourself and me a great disservice,
for a lady simply doesn't dare reveal
all she wishes, for fear that she may fail.

Lord Gui of Cavaillon

II.   10 Good Lady, your much-honored merit
makes me fearful, for it is so high.
That and no other fear prevents me
from courting you, for I'd prefer
to serve you so well that I commit no outrage.
15 I can indeed take the risk of courting
and would like actions to be messages,
and have you value service instead of pleas.
One exalted action should be worth one speech.

17. Domna and Pistoleta, "Bona domna, un conseill vos deman"

Pistoleta

I.   Bona domna, un conseill vos deman
       que me.l dones, que molt m'es grant mestier,
       qu'en una dompna ai mes tot mon talan
       ne nuill*a* ren tan non desir ni quier,
      5 e digatz me si laudatz que l'enquera
       de s'amistat o enquar m'en sofieira
       que.l reprovier*s* retrai certanamen
       qui.s cuicha pert e consec qui aten.

II.   Seingner, ben dic segon lo mieu senblan
   10 que ben o fai qui bona domna enquier,
       e cel sap pauc qui la va redoptan
       car anc domna no feri cavallier,
       mas *si* no.ill platz que s'amor li profera
       no i a plus dan e*n* neguna maneira
   15 que bona dompna a tan d'enseingnamen
       qu'ab gent parlar s'en part cortesamen.

III.   Domna, eu tem que se.ill demand s'amor
       que.m responda so que mal me sabra,
       e que s'albir son pretz e sa ricor,
   20 e que diga que ia no m'am*a*ra.
       Meill m'er, so cre, que.ill serva et atenda
       *t*ro que.il plassa que guizardon mi renda,
       e digatz me segon vostr'essien
       si farai ben o s'eu dic faillimen.

IV.   25 Seingner, totz temps fols a foillia cor,
       mas cel es fols qui la follia fa,
       e quant ho*m* serf la o*n* non a valor
       pois s'en penet que nuill gazaing non a,
       ans deu saber que ia gaire.n despenda
   30 si.n pot aver guizardon ni esmenda,
       e s'el conois qu'il aia bon talen,
       serva sidonz en patz e bonamen.

17. Domna and Pistoleta, "Bona domna, un conseill vos deman"

I.   Good lady, I'm requesting some advice
            that you could give me, for I need it badly:
            I've placed all my desire in a lady
            and there's nothing I want or wish so much;
     5 tell me if you counsel me to ask
            her friendship or refrain from asking,
            for the proverb truly says:
            He loses who makes haste; he wins who waits.

II.   Lord, I tell you: in my opinion,
    10 he does well who asks a good lady for her love;
            and he who fears her knows but little,
            for no lady ever struck a blow at a knight,
            but if the love he offers doesn't suit her
            there's no harm done anyway,
    15 for a good lady is knowing enough
            to part from him politely, with kind words.

III.   Lady, I fear that, if I ask for her love,
            she may respond in some way not to my taste,
            and that, considering her merit and rank,
    20 she may say she'll never love me.
            It will be best for me, I think, to serve and wait
            until she wants to give me my reward;
            and tell me if, as you see it,
            I'll do well, or if I'm saying the wrong thing.

IV. 25 Lord, the fool always runs after folly,
            but he's a real fool who does foolish things,
            and when a man serves where no merit lies,
            then he laments that he's had no reward;
            rather, he should know that his expense is very little
    30 if it can bring him reward and recompense,
            and if he knows she's someone of good will,
            let him serve his lady in peace and honor.

V.   Bona domna, pois aissi m'o laudatz,
            eu l'enquerai ades senes faillir,
      35   e tenc per bon lo conseill que.m donatz
            ne ia no.l voill cam*b*iar ni gequir,
            que ben sabez del don, senes faillensa,
            si vol amar o si a entend*e*nsa,
            e podetz m'en valer veraiamen,
      40   sol vos plassa ni.*l* cors vos o cossen.

VI.   Seingner, e.us prec que la domna.m digatz
            on e.us posca e valer e servir,
            e dic vos ben e voill que m'en crezatz
            qu'ie.us en sabrai la vertat descobrir,
      45   e far vos n'ai asina e cosensa
            maintas sasos, s'en leis non trob faillenssa,
            e digatz la ades de mantenen
            e non doptez ni.n aiatz espaven.

VII.   Bona domna, tant es cortes'e pros
      50   que vos sabez ben si.us am ni.us voill be,
            que tal ioi ai quant puosc parlar ab vos
            que de ren als no.m menbra ni.m sove,
            e doncs podez saber a ma senblansa
            e conoisser mon dig vas vos balansa;
      55   vos es cella vas cui mos cors s'aten,
            merce, domna, car tan dic d'ardimen.

V.   Good lady, because that's your suggestion,
           I'll ask for her right now, without fail,
  35 and I think it's good advice you're giving me,
           nor would I ever want to change or ignore it.
           For you know unfailingly whether or not the lady
           wishes or intends to love;
           and you can be most helpful to me
  40 if you wish, and if your heart consents.

VI.   Lord, I beg you to tell me who the lady is
           with whom I may help and serve you.
           I tell you, and want you to believe me,
           that I'll know how to find the truth,
  45 and am able and willing
           to help you often, if I find no fault in her.
           Now, at once, say who she is;
           have no fear or hesitation.

VII.   Good lady, you're so courteous and worthy
  50 that you surely know I love you and wish you well;
           I have such joy when I can speak with you
           that I cannot think or recall another thing;
           and so you can, by my expression, know
           and recognize: my words go out to you;
  55 you're the one my heart is longing for.
           Have pity, lady, for I speak out so boldly.

18. Ysabella and Elias Cairel, "N'Elyas Cairel, de l'amor"

La tenzon de domna Ysabella e d'En Elias Cairel

I.   N'Elyas Cairel, de l'amor
      q'ieu e vos soliam aver
      voil, si.us platz, qe.m digatz lo ver,
      per qe l'avetz cambi*at*'aillor,
  5 qe vostre chanz non vai si com solia
      et anc vas vos no.m sui salvatz un dia
      ni vos d'amor no.m demandetz anc tan
      q'ieu no fezes tot al vostre coman.

II.   Ma dom*n*'Ysabella, valor,
  10 ioi e pretz e sen e saber
      sol*i*atz qec iorn mantener,
      e s'ieu en dizia lauzor
      e*n* mon chantar, no.l ditz per drudaria
      mas per honor e pron q'ieu n'atendia,
  15 si con ioglars fai de dompna prezan,
      mas chascun iorn m'es anada cambian.

III. N'Elyas Cairel, amador
      no v*i* mais de vostre voler
      qi cambges dompna per aver,
  20 e s'ieu en disses desonor
      eu n'ai dig tant de be q'om no.l creiria;
      mas ben podetz doblar vostra folia;
      de mi vos dic q'ades vau meilluran
      mas en dreig vos non ai cor ni talan.

IV. 25 Domn'eu faria gran follor
      s'istes gair'en vostre poder,
      e ges per tal no.m desesper
      s'ans tot non aic pron ni honor,
      vos reman*r*es tals com la genz vos cria
  30 et ieu irei vezer ma bell'amia
      e.l sieu gen cor*s* graile e ben *e*stan
      que no m'a cor menzongier ni truan.

18. Ysabella and Elias Cairel, "N'Elyas Cairel, de l'amor"

I.   Lord Elias Cairel, about the love
          that you and I once had,
          I want you please to tell the truth:
          why have you turned your love elsewhere?
    5 For your song no longer comes as it once did;
          and I've never left you for a single day,
          nor did you ask a single favor so great
          that I didn't grant it totally, as you demanded.

II.   My Lady Ysabella, high worth,
   10 joy, merit, wisdom and learning you
          always used to uphold,
          and if then I spoke and sang in praise
          of them, I didn't speak because of love
          but because I expected the honor and profit
   15 that any jongleur expects from a worthy lady,
          but every day you have been changing toward me.

III.   Lord Elias Cairel, I never saw
          a lover who desires, as you do,
          to take another lady because of money;
   20 and if I spoke dishonorably of such a lover,
          when I've spoken so well of him before,
          no one would believe it. But you can go ahead
          and redouble your folly. I say my merit is increasing,
          but I have neither love nor longing for you.

IV. 25 Lady, I'd do a very foolish thing
          if I remained the least bit in your power;
          however I don't despair at all
          if I never had profit or praise.
          You will remain as people claim you are,
   30 [and] I'll go see my lovely friend
          with her fine, slender, healthy body,
          for her heart's not false or treacherous toward me.

V.   N'Elias Cairel, fegnedor
      35 resemblatz segon mon parer,
          con hom qi.s feing de dol aver
          de zo dont el no sent dolor.
          Si.m creziatz, bon conseil vos daria,
          qe tornassesz estar en la badia,
      40 e no.us auzei anc mais dir mon semblan,
          mas pregar n'ei lo patriarch Iuan.

VI.   Dom*n*'Ysabel, en refreitor
          non estei anc mattin ni ser,
          mas vos n'auretz oimais lezer
      45 q'em breu temps perdretz la collor.
          Estier mon grat mi faitz dir vilania
          et ai mentit, q'eu non crei q'el mond sia
          domna tant pros ni ab beutat tan gran
          com vos avet*z*, per q'ie*u* hai agut dan.

VII.   50 Si.us plazia, N'Elyas, ieu volria
          qe.m disesses qals es la vostr'amia,
          e digatz lo.m e no.i anetz doptan
          q*e*.us en valrai s'ela va*l* ni s'a*i*tan.

VIII.   Dompna, vos m'enquerretz de grant follia
      55 qe per razon s'amistat en perdria
          e per paor qe lauzengier mi fan,
          pero non aus descubrir mon talan.

V.   Lord Elias Cairel, a deceiver
35 is what you seem to be, I think,
like someone who pretends to suffer
over that from which he feels no pain.
If you believed me, I'd give you good advice:
go back and live in the monastery;
40 I never dared tell you what I was thinking,
but I've made this request to Ivan the Patriarch.

VI.   Lady Ysabella, in no refectory
have I ever spent a morning or an evening,
but you'll now have occasion to do so,
45 since, before long, you'll lose your youthful color.
Against my will you make me say a vicious thing,
and I have lied, for I don't think in all the world
there's such a noble lady with such beauty
as yours, which has made me suffer harm.

VII.   50 If it pleased you, Lord Elias, I would like
you to tell me who your friend is;
tell me and don't be fearful,
for I'll help out if she's so worthy and suitable.

VIII.   Lady, you ask a very foolish thing,
55 for I'd lose her friendship, and rightly so;
because of the fear I have of gossips,
I don't dare reveal my desire.

19. Domna and Peire Duran, "Midons qui fuy, deman del sieu cors gen"

P. Duran

I.   Midons qui fuy, deman del sieu cors gen
qu'es devengutz, e deman l'atressi
son ien parlar, e no.l pes si lo.l di
qu'es devengutz son bel aculhimen,
5 ni qu'esdeven son pretz ni sa cuendansa
ni qu'esdeven son ient anar en dansa
ni qu'esdeven sa graissa q'ie.l vi be
ni qu'es deven son ien cors pus no.m ve?

II.   E ia.l m'an tout siei malvat garnimen,
10 armas e draps e cavals e rossi,
e.l sieu flac cors c'anc non *si* desnoiri
ni cavalguet ni garni ni reten,
aco m'a tout lo sen e la membransa
e.l gen parlar e.l bordir e l'enfansa,
15 e.l sieu mal grat e.ls mals aibs c'a en se
m'a tout mon grais ab son malvat ale.

III.   Mais li deman de son lach cors que ten
on l'a trobat ni.l rechinhar can ri
ni.ls huelhs ronsar ni la garda guari,
20 ni on trobet tans aibs dezavinens
ni on trobet sel pieitz ab grossa pansa
ni on trobet aitan de malestansa
ni on trobet lo lach cuer c'om li ve
ni on trobet aitans enuetz can te?

IV. 25 E ia.l trobey ab un torneiamen
on richinhey can mos amicx fugi,
e.ls huelhs ronsiei denan l'ueis del moli
que.l vi *tr*iar la farina del bren,
*e*ngruysiei de dol e de pezansa
30 que.l vi cazer son escut e sa lansa,
e.l cuer ai ner car se toquet ab me:
totz los mals aibs ai de luy, per ma fe.

19. Domna and Peire Duran, "Midons qui fuy, deman del sieu cors gen"

I.   I ask milady, whom I flee, about her lovely body,
          what's become of it? likewise, I ask
          about her sweet speech and—if she'll permit me—
          her warm welcome, what's become of that?
     5 where are her merits and her charms?
          where's her graceful dancing?
          where's her roundness? for I saw it clearly,
          where's her good body, since last she saw me?

II.   Well, it's been ruined by *his* miserable equipment—
    10 his armor, banners, steeds and nags—
          and his flaccid body that was never washed,
          mounted nor held steady;
          this has robbed me of my mind and memory,
          my sweet speech, my frolicking, my childish fun;
    15 his ill will, too, plus his nasty ways;
          he's withered my roundness with his sour breath.

III.   But I'm asking her about her ugly body,
          where'd she find it? and the frown she gets when laughing
          and the knitted brows, the crabby look?
    20 where'd she get so many unpleasant ways?
          where'd she get the dugs on her fat belly?
          where'd she get so much ill-humor?
          where'd she get the ugly hide that she displays?
          where'd she get her quarrelsome behavior?

IV.   25 Well, I found them at a tournament
          where I frowned to see my lover run away,
          and knit my brows before the entrance to the mill
          where I saw him beat the chaff out of the grain;
          and I grew fat with regret and grief
    30 as I watched his shield and lance collapse;
          my hide is blackened because he touched me!
          I got all those bad things from him, by God!

20. Felipa and Arnaut Plagues, "Ben volgra midons saubes"

Arnaut Plages

I.
"Ben volgra midons saubes
mon còr ayssi cum yeu.l say,
e que.l plagues q'ieu fos lay
on es sos guays cors cortes.
5 E si dic sobransaria?"
"Diguas, e cuias qu'o sia?"
"Yeu non, que no.m sent tan ricx."
"Suefre e no t'amendicx
que de ben leu s'avenria."

II.
10 "Avenir pot? No pot ges."
"Si pot lo." "Per Dieu, no fay."
"E quom? Yeu vos o diray."
"Diguatz cum." "S'a lieys plagues."
"Plazer? A lieys, cum plairia?"
15 "Levet, s'amors o volia."
"Amors?" "Yest li enemicx?"
"Yeu no, ans estauc enicx
a quascun que la gualia."

III.
"Suefre e venra t'en bes."
20 "E cum? Que.ls mals ades n'ay."
"Mals? non ho diguas iamay."
"E per que?" "Quar non o es."
"Non es mals qu'ayssi m'aucia
languen?" "Non ges, quar un dia
25 er tos bes, si no t'en gicx,
ab sol que no la cambicx."
"E morray?" "Oc, si.s volia."

IV.
"Si.s vol?" "Oc." "Valra.m merces
ab lieys?" "Per Dieu, non o say."
30 "E per que?" "Quar non s'eschai
que trop t'iest en ric luec mes."
"Ric, per crotz, ben o sabia."
"E doncx no fezist follia?

20. Felipa and Arnaut Plagues, "Ben volgra midons saubes"

I.   "I really wish my lady knew
my heart as well as I know it;
I wish she were pleased to have me
near her fair, gracious body.
5 Is this presumptuous speech?"
"Speak! Do you think this might be?"
"I? No, for I don't feel so proud."
"Endure; don't put a friar's cloak on,
for it could easily occur."

II.   10 "It can occur? Not at all!"
"Yes, it can." "No, by God."
"How? I'll tell you."
"Tell me how." "If it pleased her."
"Please? How would it please her?"
15 "Easily, if Love willed it."
"Love?" "Are you its enemy?"
"Not I! Rather, I'm the foe
of anyone who might betray it."

III.   "Endure, and good shall come to you."
20 "But how? what I have now is evil."
"Evil? Never say that."
"And why not?" "It isn't so."
"It isn't evil that she lets me die
languishing?" "Not at all! One day
25 all will be well if you persist,
provided you don't turn from her."
"And I'll die?" "Yes, if she wills it."

IV.   "If she wills it?" "Yes." "Will she be merciful
to me?" "God, I don't know."
30 "And why?" "Because it isn't fitting
that you've presumed to rise so high."
"So high! By the cross, I knew it!"
"Wasn't it foolish on your part?

        Laissa t'en." "No m'en casticx,
35 qu'aisso no t'es mas destricx
        que ia no m'en layssaria."

V.   "No t'en laissarias ges?"
        "Non yeu." "Doncx aissi o fay
        cum *ieu* t'o ensenharai:
40 sias adreitz e cortes,
        francx e de bella paria,
        e fay so que ben estia,
        quan poiras, e no t'en tricx,
        qu'aissi deu renhar amicx,
45 oc, e mielhs si mielhs podia."

VI.   "Na Felipa, s'ieu avia
        tals rictatz don ieu fos ricx,
        atressi.us seri'amicx
        de ben dir, si cum solia."

VII. 50 Chanso, en Castella te*n* via
        al rey qui dobla.ls destricx
        qu'om pren ab los avols ricx
        quant es en lor companhia.

Give it up." "Don't reproach me for it!
35 You're only damaging your case,
   for I would never give it up."

V.   "You wouldn't give it up?"
       "Not I!" "Then do
       as I tell you:
40 be nimble and courteous,
   open and sociable;
   do what seems right
   when you can, and don't hang back,
   for that's the way a friend should act,
45 yes, and still better, if he could."

VI.   "Lady Felipa, if I had
       the high rank that would make me rich,
       then I'd be your friend
       in speaking well, the way I used to."

VII.   50 Song, go out to Castille
       to the king who doubles the injuries
       one suffers from the wicked rich
       when one is in their company.

21. Lombarda and Bernart Arnaut d'Armagnac, "Lombards volgr'eu
    eser per Na Lonbarda"

I. Na Lombarda si fo una dona de Tolosa, gentil e bella et avinens de la
persona et insegnada. E sabia bien trobar e fazia bella coblas et amoro-
sas. Don Bernautz N'Arnautz, fraire del comte d'Arma[n]hac, ausi contar de le bontaz e del valor de le; e venc s'en a Tolosa per le veser. Et
estet con ella de gra[n] desmestegesa et inqueri la d'amor, e fo molt son
amic. E fez aquestas coblas de le, e mandet le ad esa, al seu alberg; e
pois montet a caval ses le vezer, e si s'en anet in sua tera:

I.   *L*ombards volgr'eu eser per Na Lonbarda,
        q'Alamanda no.m plaz tan ni Giscarda,
        qar ab sos oiltz plaisenz tan ien mi garda,
        qe par qe.m don s'amor, mas trop me tarda,
   5   qar bel veser
        e mon plaiser
        ten e bel ris en garda,
        com n*u*ls no.l pod mover.

II.   Seigner Iordan, se vos lais Alamagna
   10   Fransa e P*e*iteus, Normandia e B*r*etagna,
        be me devez laisar senes mesclagna
        Lonbardia, Liv*o*rno e Lomagna.
        E si.m valez,
        eu per un dex
   15   valdr'e.us ab leis q'estragna
        de s*e* tot avol prez.

III.   *M*irail de Pres,
        conort avez,
        ges per *vila* no.s fragna
   20   l'amor en qe.m tenez.

Na Lonbarda se fes gran meraveilla qant ella ausi contar que Bernautz
N'Arnautz s'en era andat ses le veser et mandet le aquestas coblas:

21. Lombarda and Bernart Arnaut d'Armagnac, "Lombards volgr'eu
    eser per Na Lonbarda"

Na Lombarda was a lady of Toulouse, gracious, fair, lovely in her person, and learned. She could compose well, and made beautiful, amorous
verses. Don Bernart Arnaut, the brother of the Duke of Armagnac, heard
of her goodness and merit and came to Toulouse to see her. He lived in
great familiarity with her, sought her love, and was very much her friend.
He wrote these verses about her, and sent them to her in her house. Then
he mounted his horse, and, without seeing her, went away to his own
country.

I.   I'd like to be a Lombard for Lady Lombarda;
        I'm not as pleased by Alamanda or Giscarda.
        She looks at me so kindly with her sweet eyes
        that she appears to love me, but too slowly,
    5   for she withholds from me sweet sight
        and pleasure
        and keeps her sweet smile
        to herself; no one can move her.

II.   Lord Jordan, if I leave you Allemagna,
    10 France, Poitou, Normandy and Brittany,
        you should surely leave me, without protest,
        Lombardy, Livorno and Lomagna.
        And if you'll help me
        I'll willingly help you
    15 ten times as much with your own lady, who is foreign
        to all base values.

III.   Mirror of Worth,
        comfort is yours.
        Let the love in which you bind me
    20 not be broken for a villain's sake.

Na Lombarda was much amazed when she heard that Lord Bernart Arnaut had gone away without seeing her, and she sent him these verses:

IV.   Nom volgr'aver per Bernard Na Bernada
        e per N'Arnaut N'Arnauda apellada,
        e grans merses, seigner, car vos agrada
        c'ab tals doas domnas mi aves nomnada.
25   Voil qe.m digaz
        cals mais vos plaz
        ses cuberta selada,
        e.l mirail on miraz.

V.   Car lo mirailz e no veser descorda
30   tan mon acord, c'ab pauc vo.l desacorda,
        mas can record so q'el meus noms recorda
        en bon acord totz mons pensars s'acorda;
        mas del cor pes
        on l'aves mes,
35   qe sa maiso ni borda
        no vei, que lui taises.

IV.   I'd like to have the name Bernarda,
        and to be called, for Lord Arnaut, Arnauda;
        and many thanks, my lord, for being kind
        enough to mention me with two great ladies.
    25 I want you to say
        and not conceal it:
        which one pleases you the most,
        and in which mirror are you gazing?

V.   For mirroring and absence so discord
    30 my chords that I can barely stay accorded,
        but, remembering what my name recalls,
        all my thoughts accord in good accordance;
        still, I wonder
        where you've put your heart;
    35 in neither house nor hut
        I see it; you keep it silent.

22. Guilielma de Rosers and Lanfranc Cigala, "Na Guilielma,
   maint cavalier arratge"

La tenzon de Na Guillielma e de Lafranc Cigala

I.   Na Guilielma, maint cavalier arratge
   anan de nueg per mal temps qe fazia,
   si plaignian d'alberc en lur lengatge.
   Auziron dui bar qe per drudaria
5   se.n anavan vas lur donas non len.
   L'us se.n tornet per servir sella gen,
   l'autres n'anet vas sa domna corren.
   Qals d'aquels dos fes miels zo qe.il taignia?

II.   Amic Lafranc, miels complic son viatge,
10 al mieu semblan, cel qi tenc vas s'amia,
   e l'autre fes ben, mas son fin coratge
   non poc tam be saber sidonz a tria
   con cil que.l vic devant sos oils [presen]
   q'a rendut l'a sos cavaliers coven,
15 q'eu pres truep mais qi zo qe diz aten
   qe qi en als son coratge cambia.

III.   Domna, si.us plas, tot qan fes d'agradatge
   lo cavalliers qe per sa galiardia
   garda.ls autres de mort e de dampnatge,
20 e il mouc d'amor, qar ges de cortezia
   non ha nuls hom si d'amor no.il dessen,
   per qe sidonz deu grazir per un cen
   qar deslivret per s'amor de turmen
   tanz cavaliers, qe se vista l'avja.

IV. 25 Lafranc, iamais non razones muzatge
   tan gran con fes aqel qe tenc sa via;
   qe, sapchatz be, mout i fes gran ultratge,
   pueis bel servirs tan de cor li movia,
   qar non servic sidonz premeiramen,
30 et agra.n grat de leis e iauzimen,
   pueis per s'amor pogra servir soven
   en maintz bos luecs, qe faillir no.il podia.

22. Guilielma de Rosers and Lanfranc Cigala, "Na Guilielma,
maint cavalier arratge"

I.   Lady Guilielma, several knights voyaging
        after dark through some foul weather
        were crying out for shelter in their own language.
        They were heard by two lords who, moved by desire,
      5 were traveling at no slow pace toward their ladies.
        One lord turned back to help the travelers;
        the other speeded ahead toward his lady.
        Which of the two best fulfilled his duty?

II.   Friend Lanfranc, he who completed the voyage
     10 the best was, I think, he who went on toward his lover.
        The other one did well too, but his lady
        could not see his feelings as clearly
        as the lady who saw her man in person,
        because her knight had kept their agreement;
     15 I like a man who keeps his word
        more than one who changes his mind.

III.   Please, Lady, all the obliging things
        done by the knight who, in gallantry,
        kept other men from death and harm,
     20 he did out of love, for no courtesy
        comes to a man unless love supplies it;
        his lady should thank him a hundred times more
        than if he had seen her; for her love's sake
        he saved so many knights from trouble.

IV. 25 Lanfranc, you never reasoned so foolishly
        as the man who went on his own way.
        I'll have you know he committed an outrage.
        Why, if good service really lay close to his heart,
        did he not serve his lady before anyone else,
     30 which would have brought him her joy and gratitude?
        Then he could, for her love, do service often
        in many good places without failing her.

V.   Domna, perdon vos qier, s'ieu dic folatge,
         qu'oimais vei zo qe de donas crezia,
35   qe no vos platz q'autre pelegrinatge
         fassan li drut mas ves vos tota via,
         pero cavals c'om vol qi [biort] gen
         deu hom menar ab mesur et ab sen,
         mas car lo drutz cochatz tan malamen
40   lur faill poders, don vos sobra feunia.

VI.   Lafranc, eu dic qe son malvatz usatge
         degra laissar en aqel meteis dia
         le cavalliers que domna de paratge,
         bella e pros, deu aver e*n* bailia.
45   Q'en son alberc servis hom largamen,
         ia el no.i fos, mas chascus razon pren,
         qar sai que ha tan de recrezemen
         q'al maior ops poders li failliria.

VII.   Domn*a*, poder ai eu et ardimen
50   non contra vos, qe.us venzes en iazen,
         per q'eu sui fols car ab vos pris conten,
         mas vencut voil qe m'aiatz con qe sia.

VIII.   Lafranc, aitan vos autrei e.*u*s consen,
         qe tant mi sen de cor e d'ardimen
55   c'ab aital gien con domna si defen
         mi defendri'al plus ardit qe sia.

V.   Lady, I beg your pardon if I speak foolishly;
           now I see confirmed my belief about ladies:
35   for you, there's no other pilgrimage
           lovers should make except, by all roads, to you.
           However, if one wants horses to compete
           well in jousts, one should ride them with measure and wisdom,
           but you spur your lovers so harshly
40   that their powers fail, and you suffer the loss.

VI.   Lanfranc, I say a knight should abandon
           his ugly habits on the very day
           that a lady of noble, fine parentage
           lets him into her domain.
45   Men would have been generously served in his house
           had he not been there; each man finds excuses,
           for I know he's so cowardly
           that his powers would fail when he needed them most.

VII.   Lady, I have power and boldness,
50   though not against you, for I could beat you lying down.
           I was foolish to start a debate with you;
           I prefer to let you be my conqueror.

VIII.   Lanfranc, I concede and grant you this much:
           I feel so much courage and boldness
55   that, by the wit ladies use in their own defense,
           I will fend off the boldest of men.

23. Domna H. and Rofin, "Rofin, digatz m'ades de quors"

I.   Rofin, digatz m'ades de quors,
        cals fetz meills, car etz conoissens:
        c'una domna coinda e valens
        que ieu sai ha dos amadors,
   5 e vol q'usqecs iur e pliva
        enans que.ls voilla ab si colgar,
        que plus mas tener e baisar
        no.ill faran, e l'uns s'abriva
        e.l fag, qe sagramen no.ill te,
 10 l'autres no.l ausa far per re.

II.   Domna, d'aitan sobret follors
        cel que fon deshobediens
        ves sidons, que non es parvens
        q'amans, puois lo destreing amors,
 15 deia ab voluntat forciva
        los ditz de sa domna passar.
        Per q'eu dic qe senes cobrar
        deu perdre la ioia autiva
        de sidons cel qui frais sa fe
 20 e l'autres deu trobar merce.

III.   A fin amic non tol paors,
        Rofin, de penre iauzimens,
        qe.l desirs e.l sobretalens
        lo destreing tant qe per clamors
 25 de sidons nominativa
        noi.s pot soffrir ni capdellar;
        c'ab iazer et ab remirar
        l'amors corals recaliva
        tant fort que non au ni non ve
 30 ni conois qan fai mal o be.

IV.   Domna, ben mi par grans errors
        d'amic, puois ama coralmens,
        que nuills gaugz li sia plazens
        q'a sa domna non sia honors,

23. Domna H. and Rofin, "Rofin, digatz m'ades de quors"

I.   Rofin, now tell me from the heart
        which one does better, for you know many things:
        a charming, worthy lady I know
        has two men who love her.
    5 She wants them both to swear and pledge
        (before she lets them lie beside her)
        that they'll embrace and kiss her
        and do no more than that; one makes short work
        of it, for oaths mean nothing
   10 to him; the other simply doesn't dare.

II.   Lady, there's overwhelming madness
        in the man who disobeyed
        his lady, for it isn't fitting
        that a lover, pressed by love,
   15 should move, by force of will,
        beyond the wishes of his lady.
        Therefore I say
        that he who broke his faith
        should lose—without recovery—the high joy
   20 of his lady, and the other should find mercy.

III.   Rofin, a true lover does not let fear
        prevent him from enjoying pleasure;
        for desire and excessive ardor
        press him so that, despite the pleas
   25 of his honored lady,
        he can't contain or rule himself.
        For, as he lies with her and gazes
        at her, heartfelt love becomes so hot
        that he can neither hear, see
   30 nor know if he does harm or good.

IV.   Lady, it seems to me a lover
        errs if, loving from the heart,
        he's pleased by any joy
        that does no honor to his lady.

35 car no.ill deu esser esqiva
pena per sa domna onrar,
ni.*l* deu res per dreg agradar
s'a leis non es agradiva,
e drutz q'enaissi n*o*.s capte
40 deu perdre sa domna e se.

V.   Rofin, dels crois envazidors
aunitz e flacs e recrezens,
sapchatz qe fon l'aunitz dolens
qe se perdet en mieg dels cors,
45 mas l'arditz on pretz s'aviva
sau*p* gen sa valor enansar
qant pres tot so qe.ill fon plus car
mentre.il fon l'amors a*i*ziva
e domna q'aital drut mescre
50 mal creira cel qui s'en recre.

VI.   Domna, sapchatz qe grans valors
fon de l'amic e chausimens
qe.l fetz gardar de failh*i*mens,
esperan de sidons socors.
55 E cel fetz foudat nadiva
qe sa domna auset forssar,
e qui.l mante sap pauc d'amar,
q'amans, puois fin'amors viva
lo destreing, tem sa domna e cre
60 de tot quant ditz q'aissi.s cove.

VII.   Oimais conosc ben cossi va,
Rofin, puois que.us aug encolpar
lo fin e.l caitiu razonar:
q'eissamens obra caitiva
65 fariaz; e midonz dese,
N'Agnesina, diga q'en cre.

VIII.   De mi non cal qu'ieu o pliva
q'el ver en podetz ben triar,
domna, si.us platz, e mout m'es car

35 He shouldn't want to shun
     any pain that serves her honor.
     Nor, by rights, should something please him
     if it displeases her.
     A lover who won't be so ruled
40 should lose his lady and himself.

V.   Rofin, a cowardly invader
        is shameful, soft, and shrinking;
        be sure he was a shameful swine
        when he gave up in mid-course;
45   the bold man in whom merit thrives
        can raise his noble reputation
        by seizing all that he holds dear
        while his love is close by him;
        a lady who mistrusts that lover
50   trusts wrongly one that shrinks from her.

VI.   Lady, be sure it was high virtue
        and careful choosing
        that kept the other friend from failing,
        hoping for succor from his lady.
55   And he who dared force his lady
        acted like a born fool;
        his defender knows little of loving;
        the lover, pressed by love that's pure
        and vital, fears his lady and believes
60   all her words, for that is fitting.

VII.   Now I know just how it is,
        Rofin, when I hear you blame
        the true man and defend the loser;
        for you yourself would do a feeble job
65   of it. Now let Lady Agnesina
        tell us what she thinks about it.

VIII. Whether or not I swear,
        you yourself can find the truth,
        lady, if that pleases you; and it suits me

70 qe midons, on pretz s'aviva,
N'Agnesina, demand'ab se
Na Cobeitosa de Tot Be.

70 to have Lady Agnesina,
   in whom virtue lives, consult the Lady
   Desirous of All Good.

24. Domna and Raimon de la Salas, "Si.m fos graziz mos chanz, eu m'esforcera"

[Raimon]

I.   Si.m fos graziz mos chanz, eu m'esforcera
    e dera.*m* gauz e deporz e solaz,
    mas *a*issi.m sui a non chaler gitaz
    qu*e* ma domna, que a toz iorz esmera,
  5 ço qu'eu li dic, non deigna en grat tener,
    qu'apenas sai entre.*l*s pros remaner
    ni non sui ges cel qe era antan
    aissi me volf mos covinenz e.l*s* fran.

II.   Ha las! cum muor, quant mi membra cum era
  10 gais e ioves, alegres, envesaz,
    e quant m'albir qu'eu sui de ioi loignaz,
    per pauc mos cors del tot no.*s* desespera.
    E dunc mei hueill, cum la pogron vezer?
    Car n'ai perdut d'els e de mi poder;
  15 ço m'an ill faz, don mos cors vai ploran,
    qu'eu *non* puos far conort ni bel semblan.

III. Ha! bella domn'ar*a*s cum be.m semblera
    que, on que fos, degues humilitaz
    venir en vos que tant humil semblaz
  20 vers mi, que ia a mos iorz no.s camgera.
    Amors n'a tort, que.us fai dur cor aver
    e vos sabez, qar l'en donaz poder,
    qar si amors e vos es a mon dan,
    las! ges longas non puos soffrir l'afan.

24. Domna and Raimon de la Salas, "Si.m fos graziz mos chanz, eu m'esforcera"

[Raimon]

I.
If I were thanked for my song I'd try to sing
and it would give me joy and pleasure and solace,
but I've been cast into non-caring,
because my lady who shines brighter every day
5 does not see fit to welcome what I say
and I hardly dare stay among worthy people
nor am I at all what I used to be,
she so twists and breaks my understanding.

II.
Alas! I die when I remember how I used to be,
10 mirthful, young, happy, full of lust,
and when I realize how far I am from joy
my heart's in all but total despair.
So how can my eyes ever look at her
when I've lost my power to govern them or myself?
15 They've done this to me and filled my heart with weeping,
so I can't be comforted or seem at ease.

III.
Ah, lady, how good it would seem now
to me if, wherever you might be, humility
would find you, and you'd turn a humble glance
20 on me, one that wouldn't change for all my days.
Love is wrong if it hardens your heart,
and you know it, because you give it that power,
for if both Love and you seek my harm,
alas! I can't bear the torment for long.

[Domna]

IV.   25 Bel dolz ami*c*s, ia de mi n*o*.s clamera
          vostre bels cors cortes et enseignaz,
          si saubessez qals es ma voluntaz
          ves vos, de cui sui meilz hoi q'er non era,
          e non creaz qu'e.us me*t*'e*n* non chaler
    30 car gauz entier non puesc senz vos aver
          a cui m'autrei leialmen senz engan
          e.us lais mon cor en gauge on qu'eu m'an.

V.   Mas una genz enoi*o*sa e fera
          cui gauz ni bes ni alegrers non plaz
    35 nos guerreian, don mos cors es iraz,
          car per ren als senes vos non estera.
          Pero en mi avez tant de poder
          q'ab vos venrai quant me.l farez saber,
          mal grat de cels q'enqueron nostre dan
    40 e pesa.*m* fort car senz vos estauc ta*n*.

[The Lady]

IV. 25 Fair, sweet friend, your good, courteous, knowing heart
would never complain of me
if you knew what my desire is
concerning you, of whom I'm more fond today than ever;
don't think I've cast you into non-caring,
30 for without you I can have no total joy.
I give myself to you with loyalty, without deception;
wherever I go, I leave you my heart as pledge.

V.   But troublesome and savage people,
displeased by any joy or good or happiness,
35 make war against us, which puts my heart into a rage;
for no other reason would I remain without you.
But you have enough power over me
to make me come to you when you send for me,
in spite of those who seek our harm;
40 it crushes me to be so long without you.

25. Domna and Raimbaut d'Aurenga, "Amics, en gran cosirier"

Raimbaud d'Orenia

I.   Amics, en gran cosirier
        sui per vos e en grieu pena
        e del mal q'ieu en sufier
        non cug qe vos sentas gaire.
  5 Doncs per qe.us metes amaire
        pos a mi laissas tot lo mal,
        qar amdui no.*l* parte*m* egal.

II.   Don', amors ha tal mestier,
        pos dos amics encadena,
 10 q'el mal q'an e l'alegrier
        sen chascus so.ill es veiaire,
        q'ieu pens, e no sui gabaire,
        qe la dura dolor coral
        ai ieu tota a mon cabal.

III. 15 Amics, s'acses un cartier
        de la dolor qe.m malmena
        ben viras mon enconbrier,
        mas no.us cal del mieu dan gaire
        qe, qan no m'en puesc estraire,
 20 com qe m'an vos es comunal,
        an me ben o mal atretal.

IV.   Donna, qar ist lauzengier
        qe m'an tout sen e alena,
        so*n* nostr'angoissos gerrier,
 25 lais m'en, no per talen vaire,
        qar no.*u*s son pres, q'ab lur braire
        nos han basti tal joc mortal
        qe no iauzem iauzen iornal.

V.   Amics, nul gratz vos refier
 30 quar le mieus ditz vos refrena
        de vezer me qe.us enqier,
        e si vos fas plus gardaire

25. Domna and Raimbaut d'Aurenga, "Amics, en gran cosirier"

I.   Friend, I'm in great distress
       over you, and grievous pain,
       and of the torment that I suffer
       I think you hardly feel a thing.
     5 So why do you play the lover
       when you leave all the pain to me?
       Why don't we share it equally?

II.   Lady, this is love's way:
       when it binds two friends together,
   10 they each feel its pain and pleasure
       from their own point of view;
       for I think—and I'm not joking—
       that all the hard heartache
       has fallen on my head.

III. 15 Friend, if you'd had one quarter
       of the pain that torments me,
       you'd clearly see my burden,
       but you care little for my pain,
       and—though I can't escape it—
   20 what I go through is all the same
       to you, be it good or bad.

IV.   Lady, it's those gossips
       who've robbed my sanity and breath.
       Because they're cruel foes to us,
   25 not because of changed desire, I'm holding back
       from being beside you now; with their outcry
       they play such a deadly game
       with us that we enjoy no daily joy.

V.   My friend, I give you no thanks
   30 for letting my name prevent you
       from seeing me, as I ask;
       and if you're a better watchman

del mieu qez ieu non vueilh faire
be.us tenc per sobreplus leial
35 que no son cil de l'ospital.

VI.   Donna, ieu tem a sobrier
q'aur perdi *e* vo*s* arena,
qe per ditz de lauzengier
nostr'amo*r* tornes en caire,
40 per so deg tener en gaire
trop plus que vos, per San Marsal,
qar es la res qi plus mi val.

VII.   Amics, tan vos sai aleugier
en fach d'amoroza mena
45 quez ieu cui*d* de cavallier
siaz devengutz camiaire,
e deg vos o ben retraire,
qar ben pareis qe pensas d'al
pueis del miei pensamen no.*u*s cal.

VIII. 50 Domna, ia mais esparvier
non port ni catz ab serena
s'anc pueis qe.m des ioi entier
fui de null'autr'anqistaire,
ni no sui aital bauzaire,
55 mas per enveia.l deslial
m'o alevon e.m fan venal.

IX.   Amics, creirai vos per aital
q'aisi.us aia toztemps leial.

X.   Domna, aissi m'aures lial
60 qe ia mais no pensarai d'al.

   over me than I am,
   I'm sure that you're more loyal
35 than the Knights Hospitaller.

VI. Lady, I sadly fear
   I'm losing gold and you mere sand,
   and that from the gossips' talk
   our love has gone astray;
40 therefore I must maintain my watch
   more carefully than you do, by Saint Martial,
   for you are the one I value most.

VII. Friend, I know you take
   amorous things so lightly
45 that I think you've turned
   from knight to money-changer,
   and I must scold you for it;
   for you seem to think of something else
   as my worries are nothing to you.

VIII. 50 Lady, may I never carry
   sparrowhawk, or hunt with falcon,
   if once, since you gave me whole joy,
   I have pursued another lady.
   I'm not that kind of deceiver,
55 but disloyal people, in their envy,
   malign me and call me ignoble.

IX. Friend, I will trust you provided
   that I have you this loyal always.

X. Lady, you'll have me just this loyal;
60 I will have no other thought.

26. Domna and Donzela, "Bona domna, tan vos ay fin coratge"

Tenso

I.   Bona domna, tan vos ay fin corat*ge*
        non puesc mudar no.us cosselh vostre be,
        e dic vos be que faytz gran vilanat*ge*
        car sel home c'anc tan non amet re
    5 layssatz morir e no sabetz per que;
        pero, si mor, vostre er lo dampnat*ge*
        c'autra domna mas vos a grat no.l ve
        ni en luy non a poder ni senhorat*ge*.

II.   Na donzela, be.m deu esser salvat*ge*
   10 can el gaba ni s*e* vana de me,
        tant a son cor fol e leu e volat*ge*
        que m'amistat en lunha re no.s te,
        per que m'amor*s* no.l tanh ni no.l cove,
        e pus el eys s'a enques lo folat*ge*
   15 no m'en reptetz si la foldat l'*e*n ve,
        q'aysi o aug di*r* que dretz es onrat*ge*.

III.   Bona domna, ardre.l podetz o pendre,
        o far tot so que.us vengua a talen,
        que res non es qu'el vos puesca defendre,
   20 aysi l'avetz ses tot retenemen.
        E no.m par ges que.us sia d'avinen,
        pus ab un bays li fes lo cor estendre
        aysi co.l foc*s* que.l mort carbon e*n*sen,
        pueis cant el mor, no vo.n cal merce pen*d*re.

IV.   25 Na donzela, no m'en podetz repen*d*re
        que.l dey m'amor ab aytal covinen
        que el fos mieus per donar e per vendre
        e que tostems fos a mo*n* mandamen.
        Mays el a fag vas my tal falhimen
   30 don ies no.s pot escondir ni defendre;
        non o fas mal si m'amor li defen
        car ia per el no vuelh ma pretz dissendre.

26. Domna and Donzela, "Bona domna, tan vos ay fin coratge"

I.   Good lady, my heart is so entirely yours
      that I can't refrain from giving you some good advice:
      I say you're doing a shameful thing
      to the one who loves you more than he's loved anyone;
5   you're allowing him to die, and you don't know the reason;
      but if he dies the blame will be yours
      for no other lady besides you pleases him
      or has power or dominion over him.

II.   Maiden, I am right to be harsh
10   when he mocks me and boasts about me;
      his heart is so vain, mad, and inconstant
      that he in no way pays attention to my friendship.
      Therefore my love can't belong to him or suit him,
      and as he himself pursues a foolish course
15   don't scold me if I recognize his folly,
      for the right way, I'm told, brings honor.

III.   Good lady, you may burn or hang him
      or do anything you happen to desire,
      for there's nothing he can refuse you;
20   thus, he's yours without any reservation;
      and I don't think this becomes you at all,
      for with one kiss you make his heart swell
      as a fire kindles a dead coal;
      when he's dead, forgiving him will do you little good.

IV. 25 Maiden, you can't scold me about this
      for I gave him my love with an agreement:
      he'd be mine to give away or sell
      and he'd always be at my command.
      But he has done me a wrong
30   for which he can have no excuse or defense.
      I do no wrong if I refuse him my love;
      never for his sake would I abase my honor.

V.   Suau parlem, dona, c'om no.us entenda.
         Ara digatz que forfaytz es vas vos,
    35   mais que per far vostres plazers se renda
         so*s* cor*s* humil*s* contra.l vostr'ergulhos
         vuelh que digatz, dona, per cal*s* razos
         poyretz estar que merce*s* no vo.n prenda,
         que mil sospirs ne fa.l iorn engoysos,
    40   do*n* per un sol no.l denhatz far e*s*menda.

VI.   Si m'amor vol, Na donzela, que renda,
         ben li er obs *que* sia gais e pros,
         francx e u*mils*, c'ab nuls hom no.s contenda
         e a cascu*n* sia de bel repo*s*,
    45   c'a mi non tanh hom fel ni ergulhos
         per que mon pretz dechaya ni discenda,
         mas francx e fis, selans e amor*o*s
         si el vol qu'ie.l don lezer que mi entenda.

VII.   Aytal l'auretz, ia regart no vo.n prenda,
    50   bona dona, que.l sieu cor avetz vos,
         que el non a poder c'ad autr'entenda.

VIII.   Bon*a*.s la fin, donzela.*n* que s'atenda,
         e vos siatz garda entre nos dos
         e que.us tenguatz ab aquels que.*l* tort prenda.

V.   Let's speak softly, lady, so no one hears you.
         Now you're saying he's forfeited your love;
    35   but if, to please you, he surrenders
         his humble heart before your proud one,
         please tell me, lady, for what reason
         it could be that you won't pity him;
         for a thousand sighs torment his days,
    40   and you don't see fit to reward a single one.

VI.   Maiden, if he wants me to give my love,
         he will have to be cheerful, worthy,
         open and humble; let him argue with no one,
         and respond to every person kindly;
    45   because what suits me is not a mean or prideful man
         who would harm and diminish my worth,
         but a free and true, discreet and amorous man
         if he wants me to let him be in love with me.

VII.   You will have that kind of man, don't worry,
    50   good lady, for you have his heart
         and he's incapable of loving another.

VIII.   Maiden, the goal for which he strives is good,
         and may you be an arbiter between us,
         standing by whichever one is wronged.

27. Alaisina Yselda and Carenza, "Na Carenza al bel cors avinenz"

I. *Na* Carenza al bel cors av*i*nen*z*,
    d*o*naz conseil a n*o*s d*o*as serors,
    e ccar saubez mielç tria*r* la meilors,
    consil*h*az mi sec*o*nd vostr*'e*scien*z*.
    5 Penre marit a vostra conoscen*z*a
    o starai mi pulcela, et si m'agen*z*a,
    que far fillos non cuiç qu*e* sia bo*s*
    e ssens marit mi pa*r* trop anguisos.

II. N'Alaisina Yselda, 'nenghamen*z*,
    10 prez et beltatz, iovenz, fre*s*cas col*o*rs
    con*o*sc c'avez, cort*e*sia et val*o*rs
    s*o*bre t*o*ttas las a*u*tras conoscenz,
    per qu'i*e*.us conseil per fa*r* bona semenza
    penre marit coronat de scienza
    15 en cui farez fruit de fil*h* glorios.
    Retenguta.s pulse*l*'a *c*ui *l'epos.*

III. Na Carenza, penre marit m'agenza
    mas far infanz cuiz qu'es gran penitenza
    que las tetina*s* penden aval ios
    20 e ll*o* ventril*h* e*s* ruat e'noios.

IV. N'Alascina Yselda, sovinenza
    aiaç de mi e*n* l'umbra de ghirenza;
    quant i sireç preiaç l*o* Glorios
    qu'al departir mi ritenga pres v*o*s.

27. Alaisina Yselda and Na Carenza, "Na Carenza al bel cors avinenz"

I. Lady Carenza, fair and lovely of form,
   give advice to us two sisters,
   and, as you can better choose what's best,
   advise me according to your wisdom:
 5 shall I, in your opinion, take a husband
   or remain a virgin as it suits me?
   For making babies doesn't appeal to me,
   yet life with no husband seems to me so painful.

II. Lady Alaisina Yselda, learning,
 10 worth, beauty, youth and fresh complexion
   are yours, I know, and courtesy and valor
   above all other learned women;
   therefore I advise you: if you would have good offspring,
   take a husband crowned with wisdom
 15 by whom you'll bear the fruit of a glorious son.
   She who has him as spouse remains a virgin.

III. Lady Carenza, taking a husband suits me,
   but I think making babies is harsh penance,
   for the breasts droop way down,
 20 the belly stretches and gets ugly.

IV. Lady Alaisina Yselda, remember me
   when you are in the protecting shadow;
   pray to the glorious one
   that at parting I may remain near you.

28. Anonymous, "No puesc mudar no digua mon vejaire"

R. Jorda

I.   No puesc mudar no digua mon vejaire
d'aisso don ay al cor molt gran error
et er me molt mal e greu a retraire
quar aquist antic trobador
5 que.n son passat, dic que son fort peccaire,
qu'ilh an mes lo segl'en error
que an dig mal de domnas a prezen
e trastug silh q'o auzon crezo.ls en
et autreyon tug que ben es semblansa
10 et aissi an mes lo segl'en erransa.

II.   E tug aquist que eron bon trobaire
tug se fenhon per lial amador,
mas ieu sai be que non es fis amaire
nuls hom que digua mal d'amor;
15 enans vos dic qu'es ves amor bauzaire
e fai l'uzatge al traitor;
... que de so on plus fort s'aten
ditz mal aissi tot a prezen ...,
quar neguns hom, s'avia tota Fransa,
20 no pot ses don'aver gran benestansa.

III.   E ja nulhs hom que sia de bon aire
no sufrira qu'om en digua folhor,
mas silh que son ves amor tric e vaire
ho tuzonon (?) e s'en tenon ab lor;
25 qu'En Marcabrus, a ley de predicaire
quant es en gleiza h*o* orador
que di gran mal de la gen mescrezen,
et el ditz mal de donas eyssamen.
E dic vos be que non l'es gra*n* honransa
30 selh que ditz mal d'aisso don nays enfansa.

28. Anonymous, "No puesc mudar no digua mon vejaire"

I.   I can't help it: I must speak my mind
            about the thing that is confounding my heart,
            and it will give me pain and grief to tell,
            for I say those old-time troubadours,
     5 who are dead now, gravely sinned,
            putting the world in confusion,
            when they openly spoke ill of women;
            and all who hear their speech believe them
            and grant that such things seem true;
   10 thus they have plunged the world in error.

II.   And all these men, who were good troubadours,
            pretended to be loyal lovers,
            but I am certain that no one
            who speaks ill of love is a true lover.
   15 Rather, I tell you he is love's deceiver
            and behaves like a traitor,
            for he publicly speaks ill
            of that in which he has most hope.
            For if a man owned all of France,
   20 but had no lady, he could have no well-being.

III.   And never will a man of noble nature
            allow men to speak foolishness about this,
            but those who are deceitful, fickle lovers
            and agree among themselves.
   25 For Lord Marcabru, like a sermonizer
            in church, or a preacher
            speaking ill of unbelievers,
            speaks similarly ill of women;
            I tell you there's no great honor
   30 in maligning that from which a child is born.

IV.   Ia no sia negus meravellaire
        s'ieu aisso dic ni vuelh mostrar alhor
        que quascus hom deu razonar son fraire
        e queia domna sa seror,
35 quar Adams fo lo nostre premier paire
        et avem Damnidieu ad auctor,
        e s'ieu per so vuelh far razonamen
        a las domnas, no m'o reptes nien,
        quar dona deu az autra far *on*ransa
40 e per aisso ai.n ieu dig ma semblansa.

IV. Let no one be amazed
    if I speak this way, and even wish to prove
    that every man should argue for his brother,
    and every woman for her sister,
 35 because Adam was our first father,
    and we all have the Lord God as creator;
    if, therefore, I wish to make an argument
    for ladies, don't carp at me about it;
    one lady should do honor to another,
 40 and that's why I have given my opinion.

29. Anonymous, "Ab greu cossire et ab greu marrimen"

P. Basc

I.   Ab greu cossire et ab greu marrimen
planh e sospire et ab perilhos turmen,
can me remire ab pauc lo cor no.m fen,
ni mos huelhs vire que gart mos vest*i*mens
5   que son ricx e onratz
e ab aur fi fre*z*atz
e d'argen mealhatz,
ni regart ma corona;
l'apostoli de Roma
10 volgra fezes cremar
qui nos fay desfrezar.

II.   Sesta costuma ni sest establimen
non tenra gaire, c'an fag novelamen,
car lo rey Iacme no fo*ro*n a prezen
15 ni l'apostoli, c'absolva.l sagramen,
car nostres vestirs ricx
an nafratz e aunitz;
q*i* o tractet sia marritz,
per que cascuna entenda
20 que non port vel ni benda
mais garlandas de flors
en estieu per *am*ors.

III.   Coras que vengua lo rey nostre senhor
que es semensa de pretz e de valor,
25 per merce.l prenda c'auia nostra clamor
de la offensa que fan sieu ren*da*dor,
que.ls vestirs an naffratz
e des*en*cadenatz
e dezenbotonatz,
30 per que nostras personas
ne van pus vergo*n*hozas
prec que sian tornatz
per vos, fran*c* rey onratz.

29. Anonymous, "Ab greu cossire et ab greu marrimen"

I.   In heavy grief, in heavy dismay,
        and in dreadful pain, I weep and sigh.
        When I gaze at myself my heart all but cracks,
        and I nearly go blind when I look at my clothes
  5 (rich and noble,
        trimmed with fine gold,
        worked with silver)
        or look at my crown.
        May the Pope in Rome
 10 send him to the fire
        who untrims our clothes.

II.   I will not observe this custom,
        this law they've just made,
        for Iacme the King wasn't there,
 15 nor was the Pope; let the order be lifted;
        they've harmed and dishonored
        our rich clothing.
        May the law's author suffer
        to see every woman resolve
 20 not to wear veil or wimple
        but garlands of flowers
        in the summer for love.

III.   Whenever our lord the King may come
        (from him comes all merit)
 25 let pity move him to hear our outcry
        against the offense brought on by his stewards,
        who have torn from our clothing
        its chains
        and its buttons.
 30 See that our persons
        are no longer shamed:
        pray, have them restored
        to us, high, honored King.

IV.   Senhors dauraires e los dauriveliers,
35   donas e donzelas que es de lur mestier,
    a l'apostoli mandem un messatgier
    que escumenie cosselhs e cosselhiers
    e los fraires menors
    en son en grans blasmors,
40   e los prezicadors
    e selh de penedensa
    ne son en malvolensa
    e li autre reglar
    c'o solon prezicar.

V.   45   Vai, sirventesca, al bon rey d'Arago
    e a la papa que.l sagramen perdo,
    car vilanesca an fag, si Dieus be.m do,
    e ribaudesca, nostre marit felo;
50   ...
    quar yeu n'era pus gaia,
    la sentura m'esclaia
    que yeu solia senchar,
55   lassa! no l'aus portar.

VI.   De ma camiza blanc'ai tal pessamen,
    que era cozida de seda ricamen,
    groga e vermelha e negra eyssamen,
    blanca e blava, ab aur et ab argen.
60   Lassa, non l'aus vestir!
    Lo cor me vol partir,
    ...
    e non es maravilha.
    Senhors, faitz me esclavina
65   que aitan l'am portar
    can vestir ses frezar.

IV.   Let us, lord goldsmiths and jewelers,
35   and ladies and girls who are of their trade,
     ask the Pope in a message
     to excommunicate council and councilmen,
     and the friars minor,
     who are greatly to blame for this,
40   the preachers
     and penitentials
     who show their ill will in it,
     and other regulars
     accustomed to preach it.

V.   45 Go, my sirventes, to the good King of Aragon
     and to the Pope; let them undo the law,
     for—as God grant me grace—our ignoble husbands
     have done a vile deed.
50   ...
     that way I'll be happier.
     The girdle I used to fasten
     dismays me. Alas!
55   I dare not wear it.

VI.   I grieve for my white blouse
     embroidered with silk—
     jonquil, vermilion and black mixed together,
     white, blue, gold and silver.
60   Alas! I dare not put it on.
     My heart feels like breaking,

     ...

     and it's no wonder.
     Lords, make me a coarse cloak;
65   I prefer to wear that
     when my clothes have no trimmings.

30. Gormonda de Monpeslier, "Greu m'es a durar"

Na Gormunda

I.   Greu m'es a durar
quar aug tal descrezensa
dir ni semenar,
e no.m platz ni m'agensa,
5 qu'om non deu amar
qui fai desmantenensa
a so don totz bes
ven e nays et es
salvamens e fes,
10 per qu'ieu faray parvensa
e semblan que.m pes.

II.   No.us meravilhes
negus si eu muou guerra
ab fals mal apres
15 qu'a son poder soterra
totz bos faitz cortes
e.ls encauss'e.ls enserra;
trop se fenh arditz,
quar de Roma ditz
20 mal, qu'es caps e guitz
de totz selhs qu*e* en terra
an bos esperitz.

III.   En Roma es complitz
totz bes, e qui.ls li *p*ana
25 sos sens l'es fallitz,
quar si meteys enguana,
qu'elh n'er sebellitz
don perdra sa ufana.
Dieus auja mos precx
30 que selhs qu'an mals becx,
ioven e senecx,
contra la ley romana,
caion dels bavecx.

30. Gormonda de Monpeslier, "Greu m'es a durar"

I.   It's hard to bear it
          when I hear such false belief
          spoken and spread around;
          it doesn't please or suit me,
    5 for no one should approve
          a person who dismantles
          that from which all good
          comes, is born, and is,
          salvation and faith itself.
  10 Therefore, I will show
          what grieves me.

II.   Don't anyone marvel
          if I wage war
          against the false, wrongheaded man
  15 who does his best to cast down,
          persecute, and imprison
          all good, courtly traits.
          He is too bold,
          for he speaks ill
  20 of Rome, the capital and guide
          of those on this earth
          whose souls are good.

III.   In Rome all goodness
          is accomplished; he who disagrees
  25 lacks any sense,
          for he deceives himself;
          he will be brought down for it
          and will quit his boasting;
          may God hear my plea;
  30 let those, young and old,
          who cackle viciously
          against the law of Rome
          fall from its scales.

IV.   Roma, selhs per pecx
    35 tenc totz e per gent grossa,
      per orbs e per secx
      que lur car*n* e lur ossa
      cargon d'avols decx,
      don caion en la fossa
    40 on lur es sermatz
      pudens focx malvatz,
      don mais desliatz
      no s*o*n de l*a tra*d*o*ssa
      qu'an de lu*r*s peccatz.

V.   45 Roma, ges no.m platz
      qu'avols hom vos combata,
      dels bos avez patz
      q'usquecx ab vos s'aflata,
      dels fols lurs foldatz
    50 fes perdre Damiata,
      mas li vostre sen
      fan se*l* ses conten
      caytiu e dolen
      que contra vos deslata
    55 ni renha greumen.

VI.   Roma, veramen
      sai e cre ses duptansa
      qu'a ver salvamen
      aduretz tota Fransa,
    60 oc, e l'autra gen
      que.us vol far aiudansa;
      mas so que Merlis
      prophetizan dis
      del bon rey Loys
    65 que morira en Pansa,
      aras s'esclarzis.

IV.   Rome, I consider
  35 those men fools: crude,
    blind, dry villains
    who load their flesh
    and bone with horrid vice
    that sinks them
  40 into the pit prepared for them
    with stinking fire;
    they are never unbound
    from the burden
    of their sins.

V.   45 Rome, I'm thoroughly displeased
    that a vile man attacks you;
    with good men you're at peace
    for every one of them adores you.
    The folly of the fools
  50 caused the loss of Damietta,
    but your wisdom
    makes them wretched
    and regretful, no denying it,
    to have risen up against you
  55 and acted in evil ways.

VI.   Rome, I know for sure,
    believe, and do not doubt
    that you will lead all France
    to sure salvation—
  60 yes—and other people
    who want to serve you.
    But the thing that Merlin,
    prophesying, said
    of good King Louis,
  65 that he would die in Pansa,
    is now becoming clear.

VII.   Piegz de Sarrazis
         e de pus fals coratge
         hereti*es* mesquis
70   son, qui vol lur estatge
         ins el foc d'abis
         v*a se*.n loc de salvatge
         en dampnatio.
         A selhs d'Avinho
75   baysses, don m'es bo,
         Roma, lo mal pezatge,
         don grans merces fo.

VIII.   Roma, per razo
         avetz manta destorta
80   dressad'a bando
         et oberta la porta
         de salvatio
         don era la claus torta.
         Que ab bon govern
85   bayssatz folh esquern,
         qui sec vostr'estern
         l'angel Michel lo.n porta
         e.l garda d'ifern.

IX.   L'estiu e l'yvern
90   deu hom ses contradire,
         Roma, lo cazern
         legir, si que no.s vire,
         e quan ve l'es*qu*ern
         cum Iesus pres martire,
95   albir se lo cas
         si.s bos crestias,
         si no.s pes'en pas
         s'adoncx non a cossire,
         totz es fols e vas.

VII.   Worse than Saracens
            and more false-hearted
            are the wicked
   70 heretics. One who seeks their home
            must go into the fire
            of the abyss, into a savage place,
            into damnation.
            Rome, for the people of Avignon
   75 you reduced (and I approve)
            the wicked toll,
            for which I thank you.

VIII.   Rome, by your justice,
            you have straightened
   80 many crooked things
            and opened the portals
            of salvation
            whose door was shut.
            By good government
   85 you bring down folly.
            The one who takes your path
            is born up by Saint Michael
            and kept away from Hell.

IX.   Summer and winter,
   90 there's no doubt, a man
            should read the Word
            so that he doesn't stray from it.
            And when he sees the scorn
            that Jesus suffered,
   95 if he is a good Christian
            he should reflect on that;
            and if he doesn't meditate,
            if he fails to grieve,
            then he is a complete, vain fool.

X.   100 Roma, los trefas
      e sa leys sospechoza
      als fols digz vilas
      par que fos de Toloza,
      on d'enians certas
      105 non es doncx vergonhoza.
      Mas si.l coms prezans
      enans de dos ans
      cove que.ls engans
      lays e la fe duptoza
      110 e restaure.ls dans.

XI.   Roma, lo reys grans
      qu'es senhers de dreytura
      als falses Tolzans
      don gran malaventura,
      115 quar tot a sos mans
      fan tan gran desmezura
      q'usquecx lo rescon
      e torbon est mon
      e.lh comte Raymon,
      120 s'ab elhs plus s'asegura,
      no.l tenray per bon.

XII.   Roma, bes cofon
      e val li pauc sa forsa
      qui contra vos gron
      125 ni bast castelh ni forsa,
      quar en tan aut mon
      no.s met ni *no* s'amorsa
      que Dieus non recort
      son erguelh e.l tort
      130 ...
      don pert tota s'escorsa
      e pren dobla mort.

X.   100 Rome, the traitors
        and their dubious beliefs
        with vile, foolish teachings,
        come from Toulouse, it seems,
        where there's no shame
     105 about plain treachery.
        But the worthy count
        before two years have passed
        must leave all treachery
        and false beliefs behind
     110 to redress wrongs.

XI.   Rome, may the high King,
        lord of righteousness,
        bring dire misfortune
        on the false Toulousans
     115 who against His laws
        commit such outrage,
        for everyone hides it
        and the world is confused;
        if Count Raymond
     120 keeps supporting them
        I condemn him.

XII.   Rome, a man's undone
        and his strength has little worth
        if he grumbles against you,
     125 building or besieging castles,
        for on whatever mountain
        he builds his fortress,
        it's not so high that God forgets
        his pride and wickedness
     130 ...
        whereby he'll lose his skin
        and undergo a double death.

XIII.   Roma, be.m conort
         que.l coms ni l'emperaire,
135   pueys que son destort
         de vos no valon gayre,
         quar lur folh deport
         e lur malvat vejaire
         los fa totz cazer
140   a vostre plazer,
         q'us no.s pot tener
         sitot s'es guerreiayre
         non li val poder.

XIV.   Roma, yeu esper
145   que vostra senhoria
         e Fransa per ver
         cuy no platz mala via
         fassa dechazer
         l'erguelh e l'eretgia,
150   fals heretges quetz
         que non temon vetz
         ni cre*z*o.ls secretz,
         tan son ples de feunia
         e de mals pessetz.

XV. 155   Roma, be sabetz
         que fort greu lur escapa
         qui au lor decretz,
         aissi tendon lur trapa
         ab falces trudetz
160   ab que quascus s'arrapa;
         totz son sortz e mutz
         qu'el lur tolh salutz
         don quecx es perdutz
         q'ilh n'an capelh o capa
165   e remanon nutz.

XIII.   Rome, it consoles me
          that the Count and emperor,
     135 ever since they turned from you,
          have had little success;
          their foolish actions
          and wrong-headedness
          defeat them—
     140 it is your will
          that they can't hold out;
          warriors they may be
          but their powers don't help them.

XIV.   Rome, I hope
     145 your dominion
          and indeed that of France,
          where evil is out of favor,
          will cause pride
          and heresy to collapse,
     150 false, secret heretics
          who neither respect the bans
          nor believe the mysteries,
          they are so treacherous
          and evil-minded.

XV. 155 Rome, you know well
          that one who hears their words
          finds it hard to escape;
          they set their traps
          with false enticements
     160 by which everyone is snared;
          those who are trapped are deaf
          and dumb about the lost salvation
          that dooms them all;
          they're stripped of cape and cap
     165 and remain naked.

XVI.   Clauzis e sauputz
         naysson, senes falhida,
         crematz e perdutz
         per lur malvada vida
170   qu'anc negus vertutz
         non fe, ni ges auzida
         non avem sivals,
         e si fos leyals
         lur vida mortals,
175   Dieus, crey l'agra eyssauzida,
         mas non es cabal*s*.

XVII.   Qui vol esser sals,
         ades deu la crotz penre
         per ereties fals
180   *dechazer e mespenre,*
         que.l celestials
         hi venc son bras estendre
         tot per sos amicx,
         e pus tals destricx
185   pres, ben es enicx
         selh que no.l vol entendre
         ni creyre.ls chasticx.

XVIII.   Roma, si pus gicx
         renhar selhs que.us fan *o*nta
190   al sant esperitz,
         quant hom lor o aconta,
         tan son fo*l* mendicx
         q'us ab ver n*o* s'afronta
         no.y auras honor.
195   Roma, li trachor
         son tan ples d'error
         qu'on plus pot quascus monta
         quec iorn sa follor.

XVI.   Surely they are born,
              hidden yet known,
              consumed and lost
              by their wicked life,
      170 for they do no good thing
              (at least not
              that I've heard about)
              and if their mortal life
              were faithful
      175 I think God would have approved it,
              but it's not just.

XVII.   One who wishes to be saved
              should now take up the cross
              in order to defeat and punish
      180 the false heresy;
              for the Heavenly One
              came to stretch forth his arms
              for those who love him,
              and as he took on such suffering
      185 a person's very wicked
              who doesn't choose to hear him
              or believe his teachings.

XVIII. Rome, if you allow
              the acts of those who shame
      190 the Holy Spirit
              (when they are spoken to
              they're such mad beggars
              they won't admit the truth)
              you'll have no honor.
      195 Rome, the traitors
              are so full of error
              that each one, each day raises
              to the limit the level of his folly.

XIX.   Roma, folh labor
200   *fa qui ab* vos tensona,
          del empe*rador dic,*
          s'ab vos n*o* s'adona
          q'*en gran d*eshonor
          ne venra s*a corona,*
205   *e* sera razos.
          Mas per *o ab vos*
          leu trob'om perdos
          qui g*en sos tor*tz razona
          ni n'es an*goissos.*

XX.   210   Roma.l Glorios
          que a la Magdalena
          perdonet don nos
          esperam ben estrena;
          lo folh rabioz
215   que tan dich fals semena,
          fassa d'aital for
          elh e son thezor
          e son malvat cor
          morir e d'aital pena,
220   cum hereti*e*s mor.

XIX.   Rome, mad works
200 are done by one who fights you,
and of the Emperor
I say that if he doesn't join you
his crown will fall
into dishonor,
205 and rightly so.
But through you
he will easily find pardon
if he admits his sins
and feels remorse.

XX.   210 Rome, may the Glorious One
who pardoned Mary
Magdalene (whose gift
we surely hope for)
kill the rabid fool
215 who sows so much false speech,
he and his treasure
and his evil heart;
and when he dies may he die
in the torments
220 suffered by heretics.

31. Anonymous, "Ab lo cor trist environat d'esmay"

I.   Ab *lo* cor trist environat d'esmay,
        plorant m*os ue*lls e rompen los cabels,
        sospirant fort, lass*a*, co*mia*t pendray
        de fin amor et de totz so*n* conssells,
    5 car ja no.m platz *a*mar hom qu'el mon si*a*
        d'e*ras en*ant, ne portar bon voler,
        pus mort crusel m'a tolt cel q'eu voli*a*
        trop mais que me, sens negun mal sauber.

II.   E per aiso fauc lo captenime*n*
   10 desespera*t* e farai chascun jorn
        ab trist sembla*n,* e darai entenen
        a totz aicels que.m vey anar entorn
        qu'en me no.ls qual aver nul'esperan*sa*;
        ans podon be sercar en autre part
   15 dona q'els am o qu'els don s'amistan*sa*
        car eu d'amor e de jo*i* me depart.

III.   E si del mon pog*ue*s pendre comiat
        ab grat de Deu, axi cum fau d'amor,
        totz m*os* parens *encara m'an retrat,*
   20 plandrie.m pauc aitant vis*c* ab dolor,
        e per aiço prec la mort sans demor*a*
        *v*engua de faitz per mon las cor alcir,
        pus a mort cell de que mon cor tant plor*a*
        e fa mant dol nuyt e jorn e suspir.

IV.   25 De tots quant vey ben parats e vestits
        dençant, xentant, alegres e pagats
        a*i* gran *en*ueg e no.m plats mos delits;
        e non deu esser res maravelats,
        car pus me *son* renovellant la playa
   30 anant me.l cor en lo g*en*t aresar
        e.*l* gay vestir d'acell, a qui Deus haya,
        lo qual no crey en lo mon n'agues par.

31. Anonymous, "Ab lo cor trist environat d'esmay"

I.   With confusion wrapped around my sad heart,
        shedding tears, tearing my hair,
        sighing heavily, I, wretched woman, will say farewell
        to perfect love and all its practices;
   5 I have no wish to love or like any man
        in the world from now on,
        for cruel death has stolen the one I loved
        more than myself, with perfect pleasure.

II.   For this reason I'm acting like a person
  10 in despair, and I will spend each day
        with a dismal face, and inform
        all those I see circling around me
        that hope means nothing to me;
        and they can go seek elsewhere
  15 a lady who loves them or gives them friendship
        as I am taking leave of love and joy.

III.   If with God's blessing I could say farewell
        to the world, as I've said it to love
        (all my relations still hold me back),
  20 I'd complain but little, I live in so much pain;
        and for this reason I pray that death may come
        without delay to kill my weary heart
        since it killed the one my heart weeps for,
        and I sigh and sorrow day and night.

IV. 25 All those I see brightly adorned and clothed,
        dancing, singing, happy, and at ease
        torment me, and I desire no pleasure
        of my own; this should be no wonder,
        for at those times they renew the wound
  30 by bringing to my heart the sweet manner
        and bright clothing of the one (God keep him)
        who has no equal in the world, I think.

V.   Per que *m'es* bon de null temps amar plus
          e de iaquir amor e son hostal,
   35   car eu no crey hom de troba*r dejus*
          tan bo, tant *g*ay ne de valor aytal.
          El era franch, valent, d'onor compli*da*
          e tant ardit que ell n'es *e*stat mort,
          ... per que mon cor faria gran fallida
   40   si n'amav*a* altre apres sa mort.

VI.   Mon dolç amych, si be hom no.m sosterra,
          morta suy hey gran res, si Deu m'ajut,
          car sino mal no sent, tan fort s'aferr*a*
          dolor en me despuys que.us ay perdut.

V.   So it suits me not to love ever again,
          to abandon love and its dwelling place,
   35 for I don't think I'll find a man in this world
          as good, as cheerful, or as worthy as he was.
          He was frank, brave, completely honorable,
          and so ardent that he died because of it,
          for which reason my heart would be at fault
   40 if I loved another man after his death.

VI.   My sweet friend, if no one sustains me,
          I am long dead, God help me,
          for I feel nothing but misery, so strong is the grip
          of sorrow in me since I lost you.

32. Azalais d'Altier, "Tanz salutz e tantas amors"

*T*anz salutz et tantas amors
et tanz bens et tantas honors
e tantas fin*as* amistaz
e tanz gauz com vos volriaz
5 et tanz ris et tant d'alegrier
*v*os tramet N'Azalais d'Altier,
a vos, donna, cui ilh volria
mais vezer qe ren q'el mon sia,
qe tant n'ai auzit de ben dir*e*
10 a ceilh qe.us es hom et servire,
qe per lo ben qu'el me n'a dich
ai tant inz e*n* mon cor es*c*rich
vostre semblant que, si.us vezia,
entre milh vos conoisseria.
15 Et dic vos ben aitan en ver
qez anc donna senes vezer
non amei tan d'amor coral,
et dic vos ben, si Deus mi sal,
quez el mon non es nulla res
20 q'eu penses qez a vos plagues
qes eu non fezes volenti*e*ra
senes mant e senes prigui*e*ra,
ez ai, donna, trop gran desire
quez eu vos vis e.us pogues dire
25 tot mon cor e tot mon voler
e pogues lo vostre saber.
Aras, donna, es enaissi:
l'autre iorn s'en venc zai a mi
lo vostr'amicx trist*z* e mar*r*itz
30 com hom enchausatz e faiditz,
e d*is* mi q'en ditz ez en faitz
es vas vos mespres e forfaitz,
segon, donna, qe vos dizes,
q'eu non cuidera q'el d*i*sses
35 ni q'elh a nuilh iorn de sa vida
fazes vas vos ...
               ... am e.us obezis

32. Azalais d'Altier, "Tanz salutz e tantas amors"

So many greetings, so much love,
so many good things, so many honors,
so many perfect friendships,
and as many joys as you could wish,
5 so many smiles, so many cheerful things—
Lady Azalais of Altier sends all these
to you, lady, whom she would like
more than anyone in the world to see:
I've heard such good reports of you
10 from the one who is your man and servant
that, from the good things he has told me,
I have your face inscribed
so deeply in my heart that if I saw you
I'd know you in a thousand;
15 and I tell you truthfully
that for no lady ever, sight unseen,
have I had such heartfelt love;
and I tell you, God save me,
that there's nothing in the world
20 (if I thought it might please you)
that I would not do willingly
without hearing a command or a request.
Lady, I have such great desire
to see you so that I could show you
25 my whole heart and desire,
and could know yours.
Now, Lady, this is how things stand:
the other day your friend came here
to see me, downcast and sad
30 like a man chased away and banished;
and told me that by words and actions
he'd wronged you and failed you,
lady, according to what you said.
I could not believe what he said,
35 nor that he, a single day of his life,
committed toward you ...
... he loves and obeys you

mais que nuilla ren qu'elh anc vis.
Pero, donna, si vos cuidatz
40 q'eu n'aia mais, ben es vertatz,
qe vos aves ben tan de sen
de valor e d'ensengnamen
qe, si lo tortz granz no i fos
ja no'ilh trobaras occaiso*s*
45 per qe.l feses de vos partir
ni aissi desirant languir,
ni non potes ies per raizon
azirar lui per l'ucaison
q'eu sai, *ez* elh e vos sabes.
50 Pero s'auzire lo voles,
vostra er la perda e.l danz,
et pois per totz lo*s* finz amanz
devres en esser meinz prezada
per totz temps ez uchaiso*n*ada.
55 Ez aquilh qe non o sabran
cuidaran si qe per talan
d'autrui amar vos l'azires
e de vos amar lo lunges
ez intrares in folla bruda,
60 si ez per canzairitz tenguda,
q'esqern fai de si mal retraire
Brizeida, qar ilh fo cangiaire
sos cors, qar laiset Troilus
per amar lo fil Tideus.
65 Autressi.us er en mal retrach
si.us partes de lui se*ns* forfach,
qe.us vol e.us desira e.us ama
tant q'en moren n'art e n'aflama,
e s'a*u*tra donna l'agues mort,
70 e*u* cuidera qe molt gran tort
vos agues fait, si m'aiut Dieus,
qar ell es miellz vostre qe sieus.
E s'el, donna, per sobramar
vos vez de ren vostre pesar,
75 amors o fez e non gens elh,
per q*ez* eu conosc be qez elh

more than anyone he's ever seen.
However, lady, if you think
40 I might have more about this, it's true;
for you have so much sense,
quality, and learning,
that if the fault were not too great,
you wouldn't invent the charges
45 on which to send him away
or make him languish in longing,
nor can you be right
to hate him on account of the charge
that I know and that he and you both know.
50 However, if you want to kill him,
the loss and blame will be yours,
and then all perfect lovers
will have to cease admiring you
forever; it's you who will be charged.
55 And those who don't know
will think it was out of a desire
to love another that you hated him
and prevented him from loving you;
you'll become the subject of foolish gossip,
60 thought to be an inconstant woman;
for scorn made Briseida badly spoken of
because she was inconstant;
she left Troilus
to love Tydeus' son.
65 Likewise you will be ill-spoken of
if you leave him without provocation,
for he wants, desires and loves you so much
that he's dying, burned by the flames,
and if another lady had struck him dead
70 I'd think that she had done great harm
to you, so help me God,
for he belongs to you more than to himself.
And if, lady, from too much love,
he caused you any grief,
75 Love, no other being, did it;
for which reason I'm sure that he

    non de*u* perdre vostra paria
    ni l'amor qe de vos a*v*ia,
    ni nulla donna non es bona
80 pois q'estra ni tol zo que dona.
    Eras qon q'el sia estat,
    o per la vostra voluntat
    o per lo tort qe.us *a* agut,
    ve.l vos aissi mort e vencut
85 qez el non dorm ni non repausa
    ni el mond non es nulla causa
    qe ja.l puesca donar conort
    si doncs ab vos non troba acort,
    per q'eu vos prec, per gran merze,
90 qe vos tot per amor de me,
    li perdones e.l finiscatz
    los tortz don vos l'ucazonatz.
    Ez eu faz vos per lui fianza
    qe ja en diz ni en senblanza
95 non faza nul temps ni non diga
    ren per qe.l sias enemiga.
    E no.l sias o*i*mais avara,
    anz li sias fina e clara,
    qe.l noms ni.l semblanz no.us desmenta,
100 e prec amor qe.us o cosenta,
    bona donna.

shouldn't lose your company,
or the love he had from you.
Nor is any lady kind
80 if she withdraws or takes what she has given.
Now, whatever may have happened,
either by your own wish,
or by the wrong he did you,
behold him, so struck down and beaten
85 that he neither sleeps nor rests
nor is there anything at all
that can console him
if he doesn't find favor with you.
Therefore I beg you, in great pity,
90 that you, wholly for love of me,
pardon him and absolve
the wrongs you charge him with,
and I give you my word for him
that never in speech or in looks
95 shall he do or say
a thing that makes you his enemy.
And don't be stingy with him now;
be true and clear, so that neither
your name nor your face is belied.
100 And I pray that Love may grant you this,
good lady.

33. Anonymous, "Coindeta sui, si cum n'ai greu cossire"

I. Coindeta sui! si cum n'ai greu cossire
  per mon marit, qar ne.l voil ne.l desire.
  Q'eu be.us dirai per que son aisi drusa,
    Coindeta sui!
 5 qar pauca son, ioveneta e tosa,
    Coindeta sui!
  e degr'aver marit dunt fos ioiosa
  ab cui toz temps pogues iogar e rire.
    Coindeta sui!

II. 10 Ia Deus mi.n sal se ia sui amorosa,
    Coindeta sui!
  de lui amar mia sui cobeitosa,
    Coindeta sui!
  anz quant lo vei ne son tant vergoignosa
 15 q'eu prec la mort qe.l venga tost aucire.
    Coindeta sui!

III. Mais d'una ren m'en son ben acordada,
    Coindeta sui!
  se.l meu amic m'a s'amor emendada,
 20   Coindeta sui!
  ve.l bel esper a cui me son donada,
  plang e sospir quar ne.l vei ne.l remire.
    Coindeta sui!

IV. En aquest son faz coindeta balada,
 25   Coindeta sui!
  e prec a tut que sia loing cantada,
    Coindeta sui!
  e que la chant tota domna ensegnada,
  del meu amic q'eu tant am e desire.
 30   Coindeta sui!

33. Anonymous, "Coindeta sui, si cum n'ai greu cossire"

I.   I am lovely, and so my heart grieves
           about my husband, whom I neither love nor desire.
           I'll tell you why I am so amorous
           —I am lovely—
    5   for I am small and young and fresh
           —I am lovely—
           and should have a husband who gives me joy
           with whom I could play and laugh all day.
           I am lovely.

II.   10 God save me if I've ever loved him
           —I am lovely—
           I haven't the least wish to love him
           —I am lovely—
           in fact, seeing him, I feel such shame
    15 that I beg death to come and take him soon.
           I am lovely.

III.   But on one thing my mind is resolved
           —I am lovely—
           if my lover has restored his love to me
    20 *—I am lovely—*
           that's the hope I've given myself up to;
           I weep and sigh because I cannot see or gaze at him.
           I am lovely.

IV.   On this note I make a lovely ballad
    25 *—I am lovely—*
           and pray that people sing it everywhere
           —I am lovely—
           and that every knowing lady sing
           about the friend whom I so love and desire.
    30 *I am lovely.*

V.   E dirai vos de que sui acordada,
                    Coindeta sui!
            que.l meu amic m'a longament amada,
                    Coindeta sui!
35   ar *li* sera m'amor abandonada
            e.l bel esper qu*e* tant am e desire.
                    Coindeta sui!

V.   I'll tell you what I have resolved
          —*I am lovely*—
          Because my friend has loved me for so long
          —*I am lovely*—
     35   my love will now be offered up to him,
          and the good hope I so love and desire.
          I am lovely.

34. Anonymous, "En un vergier sotz fuella d'albespi"

I.   En un vergier sotz fuella d'albespi
           tenc la dompna son amic costa si
           tro la gayta crida que l'alba vi,
           Oy Dieus! Oy Dieus! de l'alba tan tost ve.

II.   5 "Plagues a Dieu ia la nueitz non falhis
           ni.l mieus amicx lonc de mi no.s partis
           ni la gayta iorn ni alba no vis,
           Oy Dieus! Oy Dieus! de l'alba tan tost ve.

III.   Bels dous amicx, baizem nos yeu e vos
    10 aval e.ls pratz on chanto.ls auzellos
           tot o fassam en despieg del gilos,
           Oy Dieus! Oy Dieus! de l'alba tan tost ve.

IV.   Bels dous amicx, fassam un ioc novel
           yns el iardi on chanton li auzel
    15 tro la gaita toque son caramelh,
           Oy Dieus! Oy Dieus! de l'alba tan tost ve.

V.   Per la doss'aura qu'es venguda de lay
           del mieu amic belh e cortes e gay
           del sieu alen ai begut un dous ray,
    20 Oy Dieus! Oy Dieus! de l'alba tan tost ve."

IV.   La dompna es agradans e plazens
           per sa beutat la gardon mantas gens
           et a son cor en amar leyalmens,
           Oy Dieus! Oy Dieus! de l'alba tan tost ve.

34. Anonymous, "En un vergier sotz fuella d'albespi"

I.   In an orchard under hawthorn leaves
the lady holds her lover by her side
until the watchman cries: it is the dawn.
O God, O God, the dawn! it comes so soon.

II.   5 "Would to God the darkness were not ending,
and my lover were not leaving me,
and the watchman saw no day or dawn.
O God, O God, the dawn! it comes so soon.

III.   Fair, sweet friend, kiss me and I'll kiss you
10 in the meadow where songbirds sing;
let's do all this despite the jealous one.
O God, O God, the dawn! it comes so soon.

IV.   Fair, sweet friend, let's play a fresh game
in the garden where songbirds sing,
15 until the watchman sounds his bell.
O God, O God, the dawn! it comes so soon.

V.   In the sweet wind that comes from there,
from my fair, courteous, happy friend,
I've drunk the sweet light of his breath.
20 *O God, O God, the dawn! it comes so soon."*

VI.   The lady is agreeable and lovely
admired by many for her beauty,
while her heart stays loyally in love.
O God, O God, the dawn! it comes so soon.

35. Anonymous, "Dieus sal la terra e.l pais"

> Dieus sal la terra e.l pa*is*
> on vos*tre cors* es ni estai,
> on q'eu sia, mos cors es lai
> e sai no n'es om poderos;
> 5 aissi volgr'eu qe.l cor*s* lai fos
> qi qe sai s'en fezes parliers,
> mais n'am un ioi qe fos entiers
> q'el qe s'en fai tan enveios.

35. Anonymous, "Dieus sal la terra e.l pais"

> God save the land and the place
> where you are and where you remain.
> Whatever place I'm in, my heart is there,
> for no man here has power over that.
> 5 I wish my body were there as well
> no matter who might gossip about it,
> for I'd rather have a perfect joy from there
> than have the person who so badly wants my body.

36. Tibors, "Bels dous amics, ben vos puosc en ver dir"

Bels dous amics, ben vos puosc en ver dir
qe anc no fo q'eu estes ses desir
pos vos con*osc* ni.us pris per fin ama*n,*
ni anc *no* fo q'eu non agues talan,
5 bels dous amics, q'eu soven no.us veses,
ni anc no fo sasons qe m'en pent*es,*
ni anc no fo si vos n'a*n*es iratz
q'eu agues ioi tro que fosetz tornatz,
ni anc ...

36. Tibors, "Bels dous amics, ben vos puosc en ver dir"

> Fair, sweet friend, I can truly tell you
> I have never been without desire
> since I met you and took you as true lover,
> nor has it happened that I lacked the wish,
> 5 my fair, sweet friend, to see you often,
> nor has the season come when I repented,
> nor has it happened, if you went off angry,
> that I knew joy until you had returned,
> nor ...

End Notes

1. La Comtessa de Dia, "Ab ioi et ab ioven m'apais"

PC 46.1
PC numbers refer to a widely used system of identification for works in the troubadour corpus. It was established by Alfred Pillet and completed by Henry Carstens, and was published in the *Bibliographie des Troubadours*. The first number refers to the poet, the second to the work in the poet's corpus. *Tensos* between two poets are normally identified by two different sets of numbers.

a8 b7' a8 b7' b7' a8 a8 b7'
4 *coblas doblas* and a *tornada*
derivative rhymes

The *canso* is found in the following manuscripts: A167, B104, D85, H49, I141, K126, T197, a232. It is attributed to the Comtessa de Dia in all the manuscripts except T. The *canso* is accompanied by a *vida* in ABIK and miniatures in AHIK.

This edition is based on manuscript B, the oldest and generally regarded as the more reliable manuscript of the AB group. See Zufferey, *Recherches* 35-40.

Previous editions of the work include Raynouard (1816-19), Rochegude (1819), Mahn (1846-53), Schultz-Gora (1888), Restori (1891), Santy (1893), Kussler-Ratyé (1917), Véran (1946), Hamlin/Ricketts/Hathaway (1967), Faucheux (1974), de Riquer (1975), Bogin (1976), de Casas/Cantera (1976), Farrayre (1982), Sansone (1986), Kay (1989), Kasten (1990), Städtler (1990), Rieger (1991).

The following notes are based on our reading of B and Rieger 588-91.
1. *Ab:* the capital is missing in manuscript B. The emendation is in accordance with ADHITa.
1-2. All but two couplets (ll.1-2, 9-10) in this *canso* are derivative rhymes, pairs based on the same word-root and normally marked by the alternate presence and absence of the feminine ending -*a*. While English practice

considers such rhymes "weak," in troubadour poetics, *rims derivatius* was a tour de force that enhanced the thematics of masculine-feminine relations (Kay, "Derivation"). Our translations mimic the effect of derived rhyme by echoing in the second line of each couplet a word from the first line. Lines 1-2 do not present a true derived rhyme: the 3rd person singular *apaia* comes not from the root *pascor* (to feed), like *m'apais*, but from a derivative of *pacare*, to make peaceful, to satisfy. See Kay, "Derivation" 167 and Rieger 589.

3. *que:* DHT read *car* (because, for).

4. The line is emended by modern editors to read *per q'ieu sui coindet'e gaia.* According to the fourteenth-century *Leys d'Amors*, the most complete treatise of Occitanic poetics, a phrase like *coindeta e gaia,* in which a vowel at the end of one word is followed by another vowel at the beginning of the next, should be read as a synalephe. This means that the vowel at the end of *coindeta* was blended with *e* or, more likely, was suppressed in performance (Di Girolamo, *Elementi* 12). In "Ab ioi et ab ioven m'apais" synalephe is also found in lines 22 and 26, and dialephe, where adjacent vowels function metrically as two syllables, occurs in line 8. The poets use these metrical figures whenever it is convenient to do so. We have not emended the texts at these points.

9-10. As in the case of verses 1-2, the rhyme *mais-m'aia* follows the metrical pattern but is not a derivative rhyme.

13. The referent of "he" in this line is uncertain in the original as well as in the translation. It could be the lover of lines 9-10 or the go-between of line 11.

15-16. Cnyrim (46) identifies the lines as a proverb.

20. *pois ill:* A reads *pois quill* (since).

23. *ni.ll avinen:* manuscripts ABHIKTa read *ni li valen,* which does not respect the derivative rhyme scheme. We accept Kussler-Ratyé's emendation, which is in accordance with D.

29. *crezenssa:* manuscript B reads *entendenssa,* the emendation is necessary to maintain the derivative rhyme scheme.

33. Manuscripts DHIKT read *Floris,* ABa read *Amics.* The *senhal Floris,* probably an allusion to the romance *Floris and Blanchaflor,* to which the poet makes reference in the third *canso* of this edition, represents the *lectio difficilior* (see Note on Texts).

36. *plai:* B reads *platz.* The emendation accords with all the other manuscripts.

The poet probably lived in the second half of the twelfth century, a contemporary of Azalais de Porcairagues. Metrical and intertextual evidence suggests that the two trobairitz maintained poetic relations with Raimbaut d'Aurenga, who lived in the third quarter of the century. Although the poet's *vida* states that she addressed her love songs to Raimbaut, there is no mention of a Countess of Die in extant documents pertaining to Raimbaut nor is there historical evidence of a Countess of Die who wrote poetry. See the Introduction for further discussion.

2. La Comtessa de Dia, "A chantar m'er de so q'ieu no volria"

PC 46.2

a10' a10' a10' a10' b10 a10' b10
5 *coblas singulars* and a *tornada*

The *canso* is found in the following manuscripts: A168, B104, C371, D85, G114, I141, K127, L120, M204, N229, R22, W204 (fragment), a231, b12. It is attributed to the Comtessa de Dia in most manuscripts but is anonymous in GLNW. We have included here and elsewhere, as appropriate, rubrics given in the manuscripts. They appear at the opening of the printed text in bold type (i.e. **La Comtessa de Dia**). The *canso* is attributed to *una donna de Tolosa* in M. A melody accompanies the fragment in W and there is space for musical notation in G and R. C is damaged where miniatures have been removed.

The text of the *canso* is based on B.

Editions include Raynouard (1816-21), Rochegude (1819), Mahn (1846-53), Bartsch (1855), Hueffer (1878), Santy (1893), Schultz-Gora (1888), Kussler-Ratyé (1917), Anglade (1927), Audiau/Lavaud (1928), Berry (1930), Bertoni (1937), Cavaliere (1938), Hill/Bergin (1941), Véran (1946), Gentile (1947), Piccolo (1948), Bec (1954), Frings (1957), Hamlin/Ricketts/Hathaway (1967), Roubaud (1971), Faucheux (1974), Jeanroy (1974), de Riquer (1975), Bogin (1976), de Casas/Cantera (1976), D. Rieger (1980), Farrayre (1982), Goldin (1983), Mamino (1986), Kasten (1990), Städtler (1990), Rieger (1991).

The following notes are based on our reading of B and Rieger 594-99.

5. *beltatz:* W reads *bontatz* (goodness).

6. *trahia:* B reads *trahida.* As mentioned in the Note on the Texts, the rhymes are regularized. *enganada:* L reads *vergoignada* (ashamed).

10. The poet, instead of citing analogous lovers from classical literature, names figures who were probably the hero and heroine of a contemporary romance. Note that she aligns herself with the male lover (Seguis), and her *amic* with the female beloved.

18. *acoilla:* manuscript B reads *ocoilla.* We accept Kussler-Ratyé's emendation, as does Rieger, which is based on the readings of all the manuscripts except AB. It is not possible to determine whether the verb is in the first or the third person.

21. *departimens:* L reads *descordamentz* (trouble).

26. *ez:* B reads *et.*

3. La Comtessa de Dia, "Estat ai en greu cossirier"

PC 46.4

a8 b8 b8 a8 c7' d8 d8 c7'
2 *coblas doblas* plus a *cobla* that is not doubled.

The *canso* is found in the following manuscripts: A168, D85, I141, K137, and is always attributed to the Comtessa de Dia.

The base manuscript for this edition is A, following Kussler-Ratyé and Rieger.

The text has been edited by Raynouard (1816-21), Rochegude (1819), Mahn (1846-53), Crescini (1892), Schultz-Gora (1888), Santy (1893), Gaubert/ Véran (1907), Kussler-Ratyé (1917), Berry (1930), Serra-Baldó (1934), Cavaliere (1938), Hill/Bergin (1941), Véran (1946), Gentile (1947), Marone (1948), Piccolo (1948), Roubaud (1971), Lafont (1972), Faucheux (1974), de Riquer (1975), Bogin (1976), de Casas/Cantera (1976), Farrayre (1982), Mamino (1986), Sansone (1986), Brunel-Lobrichon (1989), Kasten (1990), Städtler (1990), Rieger (1991).

The following notes are based on our reading of A and Rieger 601-04.

10. *en:* Manuscript A reads *e.* Scribes frequently left out the tilde (~) over a vowel that indicated a nasal. All the other manuscripts read *en.*

11. *s'en:* We have adopted Rieger's interpretation. Kussler-Ratyé reads *sen* (sense).

14. Again the poet compares herself and her friend to male and female lovers from contemporary romance, *Floris and Blanchaflor.* Versions of this oriental story existed in several vernacular languages, including Occitan.

16. *e ma vida:* A reads *a ma vida* but the emendation by Schultz-Gora, followed by later editors, is in keeping with the medieval taste for parallelism and *accumulatio.*

18. *cora.us tenrai:* D reads *be.us volgr'aver* (I would like very much to have you).

4. La Comtessa de Dia, "Fin ioi me dona alegranssa"

PC 46.5

a7' b7 a7' b7 c7 c7 d7' d7'
2 *coblas unissonans* and a *tornada*

A blank space large enough for an additional *cobla* is left at the end of the *canso* in D, which suggests that the scribe may have considered his source material incomplete.

The *canso* is found only in manuscript D85 where it is attributed to *La Contessa de Dia.*

The *canso* has been previously edited by Rochegude (1819), Mahn (1846-53), Schultz-Gora (1888), Santy (1893), Kussler-Ratyé (1917), Véran (1946), Piccolo (1948), Faucheux (1974), de Riquer (1975), Bogin (1976), de Casas/Cantera (1976), Farrayre (1982), Kasten (1990), Städtler (1990), Rieger (1991).

The following notes are based on our reading of D and Rieger 606-08. Unless specified, the emendations are in Kussler-Ratyé's edition and are adopted by Rieger.

6. A syllable is missing in D; we accept Rieger's emendation.

7. *m'esglaia:* D reads *esglaia.*

9. *an:* D reads *a.*

12. *qu'a ab els:* D reads *qui a bels.*

15. *solelhs:* D reads *soles* and we have emended it in accordance with the orthographic norms described in the Notes on the Texts.

18. *no.us:* Schultz-Gora emended the manuscript, which reads *nos.*

mon tarçan: the words make no sense and there is no minimal emendation that satisfactorily resolves the problem. The translation probably conveys the sense of the line.

5. Castelloza, "Ia de chantar non degra aver talan"

PC109.2

a10 a4 b6 b4 c6' d6 d6 d6 c6'
6 *coblas unissonans* and 2 *tornadas*

The *canso* is found in the following manuscripts: A169, I125, K110, N228, d311. It is attributed to Castelloza in every manuscript except N, where it is anonymous, as are 30% of the works recorded in that anthology.

The base manuscript for the present edition is A, after Rieger and Schultz-Gora. In the case of the Castelloza corpus, the texts in A are closely related to IKd and the four manuscripts present only slight variation, while N shows a significant number of textual variants (Rieger 522).

Editions of the text include Raynouard (1816-21), Rochegude (1819), Mahn (1846-53), Schultz-Gora (1888), La Salle de Rochemaure/Lavaud (1910), Véran (1946), de Riquer (1975), Bogin (1976), *Action Poétique* (1978), Paden et al. (1981), Bec (1985), Städtler (1990), Rieger (1991).

The following notes are based on our reading of A and Rieger 532-38. We follow Schultz-Gora's emendations, as does Rieger, unless otherwise indicated.

1. *talan:* A reads *talen.* As always, we have regularized the rhyme.

2. *chan:* A reads *chant* and has been emended to fit the rhyme scheme.

8. *s'en*: A reads *sin*.

13. *qe l*: A reads *qeil*. We accept Bec's emendation, as does Rieger.

16. *don*: IKd read *domna*.

23. *en*: A reads *e*.

29. *tan*: A reads *tant*. The emendation accommodates the rhyme scheme.

38. *vostre gan*: A glove in the chivalric world was an important symbol, a metonymy for the hand that gave and received challenges to combat, oaths of homage and feudal service. For the desiring woman to steal a glove from a knight who owes such service to a higher-ranking lady is a daring disturbance of the social status quo. A lady's glove may also be a meaningful token, as seen in the *razo* to the *tenso* between Alamanda and Guiraut de Bornelh (Rieger 108).

42. *d'aicella*: IKd read *de la bella* (of the beauty).

44. *lo*: A reads *li*.

46. *i fant lor dan*: A reads *que fant follatge* (who commit folly). The emendation accommodates the rhyme scheme and accords with IKNd.

47. *preian*: A reads *preon*. The emendation, in accordance with IKNd, preserves the rhyme scheme. Paden points out that the rhyme of lines 46-47 (*dan-preian*) which is found in IKNd, is merely an "eye rhyme," since the accent falls on the first syllable of *preian*. See Paden, ed. "Poems" 176-77.

55. *Na Mieils*: Rieger argues, as have Paden ("Poems" 164) and Brunel ("Almois" 462-63), that Castelloza is addressing her poem to Almuc de Castelnou. Almuc was an early thirteenth-century trobairitz whose only extant work, "Domna N'Almucs, si.us plages," an exchange of *coblas* with Iseut de Capion, is no. 14 in this anthology. An argument for this reading is found in N which reads *dompna nal murs*, and Rieger points to the paleographic similarity of *c* and *r* to explain the deformation of the name (IKd read *nalmirs*). In keeping with the norms described in the Note on the Texts, we have maintained the reading of the base manuscript.

56. *mal*: A reads *mals*. The emendation is in accord with IKNd.

According to information provided in her *vida*, Castelloza was a noblewoman from Auvergne and wife of Turc de Mairona. She addressed her love songs to Arman de Breon. Intertextual and metrical studies offer convincing evidence that the poet had relations with the court of Dalfin d'Alvernha, Count of Clermont, who lived from about 1155 to 1235. See Paden, ed. "Poems" 158-63, and Rieger 558-63.

6. Castelloza, "Amics, s'ie.us trobes avinen"

PC 109.1

a8 b10 b10 c10 d10 d10 a10 a10
6 *coblas unissonans*

The *canso* is found in the following manuscripts: A168, I125, K110, N230, d310. It is attributed to Castelloza in every manuscript except N, where it is anonymous. The texts of AIK are embellished with miniatures and contain a *vida* of Castelloza.

This text is based on manuscript A, which is the best of the AIKd group and differs significantly from the reading found in N.

Previous editors include Raynouard (1816-21), Rochegude (1819), Mahn (1846-53), Schultz-Gora (1888), La Salle de Rochemaure/Lavaud (1910), Véran (1946), Bogin (1976), *Action Poétique* (1978), Paden et al. (1981), Städtler (1990), Rieger (1991).

The following notes are based on our reading of A and Rieger 522-28.
4. *tric:* N reads *ric* (haughty).
6. *dond:* The form is a normal graphic variant of *don* in A, where the grapheme *t* alternates with *d* in the final position following an *n*. See Zufferey, *Recherches* 46.
17. *esta:* A reads *estai* and has been emended in accordance with IKNd.
20. *tan lonc pressic:* A reads *a pres de se* (by her side). The emendation, which accommodates the rhyme scheme, was suggested by Schultz-Gora and accepted by Rieger. It is based on N which reads *tam lonc pressic.*
21. *gauzir:* N reads *chausir* (to choose).
23. We accept Rieger's solution of *qe.l preiar.* A reads *qel preiar* and has been variously interpreted by editors. N preserves the variant *maing douz revenimen* ("much sweet healing," Paden, ed. "Poems" 172).
24. *greu:* N reads *gran* (great).
28. *vei:* IKd read *vit* (he saw); N reads *vi* (I saw).
37. *alegrar e:* N reads *per plam es les,* which Paden emends to *per plain e lais* ("by my lamentation and lays," Paden, ed. "Poems" 173).
38. *Convenir,* found in Ad, is a word of judicial provenance meaning to

call to justice, to summon. Although editors tend to follow IKN and emend the text to read *convertir, convenir* is valid here, given the judicial subtext of this *canso* and the inclusion of other words with legal connotations like *razonamen, falimen* and *preiar.*

47-48. Manuscript N reads "Faretz pecat, e serez n'en turmen, / e serai mos quesid'al jutjamen" ("You'll be in torment for it, and I'll be more sought after at Judgment," Paden, ed. "Poems" 173). The reading shows how manuscript variants may influence our interpretation of a work: here A warns of the harsh judgment to which her lover will be subjected by others and the poet's own impending damnation, while N recasts the lover's fault in an escatological scenario, predicting eternal damnation for the lover and salvation for the poet.

7. Castelloza, "Mout avetz faich lonc estatge"

PC 109.3

a7' b7 a7' b7 c7' d7 d7 c7' e7' e7'
5 *coblas unissonans*

The *canso* is found in the following manuscripts: A169, I125, K111, N228, d311. It is attributed to Na Castelloza in all the manuscripts except N, where it is anonymous.

The base manuscript for this edition is A, following Rieger and Schultz-Gora.

The *canso* has been edited by Rochegude (1819), Mahn (1846-1853), Schultz-Gora (1888), La Salle de Rochemaure/Lavaud (1910), Véran (1946), Roubaud (1971), Bogin (1976), *Action Poétique* (1978), Paden et al. (1981), Mamino (1986), Sansone (1986), Brunel-Lobrichon (1989), Städtler (1990), Rieger (1991).

The following notes are based on our reading of A and Rieger 541-48.
12. *vus amai:* A reads *ousai amat* and the text contains an extra syllable (hypermetric). The emendations are made by Schultz-Gora and Rieger.
15. *ganchida:* A reads *ganchia;* we have regularized the rhyme.

23. *om* could signal either the genderless, impersonal pronoun "one" or could indicate "man." The ambiguity may be intentional, as suggested by Bruckner, "Na Castelloza".

29. *calc'aondanssa:* A reads *calacom danssa.* We accept, with Rieger, a variant of Schultz-Gora's emendation (*qualqu'aondansa*), in accordance with *calcaondansa* found in IK and *calquaondansa* in N.

31. Rieger interprets *ai eu,* found in A, as a contraction of the subjunctive *aia* and the subject pronoun.

38. *Fenida,* the death knell, is also a technical term that refers to the *tornada* of a *canso.* See Van Vleck 103, 111.

43. *fan:* A reads *faz* which is grammatically problematic. The emendation was suggested by Schultz-Gora and adopted by Rieger.

47-48. Manuscripts AIKd all contain a lapsus. The scribe copied the stanza with no space left to indicate that material was missing. Paden (178-79), relying on N as the base manuscript, edits the lines to read "e prec que veingnaz a me / Depueis que aurez ausida" ("and I pray you to come to me after you hear"). Rieger completes the line with the reading from N.

8. Anonymous, "Per ioi que d'amor m'avegna"

PC 461.191

a7' b7 a7' b7 c7 c7 b7 b7 a7' b7
5 *coblas unissonans capfinidas*

The *canso* is only conserved in N where it is anonymous. Paden and Rieger have attributed the *canso* to Castelloza on the basis of metrical, thematic and codicological evidence. See Paden, ed. "Poems" 163-65 and Rieger 555-58.

Previous editors include Rochegude (1819), Mahn (1846-53), La Salle de Rochemaure/Lavaud (1910), Paden et al. (1981), Perkal-Balinsky (1987), Mölk (1989), Städtler (1990), Rieger (1991).

The following notes are based on our reading of N and Rieger 551-54.

1. Initial capitals are missing in N. Rochegude's emendation of each stanza's initial word was facilitated by the poet's use of *coblas capfinidas* (see Introduction). One of the practical effects of *coblas capfinidas* was the pres-

ervation of the proper order of the stanzas, often lost in the course of a poem's transmission.

5-6. Although melodies to only two poems in this repertoire, "Chantar m'er de so qu'ieu no volria" of the Contessa de Dia and "Si'us qier conseill, bella amia Alamanda," survive, textual references to music like those found in these lines indicate that trobairitz poems were intended to be sung like those of the troubadours. In the case of the *tenso* "Si'us qier conseill, bella amia Alamanda," Giraut de Bornelh, the first poet, would have been responsible for establishing the melody and the metrical scheme.

6. *sos:* N reads *sons* and as always we have regularized the rhyme.

9. There is a lapsus in N. Rochegude, followed by Paden and Rieger, completes the line by borrowing the verse opening *pos vei* ("since I see") of a closely related *canso* by the troubadour Peirol. See Paden, ed. "Poems" 181-82.

23. N contains a lapsus. Rochegude and Paden open the line with *Quar paor ai* ("for I am afraid"). See Paden, ed. "Poems" 181-82. Rieger suggests that the line may have begun *si m'angoissa* (so I dread), again relying on Peirol's *canso*, "Per dan que d'amor mi veigna."

34. *c'un:* N reads *cus.* Rieger's emendation correctly places the indefinite pronoun in the accusative form.

36. *los oilz ambedos:* N reads *lo oilz ambsdos.* We accept Rochegude and Rieger's emendation of the accusative plural article *los* and the emendation of *ambsdos* to the variant form *ambedos,* which is necessary to restore the metrical scheme.

40. *pot:* N reads *po.*

45. *cors:* N reads *cor.* We accept Rochegude's emendation to indicate the accusative form of *cor. ques:* the sibilant often marks a word boundary when a vowel ends one word and begins the next, but the more common grapheme is *z.*

50. *faiz:* N reads *em faiz* and is hypermetric. Rochegude and Rieger make the emendation.

9. Clara d'Anduza, "En greu esmay et en greu pessamen"

PC115.1

a10 b10 a10 b10 c10' d10 d10 c10'
3 *coblas unissonans* and a *tornada*

The *canso* is found only in C359 where it is attributed to Clara d'Anduza.

The *canso* has been edited by Fabre d'Olivet (1804), Raynouard (1816-21), Rochegude (1819), Mahn (1846-53), Charvet (1880), Schultz-Gora (1888), Mistral (1895), Portal (1896), Goût (1935), Véran (1946), Roubaud (1971), de Caluwé (1974), Bogin (1976), Albert-Birot (1978), Bec (1984), Perkal-Balinsky (1987), Mölk (1989), Städtler (1990), Rieger (1991).

The following notes are based on our reading of C and Rieger 574-76.

9. *Selh* functions as a singular and a collective plural pronoun.

15. *dir:* the word is not legible on the microfilm of C and I rely on Rieger and Schultz-Gora.

24, 28. *cors:* Troubadours, male and female, frequently play on the homophony between *cor/cors* (heart) and *cors* (body). Although we have translated body here in line 24, the heart still lingers in association. Since there is no specific word for self in Old Provençal, *cors* also functions in that sense and is an appropriate reading for line 28, where C reads *cor* (emended to *cors*).

Clara d'Anduza lived in the first third of the thirteenth century and is thought to have been a noblewoman of the house of Anduza, a court that hosted numerous troubadours in the late twelfth and early thirteenth centuries. She is the principal figure in a lengthy *razo* that accompanies a *canso* of Uc de Saint Circ (ca.1217-1253), who is known to have entertained at the court. Azalais d'Altier is probably addressing her *salut* to Clara (see no. 32, 97-99). Intertextual evidence links this work with poems by Uc de Saint-Circ, Lanfranc Cigala, Raimbaut de Vaqueiras, Guilhem d'Anduza, Pons de Capdoill, and Azalais d'Altier. See Rieger 576-83, and Poe, "Another" 329-33.

10. Bietris de Roman, "Na Maria, pretz e fina valors"

PC 93.1

a10 b10 a10 b10 c10' d10 c10' d10
2 *coblas unissonans* and 2 *tornadas*

The *canso* is found only in manuscript T208 where it is attributed to Bietris de Roman. We accept Zufferey's argument, made on paleographic grounds, that the rubric reads *bietris*, and not *bierris* or *bieiris* ("Toward a Delimitation" 32, 41).

This brief *canso* has engendered a great deal of critical discussion because it is one of the few medieval poems that might be read as an expression of lesbian love. The interpretive problems arise, at least in part, because our understanding of troubadour lexical registers is based on the standard situation in which a man addresses a woman or another man. Bec underscores the point when he observes that this poem would seem absolutely ordinary if composed by a man; if composed by a woman, its status shifts, in his view, to that of anomalous lesbian love song or *contre-texte,* that is, a travesty of a *canso* (Bec, *Burlesque* 198). Rieger rejects Bec's parameters and argues that Bietris is expressing herself in "an entirely normal, and even conventional, colloquial tone that was required by good manners between women, particularly between women of equal social position ... the author certainly conveys sympathy and affection, but ... she does not exceed the normal degree of affectivity usual between women" ("Bieris" 91).

Previous editions include Rochegude (1819), Mahn (1846-53), Schultz-Gora (1888), Monaci (1889), Bertoni (1915), Roubaud (1971), Bogin (1976), Nelli (1977), *Action Poétique* (1978), Bec (1984), Perkal-Balinsky (1987), Rieger, (1989, 1991).

The following notes are based on our reading of T and Rieger 505-09. Unless otherwise indicated, all emendations were made by Schultz-Gora and adopted by Rieger.
1. *e fina:* the line is hypermetric in T where it reads *e la fina.*
4. *solatz:* T reads *solas.*
5. *douz:* T reads *doz* and the emendation is Rieger's. *cuendanza:* T reads *acundanza.*
6. *semblan*: T reads *seblan.*
7. *qe:* T reads *ce.* In the manuscript *ce* is used for *que* in ll. 7, 9, 12, 19, 20, which we have emended. Schultz-Gora emends *ce* to *que* and Rieger keeps the manuscript reading. *en:* T reads *e.*
8. *ses:* T reads *sis.*
9, 12. *si.us:* T reads *sivos.*
14. *talan:* T reads *talen.* The line in T begins *& car* and has an extra syl-

lable.

17. *valors:* T reads *valor,* which has been emended to represent the nominative form by Rieger.

18. *no.us es*: T reads *novos evos* and is hypermetric.

19. *si.us:* T reads *se vos.*

21. *enansa:* T reads *enanza.*

22. *mas:* T reads *mes.*

23. *en:* T reads *e. gauss'e:* T appears to read *gaussa,* which may be a variant form of *gauch.* Zufferey ("Toward a Delimitation" 42) explains the form *Bietris* as "the simplification of the affricate *-tz* to *-s*," and *gaussa* presents a parallel case: the affricate *-ch* is simplified to *-ss* (cf. *gausiment* in line 10). This does not explain the final *-a,* however, and the text has been variously emended to read *sa(g)ess'* (wisdom) by Rieger, *gajess'* (gaiety) by Schultz-Gora, and *gaiez'* (gaiety) by Bec.

24. *en:* T reads *e.*

Nothing is known of Bietris de Roman and no other poet mentions her. It has been suggested that she was a sister or sister-in-law of Alberico da Romano, a Northern Italian troubadour and patron of troubadours. If so, Bietris would have lived in the first half of the thirteenth century. Intertextually the *canso* is close to "En tanta guisa.m men'Amors" by Gui d'Ussel, a troubadour of the second half of the twelfth century. See Zufferey, "Toward a Delimitation" 32-33, and Rieger 509-17.

11. Azalais de Porcairagues, "Ar em al freg temps vengut"

PC 43.1

a7 b7' a7 b7' c7 c7 d7' d7'
4 *coblas doblas* plus two *coblas singulars* and a *tornada*

Combining themes associated with the *canso, sirventes* and *planh,* this work is found in the following manuscripts: C385, D190, H57 (a fragment), I140, K125, N233, d314. It is anonymous in CHN. In H46, stanzas IV and III appear as anonymous and autonomous *coblas doblas.* In IK the work is accompanied by a miniature. A *vida* of Azalais de Porcairagues is included in IKd.

The edition in this text is based on D, after Rieger.

Previous editors include Raynouard (1816-20), Rochegude (1819), Mahn (1846-1853), Azaïs (1869), Balaguer (1878), Charvet (1880), Schultz-Gora (1888), Véran (1946), Sakari (1949), Roubaud (1971), de Riquer (1975), Bogin (1976), Sansone (1984), Bec (1985), Mamino (1986), Perkal-Balinsky (1987), Brunel-Lobrichon (1989), Mölk (1989), Kasten (1990), Städtler (1990), Rieger (1991).

" Ar em al freg temps vengut" is problematic from a textual point of view because there are two very different manuscript traditions of the work, one represented by CDIKd, the other by N. Other unusual aspects of the work include the disruption of the metrical scheme of *coblas doblas* after four stanzas and the lack of thematic unity in the work. Sakari attributes the metrical irregularities to the haste with which the poet transformed a pre-viously composed love poem consisting of stanzas III-V plus the *tornada* into a *planh* for Raimbaut; others suppose that Azalais was technically deficient. See Sakari, "A propos" 527-28. Rieger explains the thematic disunity of the poem by suggesting that the work might represent a scribe's conglomeration of several surviving fragments composed by Azalais: a *canso*, a *cobla dobla* on the *ric ome* theme and three stanzas lamenting the death of Raimbaut (Rieger 494-95).

The following notes are based on our reading of D and Rieger 484-94.
1-8. The "springtime opening" that is emblematic of earlier troubadours (and the Northern *trouvères*), becomes rare in late 12th- and early 13th-century Occitan lyric. This and the anonymous "Quan vei los praz verdesir" (Rieger 628-629) are the only extant examples by trobairitz.
3. *e.l:* D reads *e li* and is hypermetric. Rieger emends the text.
4. *s'afraigna:* N reads *se laigna* (makes an effort).
8. *l'am:* We follow Sakari who interprets *am* as *anma* (soul) ("Vers" 217 and "A propos" 525). *en:* Raynouard originally emended *e* to *en.*
9. *cor:* D reads *cors.*
11. The line appears to be proverbial (Rieger 486-87).
13-16. At this point N reads: "per qu'eu sui en gran esmai / car sai que.m aissi morai / e s'eu fos enans fenida / ben me tengra per garida" (for which I am in great distress because I know that thus I will die, and if I were already dead I would consider myself saved).

18. *plaideia:* D reads *pladeia.* The emendation accords with the other manuscripts.

21. *Veillai* refers to the home of Guilhem de Saint-Leidier, a contemporary
of Azalais whose position in the poetic debate on the *ric ome* she is citing
(see the Introduction and Sakari, "Azalais Joglar" 56-65). The reading in
N, *sai e lai* (here and there) is a *lectio facilior.* Lines 21-22 in the fragment
contained in H46 reads "qe Ovidis o retrai / c'amors per ricor non vai"
(because Ovid holds that love does not go with riches).

26. H reads *qu'en ditz d'amor seignoreia (*who dominates when it comes
to love poetry).

34. D reads *guaie.* We accept Sakari's and Rieger's emendation in accordance with CIK.

36. *outratge:* D reads *outraie.* Again the form is regularized by Sakari and
Rieger, as in CIK. *demandes:* N reads *dissessez* (speak).

41. *Belesgar* is the castle of Beauregard in the Vaucluse (Sakari, "Azalais
Joglar" 194).

43. Sakari has identified *Gloriette* as the name of the former palace of the
princes of Orange ("Azalais Joglar" 194-195).

47. *cellui* may refer to Raimbaut who died in 1173 (see Sakari, "Azalais
Joglar" 196).

49-52. *Joglar* is requested to bring the entire piece, including the *fenida* or
tornada, to Narbonne, probably designating in this fashion the Viscount-
ess Ermengarde of Narbonne, one of the most prominent women of the
second half of the twelfth century, to whom several famous troubadours
paid homage. See the Introduction for further discussion of Ermengarde
and also Sakari, "Azalais Joglar" 196-97, and Rieger 493. *Joglar* has been
interpreted as a *senhal* for Raimbaut. If the *planh* stanzas are intended to
lament his death, then the presence of the *tornada* is problematic.

53. N offers two *tornadas.* The first are lines 13-16 of the above text, the
second is the *tornada* that concludes our edition of the poem. In the case of
the second *tornada,* the final line of N offers a variant: *leis cui iois cabdell'e
guida* (she whom joy governs and guides).

According to her *vida,* Azalais was a well-educated noblewoman from the
region of Montpellier. Her love songs were written for Gui Guerrejat, "the
warrior." Sakari has discovered historical evidence suggesting that Azalais
was born in the 1140's at the castle of Portiragnes and was a neighbor of
Gui, lord of a territory that lies northeast of Béziers. Gui was Raimbaut
d'Aurenga's cousin and his name is attested in numerous documents. In
the case of Azalais, the *vida,* historical, and intertextual evidence all con-

firm her poetic ties to the court of Raimbaut d'Aurenga, one of the most important centers of vernacular poetry in the history of Occitanic verse. See Sakari, "Azalais interlocutrice" 29-36, "Azalais Joglar" 430, and Rieger 498-503.

12. Maria de Ventadorn and Gui d'Ussel, "Gui d'Ussel be.m pesa"

PC 194.9; 295.1

a8 b8 b8 a8 c10 c10 d10 d10
6 *coblas unissonans*

The *partimen* is found in A185, C389, D149, E220, H53, P48 (fragment), R78 (fragment), T83, a548. B lists the title in the table of contents. H and P contain a *razo* to accompany the work and H is illustrated with a miniature. R includes an empty staff for music. Maria de Ventadorn's name is mentioned in the rubric in ACERTa. Gui d'Ussel is named in the rubric of A, and variant spellings of the name occur there and in the text of the *partimen*.

This edition is based on A, after Rieger and Audiau.

Previous editors include Rochegude (1819), Raynouard (1820), Mahn (1846-1853), Schultz-Gora (1888), Carstens (1914), Audiau (1922), Véran (1946), Roubaud (1971), Jeanroy (1974), Bogin (1976), Bonnarel (1981), Mamino (1986), Perkal-Balinsky (1987), Kasten (1990), Städtler (1990), Rieger (1991).

The following notes are based on our reading of A and Rieger 260-62. Unless specified, the emendations are Audiau's and are adopted by Rieger.
6. *francamen:* A appears to read *fracamen*. In any case a tilde is not visible on the microfilm that I consulted.
14. *drut:* T reads *dompn* (lady).
15. *ses:* A reads *sis*.
19. *o comandar:* A reads *acomnadar*. We accept Audiau's emendation on the basis of Da. Rieger emends the line to read *e dompna deu o autrejar* (and the lady must grant it), basing her text on the reading in R.

20. The verse is missing in ADHa. Rieger emends the text to read *mas ben deu esgardar sazos* (but she should attend to the occasion), on the basis of the reading in ERT. C reads *e deu ben pregar sazos* (and she must also sometimes court). Because neither ERT nor C preserve readings of the poem that are consistently close to those in A, we have preferred not to interpolate the line.

22. *son:* A reads *son i* and the line is hypermetric.

31. *e:* a syllable is missing in A. The emendation accords with RT.

41. *es:* A reads *etz.*

45. *estara:* A reads *esta* and the emendation follows CDEHTa.

46. *finamen:* C reads *leyalmen* (loyally).

The poet and patroness Maria de Ventadorn was the daughter of Lord Raimon II of Torena, who lived from about 1143 to 1191, and the second wife of the Viscount Eble V of Ventadorn, whose family had long been associated with troubadour culture. The court at Ventadorn continued to welcome troubadours; in fact, no lady is praised in the extant corpus as often as Maria. She had two sons and entered the cloister of Grandmont in 1221 with her husband. See Rieger (262-73) and the Introduction for further details.

13. Alamanda and Giraut de Bornelh, "S'ie.us qier conseill, bella amia Alamanda"

PC 12a.1; 242.69

a10' a10' a10' a10' a10' b4 a10' b6
8 *coblas doblas* and 2 *tornadas*

This *tenso* is conserved in the following manuscripts: A18, B18, C8, D11, G70, H37, I23, K12, N181, N²22, Q87, R8, Sg66, 91, V74, a41. All attribute it to Giraut. N²22 and Sg91 contain a *razo*. The melody that accompanied this *tenso* is found in R. The *Leys d'Amors* defines this type of *tenso* as a *conselh:* "comunals entencios o prepauzamens qu'es donatz et atribuitz ad .I. o a motz, amonestan be o mal" (a common opinion or solution that is given and attributed to one or to many, recommending good or ill).

This edition is based on A after Kolsen and Rieger.

Previous editors of the text include Schultz-Gora (1888), Kolsen (1894), Appel (1895), Chaytor (1902), Hill/Bergin (1941), Véran (1946), de Riquer (1975), Hagan (1975), Bogin (1976), Perkal-Balinsky (1987), Sharman (1989), Rieger (1991).

The following notes are based on our reading of A and Rieger 188-94. The emendations are by Schultz-Gora, followed by Rieger, unless specified.

5. *desmanda:* A reads *demanda.* The emendation is in accordance with IKaNCR.

7. *pauc:* A reads *pau.*

11. The language does not permit us to say for certain whether *l'autre* is the subject or object of *coven,* that is, whether it is the transgressor or the one transgressed against who must indulge or flatter the other lover.

12. *lor:* A reads *lors.*

21. *confonda:* A reads *cofonda;* the emendation accommodates the rhyme scheme.

31. *esduia:* A reads *enduia.*

34. *primieira:* A reads *primeira.* The rhyme has been normalized in 34, 41, 44, 47, as in Rieger.

39. *Na Berengieira* has not been identified.

41. *q'ella.us:* A reads *qellas. mieira:* A reads *meira.*

44. *mainieira:* A reads *maineira.*

47. *sis:* A reads *si iaus,* and the line has an extra syllable. *sofieira:* A reads *sofeira.*

55. *enaissi:* A reads *sin aissi.*

57. *Seign'En:* CDHRSga read *senher amics* (noble friend).

62. The entire verse is missing from A, B and N. Rieger, following Kolsen, emends the text on the basis of DGIK, because all the manuscripts of this poem consistently correspond.

Since the thirteenth century, Giraut de Bornelh has been recognized as one of the most important troubadours. Most editors have treated his exchange with Alamanda as a fictitious dialogue. At least three troubadours mention Alamanda in their work, an indication that she probably did exist and was prominent in poetic circles. Lombarda (no. 21 in this edition) expresses pleasure at being named with her. Research by Rieger suggests that Giraut's interlocutor was, very plausibly, a noblewoman named Alamanda de Castelnou, who was born around 1160, who became the canoness of Saint-Etienne in Toulouse in 1223. Alamanda probably spent her girlhood, prior to her marriage to Guilhem de Castelnou, at the court of Count Raimon V of Toulouse, where she could have engaged in this poetic debate with Giraut. See Rieger 194-202.

14. Almuc de Castelnou and Iseut de Capion, "Dompna N'Almucs, si.us plages"

PC 20.2; 253.1

a7 b7 b7 a7 c7 c7 d7 d7 e7 e7
2 *coblas unissonans*

The text is found only in H45. Each stanza is introduced by a *razo* and embellished with a miniature.

Previous editors include Barbieri (ca. 1574), Rochegude (1819), Raynouard (1820), Mahn (1846-53), Schultz-Gora (1888), Stronski (1907), Bertoni (1915), Véran (1946), Boutière (1973), Bogin (1976), Nelli (1977), Liborio (1982), Dronke (1983), Perkal-Balinsky (1987), Städtler (1990), Rieger (1991).

The following notes are based on our reading of H and Rieger 168.
1. *si.us:* H reads *si ous.*
6. *languen:* H is almost illegible but according to Rieger the text reads *langrat.* Rieger has emended the text on the basis of a manuscript, no longer extant, which was consulted by Barbieri in the sixteenth century.
7. In the troubadour corpus, the spiritual connotation of terms like *perdonar, humilmen, sagramen, pentir* and *convertir* often enriches secular texts like this plea on behalf of a lover.
9. *li:* literally, "if you want to end all (this) with him."
15. *merce:* H reads *merces.* The emendation is by Rieger.

Almuc de Castelnou and Iseut de Capion were noblewomen and neighbors who lived in the late twelfth and first decades of the thirteenth centuries.

Almuc was the wife of Guigo de Castelnou de Randon, and as we have suggested (cf. no. 5, n55), she may have been an important figure in poetry circles. Although Iseut is undocumented, her surname indicates that she was a member of a prominent family. See Rieger 168-73.

15. Domna and Bertran del Pojet, "Bona dona d'una re que.us deman"

PC 87.1; 75.1

a10 a10 a10 a10 b10' a10 b10'
6 *coblas doblas* and 2 *tornadas*

The *tenso*, or *conselh*, is found in C361, D63, I122, K108, O16, S236, T70, a575 (fragment). It is anonymous in O and T. Miniatures accompany the text in IK.

This text is edited on the basis of D, after Rieger. The readings of all the manuscripts accord fairly closely, with the exception of C, which is also damaged where a miniature was removed.

Previous editors include De Lollis (1903), Bonnarel (1981), Rieger (1991).

The following notes are based on our reading of D and Rieger 322-27. All emendations were suggested by Rieger unless otherwise indicated.
3. *si.us:* D reads *suis*. The emendation accords with IKa.
4. *ves:* C reads *mais* (except). *razona:* C reads *demanda* (courts).
9. *que.l:* D reads *qeill*. The emendation is in accord with IKOSa.
11. *vos:* CIKO read *nom*.
12. The line is missing a syllable in D and is emended in accordance with IKSa and C.
13. The line in D has one extra syllable; the emendation of *dire* to *dir* agrees with IKSTa and C.
14. *mentir:* D reads *mentit*. All the other manuscripts read *mentir.*
18. The line is missing in DIK. Rieger reconstructs the line from C: *qar vos aug dir so don soi iraz* (for I hear you say what makes me angry). The reconstruction remains problematic because it is a syllable short.

19. *endomeniaz:* D reads *edoneiaçs;* C reads *endomenjaz*; O reads *endomenzatz.*

20. *maltraire:* D reads *martire* and the emendation, which restores the rhyme scheme, follows all the other manuscripts.

23, 36, 45. *Bertran:* D reads *ber.*

25. *faz:* D reads *faç.* As always, we have regularized the rhyme.

29. *feira:* D reads *feire* and the emendation is in accord with IK.

30. *vostr':* D reads *vostro.*

31. The line, a catalog of the standard attributes of a courtly lover, varies considerably in the different manuscripts. *fis:* COST read *francs* (noble, sincere). *fecels:* COSTa read *humils* (humble). *vers e dreiç:* Ca read *vertadiers* (truthful), I reads *vas vos dreitz* (true to you).

32. *venals:* D reads *leials venals.* The line has two extra syllables.

33. *non er:* IKa read *no mer* (will be ... to me).

37. *mos:* D reads *mer.* The emendation accords with Ta.

40. *ianglos:* D reads *ianglaire* (talkative). Because the line has an extra syllable, Rieger emends the word following IK.

44. *atraire:* D reads *amaire* and is emended to accord with all the other manuscripts.

45. *anar:* OST read *amar* (to love).

46. *francs:* COST read *fis* (pure, true). *trichaire:* C reads *gabaire* (braggart).

Bertran del Pojet was in the entourage of Count Raimon Berenguier V of Provence. His name first appears on a document dated September 1222. The *bona dona* has not been identified. See Rieger 327-29.

16. La Comtessa de Proensa (Garsenda de Forcalquier) and Gui de Cavaillon, "Vos qe.m semblatz dels corals amadors"

PC 187.1; 192.6

a10 b10 a10 b10 c10' d10 c10' d10 d10
2 *coblas unissonans*

This exchange of *coblas* is found in two Italian manuscripts: F47, T86. In F each speaker is identified in a rubric that precedes the appropriate stanza. T reverses the order of the exchange and does not identify the speakers.

This edition is based on F.

Previous editors include Raynouard (1816-21), Rochegude (1817), Mahn (1846-53), Azaïs (1869), Stengel (1877), Schultz-Gora (1888), Véran (1946), de Riquer (1975), Bogin (1976), Nelli (1977), Perkal-Balinsky (1987), Städtler (1990), Rieger (1991).

The following notes are based on our reading of F and Rieger 205-06.
1. *Vos:* the initial capital is missing in both stanzas.
9. *faillir:* F reads *faillr*. The emendation is made by Schultz-Gora and Rieger.
10. *Bona:* the initial capital is missing.
14. *oltrage:* F reads *oltra*ze; the rhyme has been regularized.

Gui de Cavaillon was a knight of high estate who is attested in documents dated from 1220 to 1229. Scholars have situated this exchange of *coblas* between 1200 and 1209, when Gui was at the court of Provence, an important center for vernacular poetry. Garsenda de Forcalquier, one of the most powerful women in Occitanic history, was renowned for her patronage of troubadours. Raimon Vidal and Elias de Barjols are among the troubadours who praised her. See Rieger (206-13) and the Introduction for further details.

17. Domna and Pistoleta, "Bona domna, un conseill vos deman"

PC 372.4

a10 b10 a10 b10 c10' c10' d10 d10
6 *coblas doblas* and one *cobla singular*.

This *tenso*, or *conselh*, is preserved in D202 (fragment), I138, K124, L48, O47, R73 (fragment), T71, Sg 47. IK have a miniature. The order of the stanzas is different in L, where the song is attributed to *Bertran del Poget*. The song is listed with works of Peirol in O. It is anonymous in R where there are empty staffs for music. It is also anonymous in T and in Sg, where it is copied with works by Raimbaut de Vaqueiras.

This edition is based on I, after Rieger and Niestroy.

Previous editions include Raynouard (1838), Mahn (1846-53), Massó Torrents (1907), Niestroy (1914), Véran (1946), *Action Poétique* (1978), Bonnarel (1981), Perkal-Balinsky (1987), Rieger (1991).

The following notes are based on our reading of I and Rieger 388-94.
All emendations are Niestroy's (accepted by Rieger), unless indicated.
4. *nuilla:* I reads *nuill.*
5-6, 13-14. In the first *coblas doblas* the c rhymes are not perfect.
7. *reproviers:* I reads *reprovier* but the nominative case is required here.
13. *si:* I reads *cel.* The emendation accords with LORSg.
14. *en:* I reads *e.*
20. *amara:* I reads *amera.*
22. *tro:* I reads *entro,* making the line hypermetric.
27. *hom serf:* I reads *hom fa serf* and the line is hypermetric. *on:* I reads *o;* the emendation follows D.
36. *cambiar:* I reads *camiar* (2 syllables), which makes the line a syllable short. The emended text accords with Sg.
37. *Don,* the apocopated form of *dona,* occurs in titles like *midons* and is accepted by Raynouard, although it is not attested elsewhere (Rieger 392).
38. *entendensa:* I reads *entendansa.*
40. *ni.l:* I reads *ni.*

As noted above, the attribution of the male voice to Pistoleta is problematic, but the poem does have strong intertextual connections with his corpus. It is on this basis that Rieger speculates on the identity of the lady. Pistoleta is thought to have been active between 1205 and 1228. One of his works mentions Peter II of Aragon, and Pistoleta's lady may have attended that court. Pistoleta also had ties with Maria de Ventadorn, Thomas of Savoy and Blancatz. The exchange could have been composed at one of these courts. See Rieger 394-99.

18. Ysabella and Elias Cairel, "N'Elyas Cairel, de l'amor"

PC 252.1; 133.7

a8 b8 b8 a8 c10' c10' d10 d10
6 *coblas unissonans* with 2 *tornadas*

The *tenso* is preserved in O88 and a605.

This edition is based on O.

Previous editors include La Curne (1774), Raynouard (1820), Schultz-Gora (1888), Bertoni (1915), Lavaud (1912), Jaeschke (1921), Véran (1946), Bogin (1976), Bonnarel (1981), Perkal-Balinsky (1987), Städtler (1990), Rieger (1991).

The following notes are based on our reading of O and Rieger 278-82.
4. *cambiat':* O reads *cambiant.*
9. *domn'Ysabella:* O reads *domneysabella.*
11. *soliatz:* O reads *solatz;* the text is emended in accordance with manuscript a.
13. *en:* O reads *e.* The emendation was first made by Schultz-Gora.
15. *jongleur:* here the term describes a man who performs merely for the sake of monetary gain; a jongleur was considered inferior to a troubadour because he did not compose the songs he performed.
18. *vi:* O reads *vim.*
28. *aic:* manuscript a reads *hai* (have).
29. *remanres:* O reads *remantes* and the text is emended in accordance with manuscript a.
31. *cors:* O reads *cor. estan:* O reads *istan.* The text was first emended by Schultz-Gora.
40. *Iuan:* We assume that Ysabella's words are in jest because she has just insulted Elias by suggesting that he belongs in a monastery. Apparently Rieger interprets this as an historical allusion, although she objects that there was no Patriarch Ivan in the Eastern Church in the early thirteenth century. If we were to pursue the historical perspective, Jaeschke's emendation of the name to *Joan,* the Occitanic form of *Johannes,* would be preferable because the Patriarch of Constantinople from 1199 to 1206 was Johannes X. That solution, however, creates metrical difficulties. See Rieger 280-81.
41. *Domn'Ysabel:* O reads *domneysabel.*
48. *avetz:* O reads *avet. q'ieu hai:* O reads *qieu i hai* (hypermetric); Bertoni first emended the text.

52. *s'ela val:* O reads *sala va* and Schultz-Gora emended it. *s'aitan:* O reads *sasetan* which makes no sense and results in a hypermetric line. We have adopted Rieger's emendation.

55. *e:* O reads *qe;* the text was originally emended by Schultz-Gora.

The search for the identity of Ysabella begins with our knowledge of Elias Cairel, a goldsmith by trade and a jongleur who traveled the world for many years, according to his *vida.* Elias Cairel spent much of the first decades of the thirteenth century in Italy and served the crusader Boniface I of Montferrat in Greece (hence the reference to an Eastern Patriarch?). Ysabella is thought to be either Isabella de Montferrat, widow of Conrad, a brother of Boniface, or Isabella de Malaspina, sister of Boniface and wife of Albert de Malaspina. An Isabella is mentioned in three works by Elias Cairel, which Rieger places in the first decade of the thirteenth century. See Rieger 282-289.

The poet Ezra Pound, an enthusiastic reader and translator of troubadour lyric, offers this translation of Elias Cairel's *vida* in "Troubadours: Their Sorts and Conditions," *Literary Essays* (New York: New Directions, 1935) 98: "Elias Cairel was of Sarlat; ill he sang, ill he composed, ill he played the fiddle and worse he spoke, but he was good at writing out words and tunes. And he was a long time wandering, and when he quitted it, he returned to Sarlat and died there."

19. Domna and Peire Duran, "Midons qui fuy, deman del sieu cors gen"

PC 339.3

a10 b10 b10 a10 c10' c10' d10 d10
4 *coblas unissonans*

This parodic *tenso* is preserved in R100 where it is attributed to P. Duran. There are empty staffs for music.

The work has been edited by Mahn (1856-73), Lewent (1938), Rieger (1991).

The following notes are based on our reading of R and Rieger 379-81. Unless otherwise stated, the emendations were suggested by Lewent and are followed by Rieger.

1. *Midons:* "My lady-lord," the well-known, untranslatable formula by which a troubadour presents himself as a vassal to a person who combines the status of feudal lord with that of beloved lady. *Midons qui fuy* sets the tone of the *tenso* by rendering this hallowed term ironic. R actually reads *midons dons. deman:* R reads *demans. gen:* R reads *gent;* the emendation accommodates the rhyme.

5. *esdeven:* R reads *esdeve.* Similar emendations are indicated in lines 6, 7 and 8. *cuendansa:* R reads *cundansa.* In line 5 and elsewhere in the poem, the subject of a singular verb is a logical unit composed of two or more nouns, a common practice in Occitan, especially when the verb precedes the subject (Jensen 233).

11. *non si desnoiri:* R reads *nonz desnoiri* making the line a syllable too short.

17. *ten:* R reads *te.* Rieger regularizes the word to fit the rhyme scheme.

17-20. *ten* and *dezavinens* rhyme imperfectly. Rieger (178) notes, that the declension system is often ignored in R, a manuscript copied in Toulouse in the fourteenth century. It is probably safe to assume that the *s* at the end of *dezavinens* was not pronounced by the scribe and his public and was perhaps already very weak when the work was composed almost a century earlier.

23. *om:* R reads *omz.*

24. *on:* R reads *o.*

25. *un:* R reads *.i.*

28. *triar:* R reads *tiar.*

29. *engruysiei:* R reads *e engruysiei,* making the line hypermetric.

Nothing is known of Peire Duran, but stylistic tendencies point to the early thirteenth century as the date of the work. See Rieger 381-83.

20. Felipa and Arnaut Plagues, "Ben volgra midons saubes"

PC 32.1

a7 b7 b7 a7 c7' c7' d7 d7 c7'
5 *coblas unissonans capfinidas* (except between II and III) and 2 *tornadas*

This *tenso* takes the form of *coblas tensonadas,* in which the dialogue is not distributed in blocks but broken into brief questions and responses. It has been preserved in C359, E71, M134, R88, S214, and the *Breviari d'Amor*, vv. 31,643-31,686. In CM the *tenso* is attributed to Arnaut Plages, in R to Peirol, in S to Peire Rogier.

The text has been previously edited by Rochegude (1819), Appel (1882), Mahn (1856-73), Azaïs (1862-1881), Richter (1976), Ricketts (1976), Rieger (1991).

This edition is based on C, after Appel and Rieger. Because the manuscripts contain no punctuation except for dots at the ends of lines, establishing the exchange of voices is a puzzle. We generally follow Appel and Rieger in the punctuation of the text, with the exceptions noted below. The emendations are by Appel and Rieger, unless specifically noted.

The following notes are based on our reading of C and Rieger 217-18.
6. *diguas:* M reads *veiratz* (look).
10. *no pot ges:* EM read *hom plagues* (one would be pleased), apparently playing on Arnaut's name. See also lines 3, 13, 14.
12. Appel and Rieger attribute *E quom* to the male voice, but we have interpreted it as a rhetorical question that introduces Na Felipa's response.
24. *non ges:* S reads *la noich* (at night).
39. *cum ieu t'o:* C reads *cum to.*
45. Appel and Rieger attribute the line to the male voice.
50. *ten*: C reads *tey.*
The second *tornada*, expressing dissatisfaction with the King of Castille —either Alphonse VIII (1158-1214) or Ferdinand III (1217-1252)—is only found in CM. Rieger (215, 217) emends *dobla* to read *adoba* and interprets the text to mean "zum König, der die Verluste wiedergutmacht" (to the king who restores loss). We see no reason for the emendation because hostile *tornadas* are by no means unknown in the Occitanic corpus, especially when a troubadour has failed to benefit from the largesse of a patron.

Arnaut Plagues, to whom the text is ascribed in C, is an unknown figure, although a melody he composed is mentioned in a 1226 *sirventes* by Uc de Saint-Circ. The work is linked intertextually with a poem of Falquet de

Romans, dated between 1212 and 1220. Rieger assigns this *tenso* to the second decade of the thirteenth century, in the poetic milieus of Provence or Northern Italy. The identity of Felipa, however, continues to elude us. See Rieger 218-23.

21. Lombarda and Bernart Arnaut d'Armagnac, "Lombards volgr'eu eser per Na Lonbarda"

PC54.1; 288.1

a10' a10' a10' a10' b4 b4 a6' b6
2 *coblas singulars* and a *tornada*, with 2 *coblas singulars* in response. The scribe apparently assumed that Lombarda's *tornada* originally concluded the text, since a space is left open in the manuscript.

Razos (commentaries) and *vidas* (biographies) are prose interpolations accompanying poems in the manuscripts. Many were composed in the first decades of the thirteenth century when troubadour verse was transformed from the prestigious game of memory, wit, and song cultivated in the courts and cities of the Midi, into a literature that was, for the most part, passively received in the courts and salons of Northern Spain and Italy. The prose interpolations, miniatures, and even the magnificence of certain anthologies provided this modern, vernacular, "courtly" literature with an historical context and a tradition for the new public (see Meneghetti 235-76, 323-63). A *razo* purports to explain the genesis of the song, often by creating a literal occurrence based on the poem's figurative language. We include this one brief example to show how a *razo* may fail to address the poem's thematics, but still manage to create a poignant tale (see also Poe, *From Poetry*, and Burgwinkle).

The exchange is preserved in H43 where it is embellished with a miniature.

Previous editors include Raynouard (1820), Mahn (1846-53), Chabaneau (1885), Schultz-Gora (1888), de Lollis (1889), Dejeanne (1906), Desazars, (1910), Anglade (1928-29), Véran (1946), Jeanroy (1957), Bogin (1976), Perkal-Balinsky (1987), Kay (1989), Sankovitch (1989), Städtler (1990), Rieger (1991).

The following notes are based on our reading of H and Rieger 245-47. The emendations were proposed by Schultz-Gora and are followed by Rieger, unless otherwise indicated.

1. *Lombards:* the initial is missing in H.

8. *nuls:* H appears to read *nols* but is very murky at this point. We accept De Lollis's emendation, which is also in Rieger.

10. *Peiteus; Bretagna:* H reads *piteus* and *bertagna.*

12. *Livorno:* H reads *liverno.*

16. *de se:* H reads *des;* we have emended the text.

17. *Mirail:* the initial is missing in H.

19. *vila:* H appears to read *vilia.* Since the manuscript is almost illegible, here we follow Rieger.

21. *Nom:* the initial is missing in H. *Bernada:* H reads *bernarda;* we have regularized the rhyme.

23. *grans:* H reads *gran.*

24. *tals:* H reads *tal. mi aves:* H reads *maves* and the line is hypometric.

26. *cals:* H reads *cal.*

29-32. *descorda / s'acorda; desacorda / recorda:* an involved conceit notable for interwoven derived rhymes (see above, no. 1). Three of them are based on forms of L. *chorda,* evoking the notion of strings in or out of tune, while another derivation *(recorda)* from L. *cordis,* heart, introduces line 33 in which the poet-singer refers to the elusive heart of the friend whose absence has brought discord to her thoughts.

31. *mas can:* H reads *mes cau.* De Lollis emended the text and is followed by Rieger.

The identification of Lombarda as an early thirteenth-century Gascon trobairitz is based on the historical evidence of Bernart Arnaut, second son of the Count Bernart IV of Armagnac and Fenzesac, who became count himself after his brother's death. Bernart died in 1226. His neighbor Jordan III, Lord of l'Isle-Jourdain, whom Bernart addresses in his *coblas,* is also attested in documents (Rieger 247-54).

22. Guilielma de Rosers and Lanfranc Cigala, "Na Guilielma, maint cavalier arratge"

PC 200.1; 282.14

a10' b10' a10' b10' c10 c10 c10 b10'
6 *coblas unissonans* and 2 *tornadas*

The *partimen* is preserved in I159, K145, M263 (fragment), O93, P48 (fragment), a542. P contains a *razo*. The work is ascribed to both poets in aIKO. The rubric in M merely reads *tenson*.

This edition is based on Bertoni's diplomatic edition of manuscript a. Branciforti and Rieger base their editions on manuscript a.

The text has been previously edited by Raynouard (1816-21), Mahn (1846-53), Schultz-Gora (1888), Bertoni (1915), Véran (1946), Toja (1952), Branciforti (1954), Neumeister (1969), Bogin (1976), Bonnarel (1981), Perkal-Balinsky (1987), Städtler (1990), Rieger (1991).

The following notes are based on our reading of the diplomatic edition of manuscript a and Rieger 230-33. The emendations were first made by Branciforti and are followed by Rieger.
1. Guilielma's name is spelled differently in the rubric and the text of manuscript a. The name *Lanfranc* occurs as *Lafranc* in manuscripts aIKM. O identifies the troubadour as Lanfranc Cigala.
12, 22. *sidonz* ("his lady lord"), the 3rd person form of *midons*, see no.19, note 1.
13. *presen:* a reads *prenen*. Although the aO branch of the manuscript tradition functions as the basis of our edition, we have accepted this reading from IKM branch.
22: *qe:* manuscript a reads *qel*.
24. *tanz cavaliers:* a reads *tan cavalier*. The emendation is based on M.
26. *con:* a reads *co*.
37. *biort:* a reads *baurt*. IK read *biort* from *biordar*, to joust. See note 13.
39. *los:* a reads *lo*.
43. *de paratge:* IKM read *d'aut paratge* (of high rank).
44. *en:* a reads *em*.
49. *poder:* a reads *non a poder*, which makes no sense. The emendation is in accord with all the other manuscripts.
53. *e.us:* a reads *es*.

The poem dates from the mid-thirteenth century. Lanfranc Cigala, from a prominent Genoese family, served as a judge and public servant in his native republic and is well attested in documents. He left a corpus of thirty-two poems. Guilielma could have been a noblewoman of Provence sojourning in Genoa when the poem was composed, or the *tenso* may have been composed at the court of the Counts of Provence where Lanfranc Cigala served as Genoese ambassador in 1241. See Rieger 234-39.

23. Domna H. and Rofin, "Rofin, digatz m'ades de quors"

PC 249a.1; 426.1

a8 b8 b8 a8 c7' d8 d8 c7' e8 e8
6 *coblas unissonans* and 2 *tornadas*

The *partimen* or *joc partit* has been preserved in I161, K147, O95, a545, d343. In manuscript rubrics and tables of contents the trobairitz is identified as Domna H; only d does not include the lady's initial. Rofin's name occurs as *Rofin* (IK), *Rofim* (d), *Rosin* (aIO), *Ronsin* (I) and *Rozin* (O). The name is probably a *senhal:* Bogin argues for *Rosin,* meaning "nightingale"; the variant form *Ronsin* could suggest the meaning "old hag." Rieger prefers *Rofin,* meaning "ruffian" or "libertine," which gives the debate an ironic twist (see Rieger 296, 300-01).

This edition is based on K after Rieger.

Previous editors include Raynouard (1820), Schultz-Gora (1888), Véran (1946), Bogin (1976), Nelli (1977), Perkal-Balinsky (1987), Rieger (1991).

The following notes are based on our reading of K and Rieger 296-99. The emendations were originally suggested by Schultz-Gora and followed by Rieger.
4. *que ieu:* K reads *quieu,* and the line is one syllable too short.
32. *coralmens:* K reads *coralmons;* the emendation accommodates the rhyme scheme.
37. *ni.l:* K reads *nill.*
39. *no.s:* K reads *nois.*
46. *saup:* K reads *sau;* the emendation of the preterite form is in accordance with Oa.

48. *aiziva:* K reads *aziva.* The emendation follows Oa.

53. *falhimens:* K reads *failhmens.*

The identities of Domna H. and the troubadour known as Rofin have long eluded literary historians. Rieger focuses on intertextual links between this *tenso* and a *partimen* by Aimeric de Peguihan and Elias d'Ussel, composed in Northern Italy in 1212, which suggests that the poem was composed at the court of the Este family. Another path of inquiry is provided by a *canso* by Peire Bremon Ricas Novas, composed between 1230 and 1241, which is the metrical model for the *tenso* between Domna H. and Rofin. Peire Bremon Ricas Novas served at the court of Count Raymond Berenguer IV. Attested at the court in the same period is the troubadour Blancatz, who, along with several other troubadours, praised Hugueta of Baux in his poems: Hugueta must certainly be a candidate for the elusive Domna H. See Rieger, 299-304.

24. Domna and Raimon de la Salas, "Si.m fos graziz mos chanz, eu m'esforcera"

PC 409.5

a10' b10 b10 a10' c10 c10 d10 d10
5 *coblas unissonans*

This exchange of *coblas* is found in D179, I108, K94, d340. There are miniatures in IK. The rubrics in brackets are not in the manuscripts but have been added for clarity. *Raimon de la Salas* appears as a rubric for the entire exchange in IK.

This edition is based on D, after Chambers and Rieger.

Previous editors include Schultz-Gora (1888), Chabaneau (1889), Chambers (1970), Bogin (1976), Perkal-Balinsky, (1987), Rieger (1991).

The following notes are based on our reading of D and Rieger 445-48. The emendations were first made by Schultz-Gora and are adopted by Rieger, except where noted.

2. *dera.m:* D reads *deran.* Chambers and Rieger make the emendation.

3. *aissi.m:* D reads *issim;* the emendation agrees with IKd.

4. *que:* DIKd read *que a.*

6. *entre.ls:* DIKd read *entres.*

8. *e.ls:* D reads *el.*

12. *no.s:* D reads *nom.* The emended text accords with IK.

16. *non:* D reads *fi.* The emendation accords with IK.

17. *domn'aras:* DIK read *domna res;* we have emended the text.

25. *amics:* D reads *amis.* Rieger emends the text in accordance with IKd.
no.s: D reads *nous;* the emendation follows IKd.

28. *ves vos, de cui sui meilz hoi q'er non era:* IKd read *vos es de cui sui mielz hoi que non era* (you, because of whom I am better today than I was before).

29. *met'en:* D reads *meta e.*

40. *pesa.m:* D reads *pesan.* Chambers and Rieger emended the text.

The poem probably dates from the third or fourth decade of the thirteenth century. The identification of the *domna* depends on our knowledge of Raimon, who was a bourgeois from Marseilles. He may have served in the court of Hugh II of Baux,Viscount of Marseilles (1193-1240). The only proper name given a lady in Raimon's five surviving works is an unknown *Na Raimbalda del Baus.* See Rieger 448-49.

25. Domna and Raimbaut d'Aurenga, "Amics, en gran cosirier"

PC 389.6

a7 b7' a7 c7' c7' d8 d8
8 *coblas unissonans* and 2 *tornadas*

The tenso is found in C199, D90, M139. The text is ascribed to Raimbaut in the three manuscripts.

This edition is based on M.

Previous editors include Raynouard (1816-21), Rochegude (1819), Mahn (1846-53), Schultz-Gora (1888), Santy (1893), Kussler-Ratyé (1917), Berry (1930), Véran (1946), Pattison (1952), Jeanroy (1974), Faucheux (1974),

Hagan (1975), de Riquer (1975), Bogin (1976), de Casas/Cantera (1976), Bonnarel (1981), Bec (1985), Mamino (1986), Perkal-Balinsky (1987), Sakari (1987), Kasten (1990), Rieger (1991).

The following notes are based on our reading of M and Rieger 403-09.

7. *no.l:* M reads *no. pertem egal:* M reads *partem per egal* and the line has an extra syllable. Both emendations accord with CD.

9. *dos:* M reads *.ii.*

11. *sen chascus soill es:* C reads *senta quecx a son* (each feels according to his ...).

19. *quan:* CD read *quar* (because).

24. *son:* M reads *so. nostr:* C reads *vostr* (your).

26. *no.us:* M reads *nos.*

27. *nos:* C reads *vos.*

30. D reads *car lo mieu dans* (because my harm). Our translation of M (*le mieus ditz*) stretches the literal meaning of the words in the direction of the reading found in D.

37. *e vos:* M reads *vos en* and has been emended in accordance with DC. The phrase, probably proverbial, also plays on the name of Raimbaut (Riquer 454).

39. *amor:* M reads *amors.*

41. Oaths to San Martial occur elsewhere in the troubadour corpus. Pasero (100) claims that San Martial was the patron saint of Limousin, and Rieger (407) points out that references to San Martial tend to be slightly ironic, as is certainly the case here.

45. *cuid:* M reads *cuidi.* The line is hypermetric.

45-46. The *domna* accuses Raimbaut of having become so absorbed in the appraisal of his portion that he has transformed himself from knight to money-changer. The language of economics, like spiritual and legal language, was not treated as extraneous to troubadour poetics, but absorbed and mined as a source of metaphor.

49. *no.us:* M reads *nos.* The emendation accords with CD.

Poet and patron of poets, Raimbaut d'Aurenga was a nobleman who lived from around 1144 to 1173. Despite his frequent references to Orange, he may or may not have ruled there. He certainly controlled several territories in the region (Pattison 15). Two trobairitz have been definitively connected with his court: Azalais de Porcairagues and Tibors. The Comtessa de Dia was probably also a participant in Raimbaut's poetic circle. This poem is metrically parallel to works by Azalais and the Comtessa, but such evidence is not sufficient to assign a name to the anonymous trobairitz of the work. See Rieger 409-17.

26. Domna and Donzela, "Bona domna, tan vos ay fin coratge"

PC 461.56

a10' b10 a10' b10 b10 a10' b10 a10'
6 *coblas doblas* and 2 *tornadas*

The *tenso* is preserved in R35. There are staffs for music.

The text has been edited by Selbach (1886), Schultz-Gora (1888), Véran (1946), Bogin (1976), Perkal-Balinsky (1987), Städtler (1990), Rieger (1991).

The following notes are based on our reading of R and Rieger 177-79. The emendations were proposed by Schultz-Gora and adopted by Rieger, unless specifically noted.
1. The first a rhyme in R is *-atie: coratie* (1), *vilanatie* (3), *dampnatie* (6), *senhoratie* (8), *salvatie* (9), *volatie* (11), *folatie* (14), *onratie* (16). The emended words reflect prevalent Occitanic forms.
10. *ni se:* R reads *nis,* which makes the line a syllable too short.
13. *m'amors.* R reads *m'amor.*
15. *l'en:* R reads *lin.*
16. *dir:* R reads *dire.* Schultz-Gora and Rieger read the line *qu'aissi aug dir que dretz es e onratge* (for I hear that it is right and honorable).
23. *focs:* R reads *foc. ensen:* R reads *esen.*
24. *pendre:* R reads *penre.* The emendation is necessary to accommodate the rhyme scheme.
25. *rependre:* R reads *repenre.* Again the emendation accommodates the rhyme scheme.
26. *que.l:* R reads *quiel.*
28. *mon:* R reads *mo.*
36. *sos cors umils:* R reads *son cor humil.* As has already been observed, the declension system is frequently abused in this manuscript (see no. 19,

n17-20).

37. *cals:* R reads *cal.*

38. *merces:* R reads *merce.*

39. *mil:* R reads *.m.*

40. *don:* R reads *dons. esmenda:* R reads *emenda.*

42. The line is a syllable short; Schultz-Gora proposed the addition of *que.*

43. *umils:* R reads *uuelh* (eye).

44. *cascun:* R reads *cascus. repos:* R reads *repotz,* which does not fit the rhyme scheme.

46. *per que:* the words are reversed in the manuscript.

47. *amoros:* R reads *amors.*

52. *bona.s:* R reads *bonais. donzela.n:* R reads *donzelam.*

54. *que.l:* R reads *quels.*

The anonymity of the two trobairitz remains complete (Rieger 179-81).

27. Alaisina Yselda and Na Carenza, "Na Carenza al bel cors avinenz"

PC 12.1; 108.1

a10 b10 b10 a10 c10' c10' d10 d10
2 *coblas unissonans* and 2 *tornadas*

The text is a fourteenth-century interpolation in Q42 which postdates the compilation of the anthology by half a century.

Previous editors include Bartsch (1875), Schultz-Gora (1888), Bertoni (1905), Véran (1946), Bogin (1976), Nelli (1977), Dronke (1983), Bec (1984), Perkal-Balinsky (1987), Rieger (1991).

The following notes are based on our reading of Q and Rieger 156-58.

1. *Na:* Q reads *A Na. avinenz:* Q reads *avenenç.* We have rejected the cedilla found in the manuscript only at the rhyme word. The scribe uses the *ç* and *z* indiscriminately.

2. *donaz, nos, doas:* Q reads *dunaz, nus, duas.*

3. *triar:* Q reads *triare.*

4. *consilhaz:* Q reads *consilaz. second:* Q reads *secundu. vostr'escienz:* Q

reads *vostra scienç.*

5. *conoscenza:* Q reads *conoscença.*

6. *agenza:* Q reads *agença.*

7. *que:* Q reads *qui. bos:* Q reads *bons.*

8. *par:* Q reads *pare.*

9. *nsenghamenz:* Q reads *nsenghamenç.*

10. *frescas:* Q reads *frezas. colors:* Q reads *colurs.*

11. *conosc, valors:* Q reads *conusc, valurs. cortesia:* Q reads *cortisia.*

12. *sobre tottas:* Q reads *subre tuttas. autras:* Q reads *atras.*

13. *qu'ie.us:* Q reads *quius. far:* Q reads *fare.*

14-16, 21-24. Lines 14-16 appear to have a religious meaning, but the key phrases in lines 21 and 24 are obscure. An appropriate reading depends on the interpretation of *illumbra de ghirenza* (which may or may not refer to the shelter of convent life) and *al departir,* which might indicate a temporary separation of friends, the moment of taking holy orders, or even death.

15. *filh:* Q reads *fil.*

16. *pulsel'a cui l'espos:* Q reads *pulsela da quil spuse.*

20. *lo ventrilh:* Q reads *los ventril. es ruat e'noios:* Q reads *aruat en noios.* We give Rieger's rendering of the problematic phrase.

22. *en l'umbra:* Q reads *illumbra.* Shadow as a metaphor for protection occurs in the *Psalms* and elsewhere. For example, Psalm 35:5 "et filii Adam in umbra alarum tuarum sperabant" (and the sons of Adam will take hope in the shelter of your wings). See note 14.

23. *los:* Q reads *los.*

24. *vos*: Q reads *vus.*

Interpretation of this *tenso* is difficult, given the precarious nature of its transmission and the fact that the extant version was recorded by a scribe who was apparently unfamiliar with the Provençal language. Two women appear to be speaking at cross purposes. Bogin, followed by Dronke, changes the order of the first and second stanzas, thereby dividing the playful from the serious voice. She also reads the work as a conversation among three women, Carenza and the two sisters, Alais and Yselda (see Bogin 144-45, Dronke, *Women Writers* 101-102, and Bec, who objects to Bogin's reading in "Enfants" 24-25). Anderson interprets the poem as a satire of *Midons* who would choose the convent for vanity's sake. The names, representing the three estates of women (the virgin Carenza, the noble Isolda and the peasant Alaisina) denote *Midons* as "Everywoman," in her view (Anderson 55-64). Bec also offers a unified interpretation in which Carenza recommends marriage to an educated man, a cleric who will appreciate her virginity and produce a glorious son (Bec, "Enfants" 21-30). Other critics have attempted to explain the disparate elements of the *tenso* by interpreting them from a perspective of Cathar teachings (Nelli 233).

Rieger underscores the traditional elements of this debate poem: the question of whether it is better to marry or retire to a convent and the standard formulas of praise offered by both women. In this poem, Alaisina Iselda will not choose between marriage or the convent: she wants what she views as the best of both possibilities. Intertextual allusions connect this *tenso* to the corpus of Arnaut de Maruelh, a troubadour active in Southern French courts in the late twelfth and early thirteenth century, including the court of Azalais, daughter of Count Raymond V of Toulouse and wife of Viscount Roger II Trencaval of Béziers. See Rieger 158-65.

28. Anonymous, "No puesc mudar no digua mon vejaire"

PC 404.5

a10' b10 a10' b8 a10' b8 c10 c10 d10' d10'
4 *coblas unissonans*

The *sirventes* is found only in C154 and is attributed to Raimon Jordan.

Previous editors include Raynouard (1820), Suchier (1873), Kjellman (1922), de Riquer (1975), Perkal-Balinsky (1987), Rieger (1991).

The following notes are based on our reading of C and Rieger 706-09, unless otherwise indicated.
17-18. Each line is missing two syllables but the reading found in the manuscript is coherent.
24. The first half of the line is incomprehensible but we do not find any satisfactory emendation.
26. *ho orador:* C reads *ho denant orador* and is hypermetric.
29. *gran:* C reads *grans;* Kjellman emended the text.
36. *Damnidieu:* C reads *damidieu.*
39. *onransa:* C reads *razonansa* which makes the verse hypermetric. The emendation was originally made by Suchier.

The poet criticizes not only the misogynist troubadours of old, and specifically the moralist Marcabru (ca. 1130-1149), but also the poets' public that could so easily be seduced into believing what had the mere appearance (*semblansa*) of truth, but was patently false.

Raimon Jordan, to whom the *sirventes* is attributed in C, was a troubadour active in the last quarter of the twelfth century. He is associated in the lore of the *vidas* with Helis de Monfort, sister of Maria de Ventadorn, trobairitz and patroness of troubadours. According to Rieger, it is to the circle of Maria that we must turn to identify our author, although at present she remains anonymous. See Rieger 709-13.

29. Anonymous, "Ab greu cossire et ab greu marrimen"

PC 371.1

a11 a11 a11 a11 b6 b6 b6 c6' c6' d6 d6
regular internal rhyme in I,1-4
6 *coblas singulars*

This *sirventesca* is found only in R66 where it is attributed to P. Basc. In this manuscript, "P." is the normal abbreviation for "Peire" (Rieger 694). There are musical staffs without melodic notation. Chambers sees *sirventesca* as an "author's humorous deformation" of *sirventes,* but the term is rarely attested (*Introduction* 222).

The work had been edited by Raynouard (1820), Milá y Fontanals (1861), Balaguer (1879), Appel (1890), Rieger (1991).

The following notes are based on our reading of R and Rieger 694-97. The text was originally emended by Appel; his emendations are followed by Rieger unless otherwise indicated.
4. *vestimens:* R reads *vestamens.* The emendation is in Rieger.
6. *frezatz*: R reads *frenatz (?).*
8-9. The poet rhymes *corona* and *Roma.* At this point and elsewhere in the poem the poet substitutes assonance for pure rhyme. See 34-35 (*personas - vergonhozas*) and 67-68 (*meravilha - esclavina*).

14. *foron:* R reads *fon.* The emendation, necessary to accommodate themetrical scheme, is made by Rieger.

22. *amors:* R is unclear but it appears to read *elmors* according to Rieger.

26. *rendador:* R reads *rendor.* Rieger makes the emendation, because the line is hypometric.

28. *desencadenatz:* R reads *descadenatz*, making the line a syllable short. Rieger emends the word.

30-31. Dress is not merely a question of vanity; as these lines indicate, it is a symbol of rank as well.

31. *vergonhozas:* R reads *vergonahozas.* Rieger makes the emendation.

33. *franc:* R reads *francx.*

36. *un:* R reads *.I.*

39. *son:* R reads *so.*

43. *li autre reglar:* R reads *li autre iogl. reglar* and is hypermetric.

48. *nostre marit:* R reads *nostres maritz.*

47-48. These lines may allude to a political *sirventes* entitled *Ab greu cossire,* by Bernart Sicart de Marvejols. Bernart's poem protests the Treaty of Meaux, negotiated by the French Queen Blanche of Castille and Count Raymond VII of Toulouse. This treaty, signed in 1229, signalled the end of political autonomy in the South. The specific reference is supported by a similarity in the meter, rhyme and opening of the first stanza of this work and Bernart's *sirventes.* Bernart, and our poet in turn, borrowed the metrical structure and presumably the tune from a well-known *canso* to ensure the rapid diffusion of the *sirventes* (Rieger 699).

49-51. The lines are missing in R. There is no break in the text to indicate that the scribe was aware of the omission.

58. *negra*: R reads *nega.*

62. The line is missing in R.

63. *maravilha:* R reads *maralhas.*

64. Rieger (697) cites FEW (XX, 46a): "a fur cloak of Slavic origin, adopted by pilgrims." The nugget of the poet's witticism remains unclear. She could be suggesting that she'll need to cover her unadorned clothes with fur, one luxury material that is still legal; or she could be saying that, since she's been stripped of her gold and silver adornments, she may as well go all the way and become a brown-cloaked (Slav-like? slave-like?) pilgrim.

The poem protests a sumptuary law that restricted lavish dress. Such laws, imposed for reasons of puritanical piety or as an economic measure, were associated with the Northern French royal household and the mendicant orders that supported and were supported by the French crusading army in

Occitania in the first decades of the thirteenth century. It is very likely that this work was composed at the same time and in the same milieu as that of Bernart Sicart de Marvejols (see note on ll. 51-2). Rieger suggests that the author was a noblewoman (the only women with the right to dress as they pleased), someone who could approach King James I of Aragon. The offensive law was enacted, according to the poet, while James was absent from the court, perhaps during his military campaign in Mallorca in 1230. See Rieger 698-703.

30. Gormonda de Monpeslier, "Greu m'es a durar"

PC 177.1

a5 b6' a5 b6' a5 b6' c5 c5 c5 b6' c5 (in C)
20 *coblas singulars*

The *sirventes* is preserved in C374 and R.

The extant work may be a fragment. We presume that Gormonda's original *sirventes* responded to all twenty-three stanzas of "D'un sirventes far," Guilhem Figueira's virulent attack against the Roman church. Guilhem Figueira probably wrote his *sirventes* in 1228; Gormonda's response certainly predated the April 1229 surrender of Toulouse by Count Raymond VII to the armies of French lords. This edition is based on C after Rieger. We deviate from our normal practice of avoiding the use of severely damaged texts as the basis for our edition because C is generally more correct than R.

Previous editions include Raynouard (1816-21), Mahn (1846-53), Levy (1880), de Bartholomaeis (1931), Véran (1946), Perkal-Balinsky (1987), Rieger (1987, 1991), Städtler (1989, 1990).

Städtler's translation and analysis were extremely helpful for the preparation of the English version of this poem.

The following notes are based on our reading of C and Rieger 722-24. The emendations are Levy's and are adopted by Rieger unless specified.

11. *e:* C reads *en.*

21. *que en:* C reads *quen,* making the line a syllable short.

24. *pana:* C reads *plana.*

37. *carn:* C reads *carns.*

43. C reads *no seran de la gran trossa,* a hypermetric line. We accept Rieger's emendation because *tradossa* is supported by Gormonda's method of response to Guilhem Figueira. Gormonda constructs her *sirventes* by keeping Guilhem's rhyme scheme and often his rhyme words, while at the same time transforming the context of the rhyme words. Guilhem had concluded stanza IV with the accusation: "Roma, de gran tradossa / de mal vos cargatz" (27-28: Rome you encumber yourself with a great burden of evil).

44. *lurs:* C reads *luis.*

50. *Damiata:* The loss of Damietta in 1221, an Egyptian city that had previously been conquered by crusading Christians, was still an issue in Latin political polemics when Guilhem and Gormonda composed their *sirventes.* Pope Gregory IX, in his encyclical of excommunication against Emperor Frederick II issued in October 1227, claims that Damietta was lost because God disapproved of Frederick as the secular leader of the Christians. Frederick in a Latin encyclical and Guilhem in his vernacular *sirventes* immediately reject the charge. See J.-L.A. Huillard-Bréholles, *Historia diplomatica Friderici Secundi* (Paris: Plon, 1852-1861) 3: 23-30, 37-48.

52. *sel:* C reads *sels.*

65. Gormonda is answering Guilhem's charge that the Roman church is responsible for the death of the French King Louis VIII, which occurred in 1226 at Montpensier following the successful siege of Avignon. She claims that Louis's death *en pansa* (in the paunch / in Montpensier) had previously been foretold by the wizard Merlin. Städtler's article provides an excellent overview of the relationship between the two *sirventes,* as well as a detailed discussion of the historical events mentioned in both works ("The *Sirventes*" 129-55).

69. *hereties:* C reads *heretiers.*

72. *va se.n:* C reads *vay en.* Rieger emends the text to agree with R.

74-77. Gormonda does not counter every charge that Guilhem makes: most significant is her failure to answer his repeated accusation of clerical avarice. Gormonda's sole attempt to respond to this charge may be this reference to the lowering of a road toll at Avignon.

93. *esquern:* C reads *estern* but again the rhyme word is probably determined by the opening of Figueira's ninth stanza, "Roma, be.is decern / lo mals c'om vos deu dire, / quar faitz per esquern / dels crestians martire" (57-58: Rome, the ill that men must speak of you is self-evident, because

you martyr Christians out of derision).

97. Rieger reconstructs the line based on R.

100. In stanzas X-XIV, Gormonda dismisses Guilhem's encouragement of Count Raymond VII and the people of Toulouse. The Toulousans were fighting to preserve their autonomy. At the same time, they tended to be tolerant of heretical sects. Thus, the French military action against Toulouse took the form of a crusade, and French soldiers were granted the privileges of a crusading army by the Roman Church. Gormonda also hails the excommunication of Emperor Frederick II by Pope Gregory.

106. *prezans:* C reads *plezans.* Guilhem Figueira concludes stanza X with the warning: "Mais si.l coms presans / viu ancar dos ans, / Fransa n'er dolorosa / dels vostres engans" (68-70: But if the excellent count lives another two years, France will regret your deceitful ways). There is a problem with the order of Gormonda's verses in C, which is resolved by Rieger's reversal of verses 106 and 107.

107. *enans:* C reads *ni ans.*

114. *malaventura:* C reads *malavenira.*

127. *no s'amorsa:* C reads *nos samorsa.*

130. The line has been lost in both manuscripts.

152. *crezo.ls:* C reads *cre als.*

168. *crematz:* C reads *cremat.*

169. *per:* C reads *que.* The emendation from R is in Städtler and Rieger.

176. *cabals:* C reads *cabal.*

179-180. The lines are missing in C and reconstructed on the basis of R.

189. *onta:* C reads *anta.*

192. *fol:* C reads *fols.*

193. *no s'afronta:* C reads *nossa fronta.*

200-209. A miniature has been cut from the folio in C, severely marring the stanza. Levy's reconstruction is based on R.

202. *no s'adona:* C reads *nossa dona.*

210. Gormonda's reference to God's pardon of *la Magdalena* in stanza XX may refer, as Städtler suggests (150), to one of the most notorious events of the Albigensian crusade: the massacre of the citizenry of Béziers by the crusaders, which took place on the feast of the Magdalene in 1209.

220. *hereties:* C reads *heretiers.*

The danger and power of a *sirventes* like this one can be apprehended when we consider that in 1274, almost a half century after the surrender of Toulouse, a man was accused before the Inquisition tribunal in Toulouse because he possessed a manuscript that contained Guilhem's *sirventes.* Although he denied the charge, he could recite the opening stanzas of the anticlerical work (see Aurell 226-27). Gormonda's *sirventes* is the most explicit expression in this anthology of the political and spiritual crisis in Occitania in the first decades of the thirteenth century, the drama that signaled the end of a sophisticated, prosperous society of cities and courts that had sustained troubadour culture. In the extant troubadour corpus it is rare to find any *sirventes,* especially overtly political ones, composed by women. It is surely significant that Gormonda's *sirventes* and "Ab greu cossire et ab greu marrimen" (no. 29) are only preserved in C and R, two late manuscripts copied at Toulouse and Narbonne, where a spirit of regional pride favored inclusion of pieces neglected or censured elsewhere.

Städtler proposes that Gormonda was associated with a Dominican religious community, an order founded in 1216 to combat heresy ("The *Sirventes*" 152).

31. Anonymous, "Ab lo cor trist environat d'esmay"

PC 461.2

a10 b10 a10 b10 c10' d10 c10' d10
5 *coblas singulars* and a *tornada*

The text is preserved anonymously in manuscript a167 (a fragment that ends in the middle of line 22) and "G"5.

Previous editors include Torres Amat (1836), Stengel (1877), Serra-Baldó (1932), Marfany (1966), Vidal Alcover (1982), Rieger (1991).

The following notes are based on our reading of a (1-22), "G" (22-44), and Rieger 664-74. The emendations are Vidal Alcover's, unless otherwise indicated.
1. *lo* is missing in manuscript a. Stengel first made the emendation, followed by Rieger, based on "G".
2. *mos uells:* a reads *mons uulls.* The correction is in Rieger.
3. *lassa:* manuscript a reads *lasse. comiat:* manuscript a reads *conget.*
4. *sos conssells:* manuscript a reads *sonz coussells.* Stengel and Rieger

make the corrections.

5. *amar:* manuscript a reads *aymar.* The rhyme words of lines 5, 7, 13, 15, 21 end in *e* in the manuscript and have been emended.

6. *d'eras enant:* manuscript a reads *de arc navant,* "G" reads *de res anant.* Vidal Alcovar emends the text to *d'eres anant;* Rieger proposes *deresenant.*

9. *captenimen:* manuscript a reads *capteniment.* As usual, the rhyme has been regularized.

10. *desesperat:* manuscript a reads *desesperatz.* Rieger makes the emendation.

11. *semblan:* manuscript a reads *semblans.* Rieger emends the text following "G".

13. *esperansa:* manuscript a reads *esperance.* The rhyme has been regularized in 13 and 15.

15. *amistansa:* manuscript a reads *amistance.*

16. *joi:* manuscript a reads *joie.*

17. *pogues:* manuscript a reads *polgres.* Chabaneau ("Die beiden" 139) and Rieger emend the text.

19. *mos:* manuscript a reads *mons. encara m'an retrat:* manuscript a simply reads *sequer.* The emendation is made on the basis of "G" which reads *encara ma retat.*

20. *visc:* manuscript a reads *vist.*

22. *vengua:* a reads *gengua.* Manuscript a breaks off with the words *gengua de faitz.* The Catalan origin of "G" is evident from numerous graphemes found in the text from this point on.

27. *ai:* "G" reads *ab* but the clause had no verb. *eneug:* "G" reads *amug.*

29. *son:* "G" reads *sera.* Rieger emends the hypermetric text.

30. *gent:* "G" reads *gmt.*

31. *e.l:* "G" reads *e al.* Rieger makes the emendation.

33. *que m'es:* "G" reads *quax* but the line is missing a syllable.

35. *trobar:* "G" reads *trobas.* The emendation is in Rieger. *dejus:* "G" reads *aytal* which does not fit the rhyme scheme.

36. *gay:* "G" reads *gray.*

37. *complida:* "G" reads *complit.* The emendation fits the rhyme scheme.

38. *estat:* "G" reads *stat.* The line is hypometric.

40. *amava:* "G" reads *amave.*

43. *s'aferra:* "G" reads *safferre* and is emended because of the rhyme.

Rieger suggests that this *planh* was composed in the mid-thirteenth century in Provence because it contains the standard elements of the genre (668-74).

32. Azalais d'Altier, "Tanz salutz e tantas amors"

PC 42a

This *salut d'amor,* or love poem in epistolary form, is in rhymed octosyllabic couplets.

It is found in V149. Large portions of this text are illegible and we have relied extensively on Crescini's edition.

Previous editors include Crescini (1890), Portal (1898), Perkal-Balinsky (1987), Poe (1990), Rieger (1991).

The following notes are based on our reading of V and Rieger 681-84. All emendations are by Crescini unless otherwise noted.

1. *Tanz:* V read *anz.* A space is left for the initial.
3. *finas:* V reads *fin.*
6. *vos:* V reads *quos.*
7. *a vos:* V reads *vos.* The text is hypometric.
9. *dire:* V reads *dir.* The hypometric text was emended to accommodate the rhyme scheme.
12. *en:* V reads *et. escrich:* Q reads *esrich.*
21. *volentiera:* V reads *volentira.*
22. *priguiera:* V reads *priguira.*
23. *ez:* V reads *etz.* The emendation is by Poe.
29. *tristz:* V reads *tristez. Marritz:* V reads *mariz*(?) .
31. *dis:* V reads *dixis* (?). The microfilm is almost illegible.
34. *disses:* V reads *diesses.*
36-37. V contains a lacuna in the text, identified by Crescini, but not indicated in the manuscript. It reads *fazes vas vos ... ameus obezeis.* Rieger emends the text as follows: "fazes vas vos [nuilla falhida, / mais qe vos] am'e us obezis" (harms you in any way except he loves and obeys you).
44. *occaisos:* V reads *occaisons.*
49. *q'eu sai ez elh:* V reads *qeu sai zelh.*
52. *los:* V reads *lo.*
54. *uchaisonada:* V reads *uchaisoda.*
55-68. The poet refers to the faithless Briseida, who betrays Troilus for Diomedes, the son of Tideus. According to Poe, allusions to Breseida are not found elsewhere in Occitanic literature; Azalais does so by alluding

specifically to Benoît de Sainte-Maure's *Roman de Troie* ("Another" 321).
60. *ez:* V reads *est.*
66. *sens:* V reads *senes,* making the line hypermetric.
69. *autra:* V reads *atra.*
70. *eu:* V reads *en.*
73. *E s'el:* V reads *sel.* The initial is missing.
76. *qez eu:* V reads *qeu* and the line is a syllable short.
77. *deu:* V reads *den.*
78. *avia:* V reads *ama.*
83. *a agut:* V reads *agut,* which makes the line hypometric.
97. *oimais:* V reads *omais* and Rieger emends it.
98-99. The lines suggest that Clara is the name of this poem's recipient, quite probably Clara d'Anduza (see no. 9).

Azalais d'Altier, an early thirteenth-century trobairitz, identifies herself in line six of the *salut* and her addressee, Clara (d'Anduza?), in line 98. Azalais is also mentioned in the tornada of "Anc mais non vi temps ni sazo" by Uc de Saint-Circ (PC 457.4). Poe points out the intertextual allusions between the *salut* and Clara's "En greu esmai et en greu pessamen" (no. 9), which may have been written as a response to the accusations made by Azalais in the *salut* ("Another" 322-29).

33. Anonymous, "Coindeta sui, si cum n'ai greu cossire"

PC 461.69

I. b10' b10' *respos* (refrain)
   a10' a10' a10' b10'
II-V. a10' a10' a10' b10'
Part of the refrain is repeated after the first two lines and either a part or the full refrain is repeated at the end of each stanza (Chambers, *Introduction* 226).
 4 *coblas doblas* plus one *cobla*

The *balada,* intended to accompany a dance, is preserved in Q5. Raynouard also lists a Riccardiana manuscript and Bartch lists N as sources for the text.

Previous editions include Raynouard (1816-1821), Bartsch (1875), Appel (1894), Véran (1946), Perkal-Balinsky (1987).

The following notes are based on our reading of Q. The emendations are from Raynouard.

4, 6. *coindeta:* Q reads *condeta.*

5. *ioveneta:* Q reads *iueneta.*

7. *aver:* Q reads *ave.*

12. *cobeitosa:* Q reads *cubitosa.*

17. *acordada:* here, as in Lombarda's *tenso,* the verb's etymology evokes music and harmony, which enriches the more immediate reference to the singer's state of mind.

22. *plang:* Q reads *plaiger.*

24. *coindeta:* Q reads *coideda.*

27. *coindeta sui:* Q reads *coineda.*

35. *li:* Q reads *le.*

36. *que:* Q reads *qu.*

There are no clues to the identity of the poet.

34. Anonymous, "En un vergier sotz fuella d'albespi"

PC 461.113

a10 a10 a10 b10; b is a refrain
6 *coblas unissonans*

This *alba* is only found in C383.

The *alba* is a thematically defined genre that occurs in both sacred and secular modes. The sacred *alba* has been associated with Matins, when God is beseeched to protect unsuspecting souls from the dangers of the final hours of the night (Simonelli, *Lirica* 177-207). The profane *alba* presents a mirror image: it is a song of celebration and resistance, but the lover rejoices in the pleasures afforded by darkness and curses dawn and the *gilos* who seek to thwart lovers' joy. The meter of the stanzas (decasyllables with a caesura after the fourth syllable) is the same as that of

"Reis glorios, verais lums e clartatz" ("King of Glory, true light and bright-ness" [Sharman 365, 367]) by Giraut de Bornelh, the oldest extant Occi-tanic *alba.*

The work has been previously edited by Raynouard (1816-1821), Bartsch (1875), Appel (1895), Véran (1946), de Riquer (1975), Perkal-Balinsky (1987).

The following notes are based on our reading of C.
1. *albespi,* hawthorn, etymologically "white spine." This shrub lends its color and thorniness to a series of eroticized scenes in Romance literature from the *albespi* of the "first" troubadour, Guilhem IX, "La nostr'amor va enaissi / com la brancha de l'albespi, " (Our love is just like the branches of the hawthorn [Pasero 251]), to the *aubépines* of Proust's *A la Recherche du Temps Perdu.*
17. The line is hypermetric.

It is not possible to associate this anonymous *alba* with a particular milieu or poet, since its basic elements—the orchard, spring flowers and birdsong, the watchman and his bell, the parting of lovers after a night of shared passion—are standard to the genre, however beautifully they are reinvented in this song.

35. Anonymous, "Dieus sal la terra e.l pais"

PC 461.81

a8 b8 b8 c8 c8 d8 d8 c8
1 *cobla*

The text is preserved only in H where it is embellished with a miniature. Previous editors include Gauchat/Kehrli (1891), Kolsen (1917), Zufferey (1989), Städtler (1990), Rieger (1991).

The following notes are based on our reading of H and Rieger 652-54. Kolsen's emendations are adopted except where indicated.

1. *pais:* H reads *pa.*
2. *vostre cors:* H reads *on vos es.* Literally the line means, as emended, "where your body/heart/self is (from *ser*) or remains (from *estar*)." Here as in lines 3 and 5, *cors,* grammatically, may be heart, body, or self. Paden ("Of *cors*") and others have shown how troubadours use this ambiguity to confuse and collapse physical and psychological meanings. Here, however, the trobairitz is at pains to emphasize the distinction between heart and body that makes the homophony all the more ironic: her heart is *lai,* there (lines 3 and 5) where her lover is, while her body is *sai,* here (lines 4 and 6) where she lives with her *poderos, enveios* husband.
5. *cors:* H reads *cor.* The emendation is by Rieger.
8. We follow Zufferey ("Toward a Delimitation" 38) in our interpretation of the line.

Inclusion of this text in the final folios of H suggests that it was composed in the late twelfth century or possibly the early thirteenth.

36. Tibor, "Bels dous amics, ben vos puosc en ver dir"

PC 440.1

a10 a10 b10 b10 c10 c10 d10 d10
a fragment

The partial *cobla* is found in H45 where it is accompanied by a miniature and a *vida* that identify the poet. The scribe has left enough blank space after the verse for a second *cobla.*

The text has been edited by Barbieri (ca. 1574), Rochegude (1819), Raynouard (1820), Mahn (1846-1853), Chabaneau (1885), Schultz-Gora (1888), Véran (1946), Boutière (1973), Bogin (1976), Dronke (1984), Perkal-Balinsky (1987), Rieger (1991).

The following notes are based on our reading of H and Rieger 642-44.
3. As Rieger remarks, the line is almost illegible. She accepts Barbieri's reading. Barbieri had an unbound manuscript which was apparently very close to H but is no longer extant. *aman:* H reads *amans,* which was

emended by Raynouard.

4. *no:* the word is missing in H and the line is a syllable short. Rieger and all previous editors make the emendation.

6. *pentes:* H reads *pentis*. The emendation, necessary for the rhyme, is made by Rieger, following Thomas (409).

7. *n'anes:* H reads *naves* and the emendation accords with Barbieri's reading.

8. Barbieri's text ends with this verse.

9. H ends with this verse.

This fragment may be the oldest extant work in the trobairitz corpus. Although Tibors's *vida* implies that she lived in the thirteenth century, historical research points to the second half of the twelfth century, since she was probably the sister of Raimbaut d'Aurenga. See the Introduction for further details and Rieger 644-51.

Index of Poets and Poetic Terms
discussed in introductions and notes

GARLAND LIBRARY OF MEDIEVAL LITERATURE

JAMES J. WILHELM
AND LOWRY NELSON, JR.
General Editors

Series A (Texts and Translations)
Series B (Translations Only)